C U I S I N E
V I V A N T E

The international encyclopedia of New Cuisine.

With Best Wishes _____

Frederick's

London 1987.

CUISINE VIVANTE

VIVANTE

The international encyclopedia of New Cuisine.

BY HILARY WALDEN

Dishes prepared by Jean-Louis Pollet
Photography by David Burch

WARD LOCK

A QED BOOK
Copyright © QED Publishing Ltd

First published in Great Britain in 1985
by Ward Lock Limited, 82 Gower Street,
London WC1E 6EQ, an Egmont Company.

British Library Cataloguing in Publication Data
Walden, Hilary
  Cuisine vivante.
  1. Cookery, French
  I. Title   II. Pollet, Jean-Louis

  ISBN 0-7063-6419-8

This book was designed and produced by
QED Publishing Ltd,
The Old Brewery,
6 Blundell Street, London N7 9BH

Senior Editor: Stephen Paul
Art Editor: Moira Clinch

Photographer: David Burch
Illustrators: Lynne Riding, Mick Hill

Editor: Linda Sonntag
Assistant Designer: Anthony Bussey

Art Director: Alastair Campbell
Editorial Director: Jim Miles

Typeset by QV Typesetting, London
Colour origination by
Universal Colour Scanning Ltd, Hong Kong
Printed by Lee Fung Asco Printers Ltd,
Hong Kong

CONTENTS

THE RECIPES

◆ NOTE

*Where the garnish in the photograph differs from that given in the
recipe for the dish, it is a seasonal alternative chosen by the chef.*

*Jean-Louis Pollet and Hilary Walden relaxing in
the delightful gardens at Frederick's restaurant,
London.*

FOREWORD

As a restaurant chef I have been in as good a position as any to observe the growing success and popularity of Cuisine Vivante. From somewhat elitist beginnings the movement has gone from strength to strength, attracting new followers every step of the way. However, for a number of reasons Cuisine Vivante has remained firmly within the context of restaurant food, and it has come to be regarded by many as a style of cooking that is infinitely complicated and time-consuming. This is a shame not least because it is not entirely true, but also because it has perpetuated the elitist image and has restricted the further development of the cuisine by limiting the number of people who have experience of it.

In this book I was fortunate to have been able to work with Hilary Walden on a large-scale project to introduce Cuisine Vivante to a much wider audience. The aim was not so much to 'popularize' Cuisine Vivante by reducing it to a number of common denominators, but rather to show (through the careful selection of recipes and the explanation of certain basic techniques and preparations) that the 'spirit' of Cuisine Vivante need not be solely the preserve of expensive restaurants.

Cuisine Vivante can be practised at home just as easily as any other cuisine. It can be complicated and time-consuming but it can just as easily be simple and quick. The most important principle to bear in mind is that the quality, flavour and freshness of the food must be given full expression at all times. Every step of the preparation, cooking and presentation must be made with this principle firmly in mind, and there is no reason why the home cook cannot achieve the gastronomic delights that have hitherto largely taken place within the confines of restaurants.

INTRODUCTION

Cuisine Vivante is a new and rapidly evolving style of cooking that offers unprecedented levels of aesthetic and gastronomic pleasure to the diner. It is a style of cooking in which presentation plays an integral role, with dishes receiving a precise and highly original treatment that not only looks superb but also gives full expression to the care and attention lavished on the preparation and to the individual characteristics of the main ingredients.

The essence of Cuisine Vivante lies in the selection of only the finest and freshest ingredients; cooking methods that are sympathetic to the inherent qualities of the ingredients; delicate sauces that complement the taste, texture and colour of these ingredients; and finally, a style of presentation that takes all these factors into account and visually underlines them.

The inherent logic of this culinary philosophy has seen the exclusion of traditional flour-based sauces and over-rich dishes where it is often difficult even visually to identify the ingredients let alone identify them by taste. However, Cuisine Vivante is not a slave to dogma, and there are no hard and fast rules. Innovation, experimentation and adaptation are the key concepts, and so long as the spirit of Cuisine Vivante is preserved there is no limit as to the gastronomic heights that may be attained.

The beginnings

The origins of Cuisine Vivante can be traced back to Fernand Point and the 'new-style' cuisine of the 1950s. His restaurant, La Pyramide, at Vienne in the Rhône Valley, became the centre of French gastronomic innovation as his experiments with a lighter, more delicate style of cooking that was at odds with the classical haute cuisine repertoire of Carème and Escoffier gained widespread acclaim. His ideas were seized upon by the next generation of chefs who were inspired to carry out their own experiments. Sauces were among the first techniques to be revolutionized. Instead of using flour to thicken the sauce, they boiled and reduced them. The result was a sauce that emphasized rather than masked the flavour of the food. This in turn led to a renewed emphasis on the quality of the ingredients used and on light cooking that made best use of this quality.

The presentation of food was the next technique to receive the attention of Fernand Point and his followers, Jean and Pierre Troisgros and Paul Bocuse, now the acknowledged leaders of the 'new-style'. Having so far strived to do away with the synthetic glamour of traditional haute cuisine in terms of ingredients and preparation, these 'new-style' chefs similarly strove to present the food in a different and refreshing way, and for inspiration

OPPOSITE *Paul Bocuse (top) and Jean and Pierre Troisgros (bottom), widely recognized today as the leaders of the 'new style'. Taking their lead from Fernand Point and incorporating concepts of food presentation from Japan, they have developed a style of cooking worthy of the highest regard.*

Cuisine Vivante aims to stimulate both the eye and the appetite, and this concept is applied to the individual dishes and to the meal as a whole. This selection of dishes — Oysters with watercress, Veal tournedos with mixed peppers, Strawberries and orange crème and a light side salad — demonstrates the qualities of balance, colour and flavour progression that are the hallmarks of Cuisine Vivante.

ABOVE *Michel Guérard*
originator of the Cuisine Minceur
that provoked a widespread
reappraisal of food and its
presentation by chefs and
restaurant owners throughout
the world.

they turned to Japan. From the Japanese, the frontrunners of the 'new-style' adopted and adapted the precise and ornamental arrangement of dainty portions of food. To these they added a sauce — or even three — not poured over the food to hide it, but to provide background colour, a pool of green or pink beneath a white fillet of fish, and to expand the symphony of flavours. The finishing touch was perhaps a scattering of fragrant leaves or a display of colourful vegetable julienne.

Having established the principles of light, sympathetic cooking and subtle saucing, the originators of Cuisine Vivante turned to Japan again for further inspiration — and they found it in the Japanese art of *sashimi* (raw fish). The preparation and serving of raw fish was an explicit manifestation of the spirit of Cuisine Vivante, and was quickly assimilated into the new philosophy. Further inspiration came from South America, where the technique of 'cooking' fish by the action of lime or lemon juice was discovered. Slivers of fish were marinated in the juice until they turned opaque — a famous and increasingly popular technique known as Seviche.

Michel Guérard

The development of the 'new-style' cuisine continued apace but knowledge of it remained the privilege of a gastronomic élite until Michel Guérard launched his Cuisine Minceur in the mid-1970s. With its abandonment of all fats and its intensive use of ingredients both expensive and rare, it was too extreme to become a way of eating for many, but because it was extreme it attracted enormous publicity. It started a general revival of interest in food and its preparation, and it caught the imagination of chefs and restaurant owners everywhere. Creativity, originality and individuality in the kitchen were suddenly the order of the day. Chefs hit on new combinations of tastes and textures that often surprised, though at first perhaps did not consistently delight, their customers.

As interest grew and the art mellowed, books and articles were produced and knowledge rapidly spread to a much wider audience. This spreading of knowledge in turn helped to consolidate the foundations of Cuisine Vivante, and went some way toward giving it the international 'flavour' it now enjoys. Cuisine Vivante is for people who take a serious interest in their food and who regard cooking as an art itself and not just a laborious means to an end. It calls for a meticulous attention to detail at every stage, from shopping to serving, and it is a style of cooking that can transform the quality of any meal, whether it be breakfast or a bedtime snack.

Cooking and serving a Cuisine Vivante meal perfectly requires a considerable amount of time and thought — and it is this careful attention to detail that will show in the dishes placed before the diner. Although there are no set rules for the combination of dishes and ingredients, experiments are only welcome if they are pleasant to eat. The best way to develop the skill of combining flavours is to experiment on yourself on a small scale.

The aims of Cuisine Vivante

A Cuisine Vivante meal aims to stimulate both the eye and the appetite and should ideally include something that is light and airy, something that has a little more substance, something smooth, something crisp, something creamy, something refreshing, something moist and something dry. A variety of tastes, textures and colours that complement and do not swamp one another is most likely to satisfy the diner. This theme should be carried on throughout the meal — that is in adjacent courses as well as within the same course. Sauces, vegetables and garnishes need to be chosen with care to give balance and aid the progression of flavour, and the meal should have its base in the season's best produce.

The worst sin in Cuisine Vivante, as in any other style of cooking, is monotony. No matter how perfectly it is cooked and presented, a menu of sole timbales with white

BELOW Michel and Albert Roux, widely acknowledged today as the leaders of the 'new style' movement. With over 50 years' experience of cooking in grand houses and in the world's top restaurants, the Roux brothers embody the spirit and excitement of Cuisine Vivante.

Thoughtful yet innovative
presentation is an integral part of
Cuisine Vivante. The quality of
the food is given full expression in
this varied selection of dishes.

15

wine sauce followed by poached chicken breasts with potato purée and celeriac purée, and a dessert of vanilla bavarois, will be uninspiring and forgettable. It provides no colour to excite the eye, no distinct contrast of flavour and a uniform smooth creamy texture broken only by the tender flesh of the poached poultry.

With a little thought, the same main elements of sole, chicken and bavarois could be turned into a memorable gastronomic experience. A watercress or spinach sauce with the sole would add colour, a pleasant sharp edge and slightly more body; crisp mangetout and carrot julienne would lift the chicken in colour and texture; and the bavarois could be served with a sauce of raspberry coulis, a garnish of fresh fruit and langues de chat, to give brilliant colour, juicy freshness and extra bite, and bring the meal to a mouthwatering close.

Balance is perhaps the first consideration in planning a meal, but there are others that should be taken into account. The time of year affects not only the availability of fresh produce, but the heartiness of appetite, which tends to diminish in hot weather. The activities and tastes of your guests need to be borne in mind. If you are planning an evening meal for someone who has sat at a desk all day and eaten a business lunch, it will need to be lighter than one you would set before someone who had spent an energetic day outdoors. First-time guests will appreciate being asked whether there are any foods they avoid eating for reasons of taste, diet or religion.

Finally, but most importantly — consider yourself. You will need to calculate shopping and cooking time and choose as many dishes as possible where all or most of the preparation can be done in advance. Dishes like cold terrines and ice cream can be made beforehand and you can also pre-prepare the base for a mousseline or purée, leaving only the final stages and the decoration for the last minute. It is impractical to imagine that you can cook and present a main course for six and six individual plates of vegetables single handed. Unless you have help, keep the last-minute tasks to a minimum and arrange just one large platter of vegetables, making sure that it includes at least one purée that you can prepare in advance.

Organization of equipment plays a major role in the creation of any meal, and is especially vital with a complicated Cuisine Vivante menu. Before you start to cook, have all the ingredients out and weighed and the equipment ready — the ramekin dishes in the roasting tray, a sheet of greaseproof paper nearby, and the kettle filled with water to pour into the roasting tray or to blanch vegetables and take the pressure off the hob. Put all you need, including tongs and cling film, out on the work surface or in a handy cupboard if space is short. The moment you have finished with something, clear it away — if you are using the sink, fill a large plastic bucket with hot soapy

SPRING AND SUMMER MENUS

For Two People

ASPARAGUS GATEAUX

BREAST OF CHICKEN WITH
LETTUCE SAUCE AND
THYME

STRAWBERRY BISCUIT
GATEAUX

For Four People

GINGER AND LIME SORBET
WITH MELON

SCALLOPS WITH MUSSEL
PARCELS

SLICES OF LAMB WITH
ASPARAGUS

WINE JELLY WITH PEACHES

For Four People

DUO OF BROCCOLI WITH
LEMON SAUCE

PARCELS OF TURBOT WITH
SCALLOPS

STRAWBERRIES AND
ORANGE CREME

For Six People

TRIPLE VEGETABLE
TIMBALES

NOISETTES OF LAMB WITH
TARRAGON

NOUGAT GLACE WITH
PASSIONFRUIT

For Two People

EGGS WITH LETTUCE AND
SORREL AND CHAMPAGNE
SAUCE

STEAK WITH OYSTER AND
MUSHROOM FILLING

BLACKCURRANT RINGS

For Four People

CRAB AND FINE JULIENNE
OF VEGETABLES SET IN
LIGHT ASPIC

MEDALLIONS OF HARE
WITH BEETROOT

MANGO SORBET

For Six People

CHILLED BEETROOT
CONSOMME

MEDALLIONS OF VEAL
WITH COURGETTES AND
LEMON

PILLOWS OF FRESH PEAR

For Four People

PEAR VINAIGRETTE WITH
SMOKED SALMON MOUSSE

FILLET OF BEEF WITH
PARSLEY

KIRSCH ICE CREAM IN
COUPELLES

water and stand it in the corner of the kitchen. Clearing clutter and vanquishing chaos eases tension, as well as making valuable space for the plates to be laid out when you come to arranging the food.

Even perfectly cooked food can look unappetizing unless it is presented with neatness and a touch of flair. Choose plain rather than patterned plates, so the eye is not distracted from the food. A sauce slopping clumsily over the edge of a plate is an appetite depressant, as is an overabundance of garnishes. Cuisine Vivante favours understatement — the bunch of watercress gives way to one or two strategically placed leaves.

Garnish is often minimal as the ingredients of the dish themselves are arranged to form an attractive pattern, as in Loin of venison with pears and cranberries (p.295). Complementary vegetables can also be used to decorative effect, eliminating the need for indiscriminate handfuls of parsley that serve no purpose other than to relieve the monotony of the food they conceal. Only use garnishes that are relevant to the food and that are edible. But beware of spending too much time on the finishing touches or the food will be cold before you take it to the table. The most attractive effects can be achieved with the minimum of effort — for example in the judicious placing of a few leaves of herbs on the sauce or around the border of the plate. Cuisine Vivante lends itself to delicacy of presentation because it avoids gargantuan portions, so that the plates don't need to be cluttered with food.

Serving and choosing wines

Serve wines in the logical pattern of light before full-bodied, dry before sweet, young before old and lesser quality before the best, and serve them at the temperature that brings out their particular character. Serve white wines chilled (about 6-10°C/40-50°F). The more full-bodied and better quality wines need less chilling. Red wines should be served at room temperature (16-18°C/60-65°F). There are one or two exceptions to this general rule — for example, a red Loire is more enjoyable served cool. To trap the aroma of the wine, the bowl of the glass should taper gently inwards to the rim. Glasses should be filled to two thirds full and should generally be topped up after half this amount has been drunk.

Choose a wine that complements the food — unless you are serving fine wines of particular note, when the food will be chosen for its restrained elegance, lightness and purity, to complement the wine. A delicate red wine is the ideal partner for a dish of young lamb, and a more full-bodied wine better suits a beef or game dish with a more pronounced character. But complementary does not always mean similar, except in quality. A dish with rich and complex flavours is best set off by a wine of a simpler, more subdued character.

BATTERIE
DE CUISINE

♦ *A good selection of carefully chosen, well made kitchen equipment will bring pleasure as well as efficiency to cooking. Expand your batterie de cuisine as your repertoire grows. When buying equipment a useful rule for the big items is buy the best you can afford. They should last for about 15 years. But when buying small or specialist equipment that may only be used once or twice, be as economical or extravagant as your budget dictates.* ♦

BASICS AND OPTIONAL EXTRAS

For ease of reference the equipment covered in this section has been divided into two groupings — basics and optional extras. The basic kitchen tools used in the preparation of the majority of the recipes in the book are not all vital, and it is perfectly possible to improvise if you don't possess the whole range.

The optional extras are items that make life a great deal easier if your repertoire is more extensive. Even then, they may not all be necessary — if pasta is not something you enjoy, then there is no point in buying a pasta-making machine. Whatever you buy, from a knife to a sorbetière, should be well made and durable.

Knives

A set of good knives can spell the difference between success and failure in the kitchen. The blade of a good quality knife is forged (hammered into shape from hot metal), and not stamped out of a sheet. The blade should be ground all over so that it tapers from the back to the edge and from the handle to the point. It should extend the length of the handle (the extension is called a tang) and be held in place by rivets.

At one time, carbon steel was considered the best material for knife blades because it could be sharpened to a razor-like edge. Unfortunately, it rusts easily and needs care and attention to be kept in good condition. Stainless steel knives, though less demanding, could not be sharpened to a sufficiently sharp edge in the early days, but this drawback has since been overcome and there are now stainless steel knives around that can carry out any chopping or cutting task with proficiency.

Balance and weight are also crucial factors in the selection of kitchen knives. It is impossible to use a knife efficiently if it does not feel right in the hand.

SHARPENING KNIVES

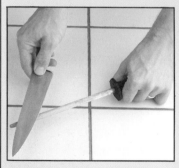

1 Hold the blade at a 30° angle.

2 Draw down to the steel's handle.

There are basically two methods for sharpening knives — a sharpening steel or an oilstone.

To sharpen a knife with a steel, hold the blade at an angle of 30° to the steel (starting at the tip) and draw down to the steel's handle making sure that the whole length of the blade comes into contact. Sharpen both sides of the blade in the same way.

1 Clean the stone with oil.

2 Rub in a circular motion.

To sharpen a knife on an oilstone, first clean and lubricate the stone with cooking oil. Place a cloth under the stone to stop it slipping about. Tilt the blade at a 20° angle to the stone and slowly rub the whole length in a circular motion.

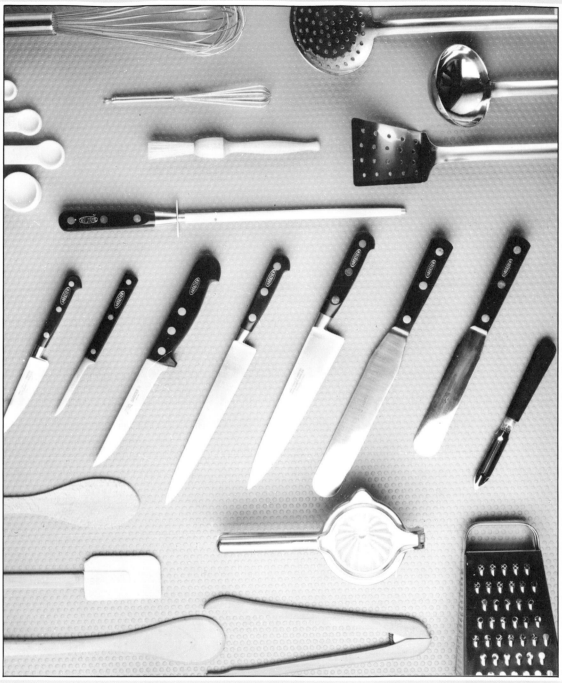

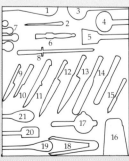

BASIC HAND UTENSILS

1/2 *Large and small wire whisks*
3 *Skimmer*
4 *Ladle*
5 *Fish slice*
6 *Pastry brush*
7 *Measuring spoons*
8 *Knife sharpener*
9 *Small paring knives*

10 *Flexible boning knife*
11 *Flexible filleting knife*
12 *Heavy bladed cook's knife*
13/14 *Palette knives*
15 *Potato peeler*
16 *Grater*
17 *Lemon squeezer*
18 *Tongs*
19/21 *Wooden spatulas*
20 *Flexible spatula*

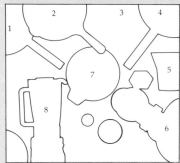

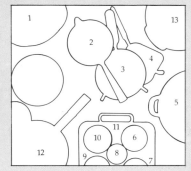

BASIC UTENSILS
(above)
1/2 Heavy, flat-bottomed
 sauteuses
3 Chopping board
4 Non-stick frying-pan
 with lid
5 Plastic measuring jug
6 Balance scales with
 metric and imperial
 weights
7 Heat-resistant mat
8 Liquidizer

BASIC UTENSILS
(right)
1 Mixing bowls
2/3/4 Sieves
5 Colander
6/7/8/9/10 Selection of
 different sized ramekin
 dishes
11 Roasting tin for cooking
 ramekins
12 Stock pot with lid
13 Large saucepan
14 Pudding basins

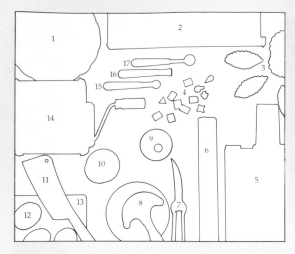

OPTIONAL EXTRAS

1 *Steamer*
2 *Mandolin slicer*
3 *Tartlet tins*
4 *Set of aspic cutters*
5 *Food processor*
6 *Rolling pin*
7 *Poultry shears*
8 *Small mezzaluna and*
  bowl

9 *Set of plain cutters*
10 *Flour dredger*
11 *Meat cleaver*
12 *Set of dariole moulds*
13 *Baking tin*
14 *Pasta-making machine*
15 *Canelle knife*
16 *Zester*
17 *Melon baller*

INGREDIENTS

◆ *Quality and freshness are the by-words for all Cuisine Vivante ingredients. Even store-cupboard staples, which are not used extensively, should not spend long on the shelves.*

When buying fresh ingredients, shop around for the best. Ask for advice and discuss your requirements with the supplier. Don't be afraid to insist on getting what you want. Make a careful selection of fruit and vegetables. If you want the tomatoes from the box on display, don't allow yourself to be served out of a box at the back of the shop you can't see. Ask to inspect the meat that has been cut for you, and ◆ *if it is not quite right, say so.*

VEGETABLES

Vegetables feature prominently in Cuisine Vivante. Their textures and colours make them ideal material for using to decorative effect, and so quality is of paramount importance. Second-rate vegetables can ruin a Cuisine Vivante meal.

Spotting top vegetables is not difficult — but tracking them down can cause a problem. Try to be flexible in your choice and pick the vegetables that look the best rather than the ones you had planned to use if these happen to be inferior. Firm tubers, plump juicy tomatoes, crisp hollow peppers, tight headed cauliflower, leafy spinach, should all look fresh, have a good bright colour, be unblemished and undamaged. Avoid specimens that are limp or wilting, discoloured or damaged and look generally dull and tired.

Flavour is more difficult to determine from appearance than freshness, but the general rule that small equals young, tender and sweet is nearly always a sound one. Buy a vegetable in its natural season and avoid the 'forced' varieties. They will almost inevitably be lacking in flavour.

Picture: page 32
1 Pumpkin
2 Leeks
3 Shallots
4 Cherry tomatoes
5 New carrots
   with leaves
6 Oyster
   mushrooms
7 Butter
   mushrooms
8 Asparagus
9 Red pepper
10 Green pepper
11 King Edwards
   potatoes
12 Jersey new
   potatoes
13 Courgettes
   with flowers
14 Salsify

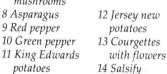

Asparagus
There are two main contenders for best asparagus — the fat white Argenteuil from France and the slim, green English variety. Both are delicious, but the tips of the slim green English asparagus are better for presentation purposes.

Carrots
Choose slim young ones with their feathery green leaves still intact. They will taste fresher and part of the green stem can be left on to preserve the flavour of the cooked carrot and to make it look more interesting. The leaves can be used separately both for garnishing and for flavour.

Leeks
For flavouring delicate sauces, for garnishing or for serving as a vegetable, use only tender slim leeks. Slightly fatter ones can be used as a flavouring in stocks and more full-bodied meat sauces. Unless specifically called for, remove the green part.

Mushrooms, cultivated
Tiny, tightly closed button mushrooms are useful for garnishing, either sliced or turned, but are very mild in flavour. Flat or open mushrooms have more flavour, but they darken when cooked and give off quite a lot of dark juice. They can be used instead of wild mushrooms when these are not available.

Mushrooms, wild
With the exception of morels, wild mushrooms are one of the treats of autumn. Morels show due consideration and come out in the spring. Very few people pick their own wild mushrooms but rely on specialist greengrocers and some of the better supermarkets.

Ceps vary in size. They have a strong brown cap and a thick stem. They do not collapse to the same extent as other mushrooms when cooked. They have a meaty flavour and a meaty texture.

Chanterelles or girolles are bright yellow trumpet-shaped mushrooms with a smell that has a hint of apricots to it and a fine delicate flavour. Their slightly chewy texture easily becomes tough if they are not cooked with care.

Morels have caps that look rather like sponges — they are covered with holes. Because of this particular care is needed when cleaning these delicious mushrooms to make sure all the grit is removed.

All these mushrooms are available dried. They must be soaked before they are used and will usually have a stronger but less fresh flavour and a more chewy texture.

Potatoes
Potatoes can be chosen intelligently so that their variety is best suited to the dish you intend to make. More and more greengrocers are marking potatoes with their name, if not their use, so choosing the most appropriate type is now at least a little easier. For purées choose King Edwards, for potato baskets choose Maris Piper.

Salsify
Buy salsify and its close cousin scorzonera whenever you can.

They have a delicious delicate flavour and it is always nice to serve something a little different. Both are long slim roots, salsify having a white skin, scorzonera a black one.

Shallots

If you have ever thought that to use shallots rather than onions was merely an extravagance, prepare two simple sauces, one using shallots, the other using onions. Now taste. Shallots will have imparted a sweet delicate flavour, where onions are heavy and dominant. Shallots must always be cooked gently as browning makes them slightly bitter.

Tomatoes

Whenever tomatoes are to be puréed or used in a sauce, make sure that they have plenty of juicy flesh and few seeds and, most importantly, have been basking in the sun. Merely selecting a type that is traditionally grown in the sun is not enough — irregular ridged Mediterranean tomatoes can be as tasteless as any other tomato when grown in a cool English summer.

Turnips

Avoid the cannonball sized, harsh-flavoured variety that smacks of institutional cooking in favour of the glowingly white, sweet flavoured baby 'navets' of France that appear on spring and early summer tables as 'primeurs'. As with baby carrots, buy the ones that still have their tops intact.

SALAD LEAVES

The most delicately flavoured and textured salad leaves are those that are picked when young. As they grow older they increase in coarseness, their flavour becomes harsher and any tendency towards bitterness more pronounced. With their increase in popularity, many varities are being cultivated under glass. This has the advantage of increasing the yield and extending the natural season, but the disadvantage of producing plants that lack the character of young specimens grown outside.

Picture: page 33
1 Round lettuce
2 Watercress
3 Radicchio
4 Mignonette
*   lettuce*
5 Cos lettuce
6 Belgium endive
7 Corn salad
8 Curly endive
9 Iceberg lettuce

Batavia

Sometimes called batavian endive or escarole, this has broader leaves than curly endive. The edges of the leaves have varying degrees of curl to them but they are never as crinkly as those of the curly leaved variety. It has quite a substantial texture with a mild bitterness and a slight pungency. Available in winter.

Chicory

Chicory is called endive in America and witloof in France. It has blanched white tightly packed cigar-shaped leaves that should be pearly and translucent. The bitter note that is a characteristic of the flavour of chicory is at its finest and most delicate in small leaves. Chicory is available from autumn through to spring.

Corn salad

This is also known as lamb's lettuce, or mâche in France. It has elongated slightly spoon-shaped leaves that are soft rather than crisp and have a slightly velvety feel to them. They do not form a heart. Corn salad should have a subtle, bitter, earthy flavour. Available from late autumn, through winter to the early months of spring.

Cos or Romaine lettuce

This type has long, coarse, crisp leaves with a slightly more pronounced flavour that is sometimes described as nutty.

Curly-leaved endive

This is called chicorée frisée in France. It has a mop of frizzy, crinkly leaves. The outer ones are bright green and the inner ones are almost white. Available in winter.

Iceberg lettuce

The tight, light-green compact head of this crisp lettuce is best for cooking as it retains its texture. Available from spring to early autumn.

Radicchio

This is really a red chicory. The leaves are dark red or maroon in colour or streaky with red and cream. The heads are the same shape as ordinary chicory or they may fall more openly. Available from autumn through to spring.

Round lettuce

Also known as butterhead or cabbage lettuce, it has soft coarse loose leaves and a mild flavour. Available nearly all the year round.

Watercress

Cuisine Vivante has brought new life to watercress. No longer merely a minor salad vegetable or useful greenery for garnishing, watercress is puréed to add colour, texture and a pleasant, slightly piquant flavour to sauces and stuffings and the leaves are used individually to add a simple touch of colour.

Watercress becomes limp very quickly so buy it as near as possible to the time it is to be used and keep it cool.

31

HERBS

Herbs are one of nature's flavourings and therefore have an important role to play in Cuisine Vivante. But they are used with discretion and not allowed to become too dominating. Even when a herb is the main flavour in a sauce, such as the basil sauce with the medallions of rabbit, its use is carefully regulated. Its character shows, but with subtlety.

Successful traditional combinations, such as mint with lamb, are regarded with respect by Cuisine Vivante, but treated to a fresh approach. Instead of being added to a sharp vinegar dressing (a killer for any wine), the mint appears as an attractive highlight in a warm velvety sauce. Cuisine Vivante cooks are constantly developing original and perhaps surprising combinations of herbs with meat or fish, such as Duck breasts with tarragon sauce (p.268).

There is no comparison between the flavour of dried and fresh herbs. For the very best results, pick small tender sprigs early in the morning after they have spent a brief life basking in warm sunshine with just the right amount of water. Grow them yourself in the garden, a window box or a pot behind a sunny window, but don't pick them while they are hot from the sun. Failing this, buy from a supplier who has a good turnover. Even fresh herbs lose their flavour after a few days. Once picked or bought, keep the herbs cool and moist. Larger sprigs can be placed in a container of cold water, small sprigs and leaves placed between sheets of damp absorbent paper inside a plastic bag and stored in the salad drawer of the refrigerator.

BELOW *Frozen herbs should normally be finely chopped before freezing. However, if the stems are also required they may be left whole.*

Fresh herbs can be dried at home, but they cannot be dried successfully. A more successful way of preserving them is by freezing. Chop the herb finely, spread it out on a tray, quickly open-freeze, then wrap in polythene bags.

Quantities of herbs specified in recipes can only be approximate because even fresh herbs can vary in the intensity of their flavour. Tasting just before serving is therefore vital.

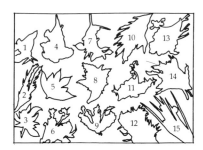

Picture: page 36/7

1 Mint	9 Lemon thyme
2 Rosemary	10 Lemon verbena
3 Sage	11 Marjoram
4 Parsley	12 Tarragon
5 Bay leaf	13 Chervil
6 Summer savory	14 Dill
7 Basil	15 Chive with
8 Fennel	flowers

Basil
The shiny green leaves of basil have a slightly clove-like, warmly pungent flavour. Pick when young and handle gently as the tender leaves bruise and discolour easily. For this reason the leaves should be torn rather than chopped.

Bay
The sweet, resinous, warm and spicy flavour of bay is an indispensable part of a bouquet garni.

Bouquet garni
A bouquet garni is a number of herbs tied together in a bundle in a small muslin or cheesecloth parcel with a string attached so that they can be removed easily at the end of cooking. It is used in soups and stocks to give an all-round flavour. The traditional herbs in a bouquet garni are parsley, bay and thyme, but they can be varied according to the dish being cooked, eg a sprig of rosemary can be added if the stock is to be used for a lamb dish.

Chervil
The delicate flavour of chervil with its hint of aniseed is so subtle that it has to be used in fairly large amounts. The feathery leaves are popular for garnishing as they look attractive yet do not upset the balance of flavouring within the dish.

Chives
Only the most slender, tender green leaves should be used for a flavour that is mild and delicate with just a suggestion of onion.

Dill
Feathery dill leaves impart an aromatic, slightly sharp yet sweet flavour that has a particular affinity with fish.

Fennel
Sweet herb fennel should not be confused with the bulbous vegetable, Florence fennel. The feathery leaves look very much like dill leaves but have a totally different flavour, having a sweet aniseed note to them. But like dill, fennel goes well with fish.

Mint
Unless the type of mint is specified in a recipe, such as apple mint, use the type that grows so profusely and completely unaided in many gardens. This is spearmint. Use it judiciously as it can be all-pervading.

Parsley
Parsley is the best known herb and the most adaptable. The flat leaved variety has a finer, more pronounced flavour that stands up to cooking in stocks better than the curly leaved type. Use only the leaves to garnish a dish. Keep the stalks for flavouring.

Rosemary
The sweet, spicy flavour of rosemary has an intensity that can be overpowering if it is not used with care. The spiky leaves are much tougher than those of other herbs and must be chopped very finely.

Sage
Use only young, small tender sage leaves, as the fragrant, aromatic flavour becomes more harsh and dominating in larger, older leaves.

Summer savory
Summer savory has a smell that is redolent of thyme but it has its own particular mild aromatic flavour with a pleasant hint of bitterness.

Sweet marjoram
Sweet marjoram (not pot or wild marjoram) is used for its pungent, yet mild, warm, sweet flavour.

Tarragon
The variety with the familiar warm, sweet, vanilla-aniseed flavour is French tarragon. Russian tarragon is altogether different and is dull and disappointing in comparison.

Thyme
The tiny leaves of thyme have a fairly strong, warm, sweet flowery earthy flavour and smell that stands up well in the cooking of stocks.

FRUIT

The affinity of some fruits with some savoury foods has long been exploited, both in classical haute cuisine and traditional country cooking. But fruits are used more frequently in Cuisine Vivante than in either of these. Fortunately the initial craze for using fruit with almost anything with seemingly little regard for what a dish was actually like to eat has died away and given way to more thoughtful, and consequently more enjoyable, combinations. A fruit is used when it contributes something — a pleasant contrast of colour or flavour, whether it is a juicy sweetness, a tang or a sharpness.

And, of course, fruits are vital in Cuisine Vivante desserts. Simply puréed or sieved they provide sauces that are light, fresh, clean and delicate. They form the basis for ice creams, sorbets and mousses and the filling for pastries. There is now a very wide variety of fruits quite readily available at every season of the year. This is not always a good thing. Strawberries, for instance, are delicious when opened naturally by a warm summer sun, but tasteless in winter when forced by a grower. Many other fruits suffer from not being enjoyed where they are produced. A lemon straight from a tree has a rich, warm, full, tangy aroma and flavour undetectable in a lemon bought in a shop hundreds of miles away. Though it is not always desirable to limit your purchases to local fruit or fruit in season, it is best to buy from what is plentiful, as it is then less likely to be an exclusive, out-of-season crop.

The condition and quality of fruit is easy to assess. There should be no blemishes, it should be undamaged, have a bright clear colour and feel heavy for its size.

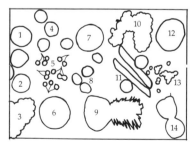

Picture: page 40/1
1 Red apple
2 Cox's, Golden
  Delicious and
  Granny Smith
  apples
3 Black/Cape
  grapes
4 Limes
5 Cherries
6 Ogen melon
7 Charantais
  melon
8 Passionfruit
9 Pineapple
10 Seedless white
   grapes
11 Rhubarb and
   apricots
12 Mango
13 Cranberries
14 Pears

Apples
A common enough fruit but of the dessert varities, pick Cox's Orange Pippins and French Reinettes for the best flavour; of the cookers, the choice lies with Bramley's Seedlings.

Apricots
A great deal of care is required when buying apricots as all too often the fruit that is offered for sale is hard, dry and lacking in flavour. Apricots should be picked when they have just reached their optimum ripeness. However, at this point they are very fragile and do not travel well, and are consequently harvested when immature.

Depth of colour is not necessarily a sign of ripeness as some varieties are always pale-skinned. There should not, however, be any tint of green in the colour. The fruit should feel heavy for its size, yield slightly to light pressure in the palm of the hand and have a faint, warm, fruity smell. If in any doubt, buy the smallest quantity you can and taste one before buying the full amount required.

Cherries
Cherries are available in a variety of colours, so bear in mind the colour of the dish in which they are to be used and select those that will look most effective. However, do not use dark morello cherries unless they are specifically called for since they have a sour taste.

Cranberries
A small American fruit similar to

bilberries, cranberries have a lustrous skin which varies in colour from pink to dark red. The berries have a sharp, slightly bitter flavour and should be firm and smooth. Cranberries are one of the very few fruits that it is worthwhile buying frozen.

Figs

These squat pear-shaped fruits are soft to the touch when ripe, and the skin, which is either white, red or purple, has a bloom to it. The juicy pulp is sweet, deep red and heavily seeded. Fresh figs are available from August to December.

Grapes

Whenever possible buy grapes in bunches and be sure to avoid any with shrivelled, split or squashed berries, or those which show mould near the stems. The juicy, thin-skinned grapes most widely used in Cuisine Vivante recipes should have a distinct bloom to them.

Kumquats

The sweet/sharp flavour of this small (4-5 cm/$1\frac{1}{2}$-2 in long) fruit combines well with both sweet and savoury dishes, and its bright orange flesh and skin add a splash of colour.

The skin is very thin and does not need to be removed before the fruit is eaten as it has a delicious sweet, slightly aromatic flavour.

Mangos

Mangos have the reputation of being the most delicious of fruits. There are several different types of mango with different coloured skins, coming from different parts of the world. They may be green, deep yellow, red or dappled.

Melons

When buying melons always insist on touching them to check for ripeness; a ripe melon should yield to gentle pressure applied at the stalk end.

Ogen melons have a yellow/orange skin with faint green stripes. The sweet and juicy flesh is pale yellow.

Charentais melons are small and perfectly round. The skin is yellow/green and slightly rough. The deep orange flesh is faintly scented.

Passionfruit

The skin of this vine fruit should be hard and wrinkled — the wrinkles are a sign of ripeness. The seeds of the passionfruit and the pomegranate are eaten, but those of the pawpaw (papaya) are not.

Pears

Pears, like apples, are divided into dessert and cooking varieties. They are easily bruised and should be treated very gently. Ideally pears should be purchased before they are fully ripe and should be kept in an airing cupboard for 2-3 days. To test for ripeness gently squeeze the stalk end to see if it yields.

Of the dessert varieties Doyenné du Comice, William's Bon Chrétien and Beurre Hardy are probably the best.

Pineapple

Smell a pineapple to judge if it is ripe — if it smells warm, fragrant and fruity it will be ready to eat.

Pineapples are one of the few fresh products that can be bought a day or so in advance as they will safely continue to mature. Generally speaking a pineapple that feels heavy will be the most succulent, and likewise one that is small will generally have the sweetest flavour and the most tender flesh.

Rhubarb

Select slim, pink, crsip sticks of rhubarb as these will have a delicate flavour and flesh that almost smells when cooked. Large sticks tend to have an acidic taste and flesh that is coarse, watery and fibrous.

Strawberries

Although strawberries are available at Christmas and other unusual times of the year, they are best avoided. Likewise strawberries picked at the very beginning of the season should be avoided if possible, since they will not have had sufficient sunshine in which to develop their true flavour.

Choose from fruit that has a bright, clear, uniform colour — depth of colour is not necessarily an indication of depth of flavour — and that is firm and unblemished with the hulls still intact. Strawberries are extremely perishable and should only be bought from a sup-plier who keeps them in a cool place away from strong light. Try to buy as near as possible to the time they are to be used and keep them in a cool place after purchase. Remove the hulls at the last moment and avoid washing if possible; wipe it very carefully with a damp cloth.

FISH

Shopping around for fish is a luxury few of us can indulge in. In some areas just finding one fishmonger is enough of a problem. Whether he is good or bad, encourage him, and query poor quality politely. Talk to him about the more unusual varieties, especially if he does not stock them, and keep asking when he is likely to get them.

The first consideration in selecting fish is freshness. Whole fish should be stiff but not frozen rigid, the skin bright and shining with scales that are close together and lying flat against the body. The gills should be hard to open and their insides should have a clear pink-red colour. The eyes should be full and bright with black pupils and transparent corneas. When buying pieces of fish look for flesh with a pearly translucency that doesn't show any signs of milkiness.

Picture: page 44
1 Red fleshed trout
2 Brill
3 Pike
4 Wild salmon

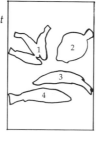

Bream (daurade)
There are many fish bearing the name of 'bream' but the one that is generally considered to have the finest flavour and texture is the true French daurade, the gilt-headed bream.

Brill (barbue)
Brill belongs to the same family as turbot, but the fish are smaller and their flesh softer and less finely flavoured, although still good.

John Dory (St-Pierre)
This fish is rarely sold whole by fishmongers because its somewhat large ugly head deters people from buying it. If you do manage to buy a whole fish, you will find that the amount of edible flesh in relation to its size is small, but the rest does make very good stock.

Monkfish (lotte; baudroie)
This is an even uglier fish than the John Dory. It has a large head and a tail that provides firm very white flesh with a texture and taste often considered to be more like lobster than a white fish. Monkfish has a sufficiently good flavour and texture to be judged on its own merits. To see it merely as a substitute for lobster is to do it an injustice.

Pike (brochet)
Pike appears most frequently in Cuisine Vivante as an ingredient in recipes for quenelles, as the flesh has a gelatinous quality that helps to bind the mixture together without making it heavy.

Salmon (saumon)
The best salmon is wild salmon from Scotland, and should be cooked quite simply. Less delicate farmed salmon is also delicious poached in a well-flavoured court bouillon.

Salmon trout (fruite de mer)
As the name suggests, this fish combines the characteristics of the salmon with those of the trout. The flesh has the fine flavour and the pale pink colour of salmon, but it is softer and more succulent.

Sea bass (loup de mer; bar)
As with bream the name bass encompasses a number of different fish but the one to use in the context of Cuisine Vivante is the common sea bass.

Sole (sole)
Dover sole has a subtle flavour and beautiful firm white flesh. The light cooking and delicate light sauces placed under the fish in Cuisine Vivante recipes enhance its fine flavour and texture.

Trout (truite)
Rainbow trout is readily available. The wild brown trout is almost exclusively the perogative of fly-fishermen. Nearly all the rainbow trout on sale are farmed, but it is still important to buy only from suppliers who are known to take particular care over their stock as their flesh easily becomes tainted if the fish feeds off strange-tasting, stagnant or muddy matter.

Turbot (turbot)
The flesh of these large flat fish is creamy white and well flavoured. It is delicate yet firm, one of the more substantial fish.

SHELLFISH

Whereas fish should look as if they are almost alive when they are bought, crustaceans (lobster, crab, prawns, crayfish etc) should actually be alive if at all practical and possible, as they deteriorate very quickly. Live shellfish should be animated and should feel heavy in relation to their size.

Molluscs (oysters, clams, mussels etc) must be alive when they are bought, and any specimens that are open should not be bought at all.

Picture: page 45
1 Clams
2 Crab
3 Scallops
4 Lobster
5 Dutch mussels
6 Fine oysters
7 Pacific oysters

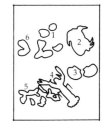

CRUSTACEANS

Crab (crabe)
The male crab is generally considered to be the better buy as it contains a higher proportion of white meat. But, like the hen lobster, when female crabs are in season they will provide coral. To distinguish between the sexes, look at the tail flap on the underside — the male's is smaller than the female's.

Crawfish (langouste)
These are lobster-like creatures, but with small claws. There are also some other differences. When live, crawfish are reddish, lobsters dark bluish. When cooked, crawfish are a less brilliant colour than the lobster.

Crayfish (écrevisse)
These look rather like miniature lobsters. They are very good for eating on their own — they have delicate, sweet flesh — and also provide a useful and popular garnish for many other fish dishes.

Dublin Bay Prawn (langoustine)
The tails of these miniature lobster-like creatures, also known as Norway lobsters, provide the ubiquitous frozen scampi. But don't let that put you off buying fresh langoustines, as they can be one of the most delicious of seafoods.

MOLLUSCS

Clams (praires)
The best clams are the palourdes of France. Open them in the same way as oysters. Remove and discard the black intestinal tube and keep the liquor for fish stock and sauces. Clams are available all the year round but are best during the summer months.

Mussels (moules)
Bouchots from the coast of Northern France and the Netherlands are generally considered to be the best mussels, but if they are not available, substitute local ones. Mussels are available from the autumn through to the spring but they are at their best during the winter.

Oysters (huîtres)
Oysters are now available all the year round. However, the ones on sale during the summer months without an 'R' in them are not the superior natives (Colchesters, Helstons etc.) or Belons or Marennes, but inferior Pacifics and Portugueson. Their lower price might tempt you to buy them. But if you do succumb, do not expect them to have the fine flavour and texture of their more costly cousins. The different varieties are distinguished by their shells. Which size oyster to buy depends on how prominent they are in a dish. Oysters have extremely delicate flesh so any cooking must be kept to an absolute minimum.

Scallops (coquilles Saint-Jacques)
Scallops are frequently used in Cuisine Vivante dishes because both the delicate bright white body and the tender brilliant orange coral are delicious to eat and attractive to look at. In theory scallops should be available all the year, but supplies can be erratic as they are affected by the weather. Scallops are opened in the same way as oysters. Once opened, remove and discard the fringe and black intestinal thread, then gently lift the flesh from the shell with a rounded soup spoon. The flesh is almost as delicate and fragile as that of an oyster, so must be cooked with the same degree of respect. The coral cooks more quickly than the body, so the two are often separated.

POULTRY AND GAME

'Poultry' is the term used for birds that are bred in captivity for the table. Poultry can be bought from a poulterer and game dealer, a poulterer and fishmonger, a market stall or a supermarket. From all but the last outlet fresh poultry, especially chicken, may be on sale resplendent in its feathers and undrawn, although the plucking and drawing should be done for you if you ask. A good supplier will automatically include the giblets with the drawn bird.

'Game' is the term used for wild animals and birds that are hunted for food. The majority of game are protected by law and can only be hunted during an 'open' season. This period varies from species to species and from country to country. But most people's source of game is not the shoot but the game dealer. If you are lucky, your butcher may also be a game dealer. A reliable supplier is as vital for game as for ordinary meat. The critical points that can make or mar a game dish are the age of the bird or animal and the length of hanging. Only the flesh from young animals is suitable for Cuisine Vivante recipes, as older animals need longer and slower cooking. However, they should not be too young as their flesh would not have had a chance to develop any character.

The game dealer will tell you how long the game has been hung. If you order game in advance he should hang it for you in just the right conditions — if you live in a centrally heated flat you will not have anywhere suitable at home — and for the length of time you specify. After hanging he will also skin or pluck and draw for you, possibly for a small fee.

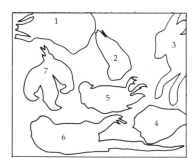

Picture: page 48/9
1 Mallard
2 Teal
3 Hare
4 Wood pigeon
5 Red-legged
 partridge
6 Cock pheasant
7 Quails

POULTRY

Chicken

Fresh whole chickens and chicken portions are coming back into fashion. But 'fresh' does not necessarily mean that the bird has spent its life ranging free and searching for its own food and therefore has superior flavour. 'Fresh' may simply mean that the bird has come direct to the supplier from a battery farm. Nevertheless, it should still be more tasty than its frozen cousins because its flavour will be unimpared by the freezing process — indeed it will have been given a boost by hanging.

Tasty, yellow fleshed maize-fed chickens are becoming easier to find in Britain, but the highly prized Bresse chicken is unfortunately not available, at least, legally. The laws governing the sale of poulet de Bresse and British import controls are not compatible.

With the exception of poussins (young birds weighing only about 450-700 g/1-1½lb) only the breasts of the bird are popularly used in Cuisine Vivante and although these can be bought as portions, buy whole birds whenever possible and remove the breasts yourself. The legs can be used in more everyday cooking whilst the carcasses will be the foundations of a stock.

Duck

Like chicken, fresh duck is beginning to make a comeback, though, as with chicken, 'fresh' does not necessarily mean free range. Again, it is possible to buy the breasts separately, but it makes more sense to buy a whole bird.

An English (Aylesbury) duck breast is not the same as the French magret. These come from specially fattened ducks and are firmer, more meaty and tasty. Also, whereas English duck are being bred with less and less fat on them, the magret will have a layer of fat between the skin and flesh.

Magret are slowly appearing in a few more shops but if you are unable to find them, substitute ordinary duck breast. The ratio of flesh to carcass on Aylesbury duck is low, so the best buy is not the smallest and youngest. For a reasonable portion of meat buy a duck weighing about 2 kg/4 lb. This is not so true of the French Nantais and Chalon breeds. They are more meaty.

Guinea fowl

These are a relative of the pheasant and at one time were classed as game. But now, with very few exceptions, all the birds offered for sale have been specially reared for the table and are considered as poultry.

Guinea fowl are about the size of a pheasant or a small chicken and may be hung for 2-3 days so that they develop a flavour that is a cross between the two.

GAME

Grouse

References to 'grouse' invariably mean the red grouse of Scotland and the moors of the far north of England. Grouse should be eaten in the year of their birth. Young grouse have soft, downy feathers on the breast and under the wings. The outermost large flight feathers should have pointed tips. Hang young grouse for 3-4 days.

Hare

Young hare of under a year is easy to recognise as it will have a white belly, pliable ears that split easily, a very small hare lip and short claws. Hare and rabbit should be hung by the feet of their hind legs (birds are hung by their necks) so that the blood will drain away from the intestinal areas of the body and escape through the mouth. Only the saddle, divided into its two fillets, is used in Cuisine Vivante. It may be sliced along its length or cut into round medallions. Hang for about 3 days.

Partridge

The grey-legged variety is more interesting to eat than the French or red-legged. A bird of about 400 g/14 oz in weight should give the right balance of tenderness and flavour. As with pheasant, look for plump breasts, which provide the majority of the flesh of a partridge, supple skin and smooth, securely attached feathers. The legs of a young grey-legged partridge will have a yellowish colour, becoming slate grey with age, and the outermost large flight feathers will have pointed tips. Hang young partridge for about 4 days.

Pheasant

The male (cock) pheasant steals the show for looks when alive but it is the female (hen) who makes the best eating. She will generally be more plump, succulent and tender. Young birds will have smooth, pliable feet and light plumage, the first wing tip feather will be pointed (it is rounded in an older one) and the spurs of a young cock will be short and rounded. Also look for plump firm breasts, supple skin and smooth, securely attached feathers. Hang young pheasant for about 5-6 days.

Pigeon

There is no 'open' or 'closed' season for wild pigeon, but they are at their best during the summer months when they are feeding on young shoots and leaves. These wild birds have a darker flesh with a more 'gamey' flavour than birds that are bred for the table. They will become tough with age, so it really is important to select young birds if serving wild pigeon, although in Cuisine Vivante only the more tender breast meat is used. If you prefer or if the other flavours in a recipe dictate, use a mellow flavoured bred bird instead of a wild one. If you have the chance, opt for a maize-fed pigeon, which is tender, with a delicate yet distinctive flavour.

Quail

Wild quail are a protected species in Britain, so we have to rely on farm-bred birds for the table. Choose fresh birds with plump breasts and a pliable skin that shows no signs of dryness.

Quail have a delicate flavour and are not hung before being eaten.

Rabbit

Much of the rabbit that is on sale is not game, but farm bred. The flesh of an animal that has frolicked in the fields will have more colour and flavour than a cosseted creature. If you have the choice, which to select is really a matter of taste, but always look for the same signs of youth as in a young hare. A wild rabbit will benefit from a short hanging.

Just the fillets from the saddle are used in Cuisine Vivante. This has a similarity to chicken, but is less dry with a slightly more distinctive flavour.

Venison

Venison is beginning to be more widely available in the shops as attempts to farm it commercially are showing dividends.

The prime cuts are the fillets from the saddle and the loin. The flesh from the small roe-deer is generally considered to be finer than that of the large red deer, but any good quality venison should be a rich dark red and finely grained. The male (buck) is better for eating than the female. Both are at their best when between 18-24 months of age. Hang venison for about a week.

Wild duck

There are several species of wild duck — small teal, slightly larger widgeon and the largest, most commonly used, mallard.

MEAT AND OFFAL

A good butcher who can be relied on to sell only top quality meat is vital. Undue amounts of fat and gristle are immediately visible, but toughness and flavour, or the lack of it, are a different matter. A sauce may be sublime, but if the meat with which it is served requires more than a moment or two's chewing and tastes of nothing, the whole dish will be doomed to failure.

Given the Cuisine Vivante treatment, offal — liver, kidneys and sweetbreads — provides some of the most delicate, succulent and appetising of dishes. To make good enjoyable eating it really must be fresh and it must be cooked lightly. Overcooking is often responsible for the ruination of offal.

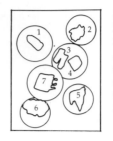

Picture: page 52
1 Veal steak
2 Veal kidneys
3 Pork fillet
4 Beef fillet
5 Calves liver
6 Sweetbread
7 Rack of lamb

Beef

Aberdeen Angus and the French Charolais (though rarely seen in Britain) are higly prized for the quality of their flesh. The flesh of good quality beef has a fine grain and appears moist but not wet. When freshly cut, the colour will be bright red, but it becomes dark red, even brownish after several hours. Avoid meat that shows any sign of dryness. The fat should be firm, fresh looking and yellow, but the shade of yellow depends on the diet of the animal. Grass produces a deeper yellow fat than barley.

Kidneys

Although larger than other kidneys, veal kidneys are the most tender and delicate. They are not kidney shaped, but have a unique shape and structure consisting of many small segments joined to a central core. Lambs kidneys weigh only 25-50 g/1-2 oz each. Soaking in milk for an hour or so helps to remove the blood. After soaking, rinse and dry the kidneys thoroughly.

Lamb

The most meltingly tender, delicately flavoured lamb comes from milk-fed animals, but they are only available during the early spring months. As the year progresses and the animals become larger, their flesh will gain flavour and colour but it will also get tougher. The late spring and early summer are considered to be the time of year for the optimum balance between flavour and tenderness.

Because of these differences, the method of cooking the lamb and the flavour of the sauce must be chosen carefully if a dish is to work successfully as a whole.

The most frequently used cuts are loin, which is usually rolled and boned, best end of neck and fillets cut from the saddle. Noisettes are cut from the boned and rolled best end of neck. Medallions are cut from a boned best end of neck. The fat is trimmed off, the meat is rolled up firmly with the eye inside and tied in shape with string. The size of the cuts and the number they serve change noticeably throughout the year.

Liver

Calves liver is the finest of all. It has an excellent flavour, a smooth texture and is exceptionally tender. However, it is always expensive and not always available. More accessible is lambs liver. Its more pronounced flavour can be complemented by a fuller flavoured sauce.

Sweetbreads

Calves sweetbreads, and in particular those from milk-fed veal, are the sweetbreads to choose for the finest flavour and texture. To get fresh sweetbreads it is usually necessary to order them in advance from the butcher, who will probably sell them in pairs rather than by weight. Allow one pair per person. When they arrive they should be pale, creamy, moist and plump. Frozen sweetbreads are sold in pre-weighed packs, usually of 225 g/8 oz, by some supermarkets.

Soak sweetbreads in frequent changes of cold water to remove all traces of blood, then blanch them in water acidulated with lemon juice to keep them white, enabling the covering membrane and pieces of gristle to be removed easily. After cooking, they should be pressed to help them to keep their shape.

Veal

Milk-fed veal from calves slaughtered when they are between 8 and 12 weeks is preferred by Cuisine Vivante chefs. Until recently, Holland has been the source of this type of veal, but now two or three farms in England are also producing it. The flesh of tender milk-fed veal is a pale pearly pink, whereas the flesh of older, more highly flavoured and slightly tougher veal is a darker pink. All veal flesh should be firm and moist, though not wet, and the bones should be bright and translucent.

The cuts that are used are the loin and the fillet. Medallions are cut from the fillet. They should be about 2.5 cm/1 inch thick, trimmed and tied into neat round shapes. Escalopes are cut across the grain and come from the top of the leg. They are generally beaten firmly, but not heavily, between two sheets of clingfilm to flatten them to about 6 mm/1/4inch, then trimmed to a neat shape.

MISCELLANEOUS

Picture: page 53
  (top)
1 Fine olive oil
2 Virgin olive oil
3 Sunflower seed
  oil
4 Walnut oil
5 Hazelnut oil

(bottom)

1 White wine vinegar	*4 Lemon wine vinegar*
2 Pure red wine vinegar	*5 Raspberry vinegar*
3 Rosemary vinegar	*6 Tarragon vinegar*

Butter
The butter used in Cuisine Vivante is always unsalted. This is partly because it allows for more control over the amount of salt used in a dish, but more importantly for reasons of quality. Only the best quality butter is left unsalted. It will usually taste fresher than salted butter and have a sweeter, more delicate flavour.

Caul
Caul is a lace-like membrane that is wrapped around foods when they are cooked for two reasons. It holds ingredients together which might otherwise disintegrate during cooking and keeps them moist by protecting them from the heat and gently basting them. If it does not melt away during cooking once it has served its purpose, it can be peeled off easily before the food is served. Caul can be ordered from good butchers.

Crème fraîche
Crème fraîche, with its light texture and slightly acidic flavour, gives delicious, fresh tasting results. Many supermarkets and smaller specialist food shops now sell crème fraîche but if you are unable to buy it, a reasonable imitation is easy to make. Blend double cream with twice the amount of soured cream or full-fat plain yoghurt. Heat the mixture gently to 90°C, pour into a container, cover and keep in a warm place (about 75°C) overnight. Stir, then keep in the refrigerator.

Oils
Sunflower oil can be used to sauté ingredients for particularly light, delicately flavoured dishes, and it may also be blended with olive oil to produce a salad dressing with a slightly less characteristic flavour.

Olive oil should be your first choice for all fine cooking but it is important to select the right grade of oil for the particular task in hand. The lighter, mildly flavoured, less expensive grades are suitable for the majority of Cuisine Vivante recipes but for salad dressings use the rich, green virgin oil from the first pressings of the olives. The very best of these come from Provence and Tuscany — those from Provence have a slightly fruity flavour, while those from Tuscany have a slightly nutty note.

The use of nut oils such as walnut and hazelnut can add an interesting dimension to salads. For a subtle effect they may be blended with a little olive or sunflower oil.

Peppercorns
Buy in quantities that you will use up fairly quickly and grind freshly each time you require pepper as it does lose its strength. Black pepper is more often used because it has a finer, more aromatic flavour than white, which is hotter. White pepper is preferred when specks of black would spoil the appearance of a dish.

Green peppercorns, which are unripe berries, can occasionally be bought fresh, but are more usually sold in cans or bottles in brine. They must be rinsed before they are used. Green peppercorns are crisp and tender with a mild flavour.

Pink peppercorns come from a plant of a different species. They are soft with a surprisingly subtle flavour that lacks the hotness or spiciness of pepper. Pink peppercorns imported from Madagascar are generally considered the best.

Vinegars
Different flavoured vingears have joined the ranks of sherry vinegar, red and white wine vinegars, cider vinegar and tarragon vinegar in the preparation of a number of sauces for meats and fish as well as salads. The most notable are the fruit vinegars, especially raspberry, but there are other herb ones as well. These can easily be prepared at home by steeping the required herb in a good quality white wine vinegar for about two weeks.

Wild rice
Wild rice is not actually a rice but a grass with a deliciously distinctive flavour that to some people is reminiscent of nuts. It is expensive, but well worth using for the right dish on the right occasion. To make the wild rice go a little further mix it with a little brown rice cooked separately. Wild rice is available from delicatessens, specialist food shops and good supermarkets.

Wines, spirits, eau-de-vie
When choosing a wine for cooking, select one that you would be more than happy to drink. A thin acidic wine cannot produce a rounded, well flavoured sauce. It is for this reason that medium-bodied white wine is frequently specified in the recipes. Too many wines from the lower end of the price scale are too light and unbalanced to withstand boiling down satisfactorily. The same applies to vermouth — do not shop around for the cheapest you can find, but look for flavour and body.

Cognac is usually specified rather than brandy, because not only does this guarantee a certain level of quality, but also a certain type of flavour. There are other brandies of equal quality, but they often have different, individual flavours.

When 'Framboise' or 'Fraise' are called for, this means the dry, colourless, eau-de-vie — not the sweet, coloured liqueur.

TECHNIQUES

AND BASIC

PREPARATIONS

The techniques and basic preparations of Cuisine Vivante are not overly complicated, but it is important that they are carried out correctly. The following section details the methods of preparation and cooking that characterize Cuisine Vivante and that are designed with one aim in mind — to preserve and give expression to the quality, flavour and freshness of the food. In addition, recipes are given for the most commonly used basic preparations referred to throughout the main recipe section.

BASIC PRINCIPLES

◆ The overriding objective when preparing and cooking foods for Cuisine Vivante is always the preservation of the quality and natural flavour and freshness of the food.

◆ The preparation of all ingredients is left to the last possible moment.

◆ All equipment for cutting is sharp.

◆ Meat, if kept temporarily in the refrigerator, is transferred to room temperature about half an hour before cooking.

◆ Nothing is cooked until the last possible moment.

◆ Cooking is light and quick.

◆ A fish slice, spatula or tongs are used to turn or lift meat during and after cooking to avoid piercing the surface and allowing the juices to escape.

◆ Food is served as soon as it is ready.

MEAT, POULTRY AND GAME

With meats, poultry and game the aim is to cook them so they remain moist and, generally, pink in the centre. The exceptions are pork and sweetbreads, but this certainly does not mean they should be overcooked, especially in the case of sweetbreads. The source of heat must be preheated and it must be high and the cooking must be brief. The methods favoured are roasting and steaming, sautéeing or frying. If a meat is to be cut before it is served it must be left to rest for 10-15 minutes to allow it to settle and the juices to run evenly throughout the meat. In the majority of dishes the meat will be resting while the sauce is prepared. Cut meat cools very quickly, so to keep it warm while the plates are prepared with the sauce and garnish, the slices are put back together and covered with clingfilm.

Roasting

The meat is usually cooked very briefly on either side, often in a little fat in a hot pan to sear the outside and keep the flesh moist by sealing in the juices before it is put into the hot oven. Leaving the flesh on the bone also helps to keep it moist or, as in the case of veal, it may be cooked in a heavy casserole dish that the piece of meat just fits. Meats that have a tendency to dryness, such as game, can be covered with grease-proof paper during cooking.

Steaming

This gentle method of cooking is sometimes used for small pieces of meat that are very lean, tender and delicately flavoured, such as baby lamb and chicken breasts. The water in the steamer must be boiling so that the meat immediately comes into contact with a high temperature and a steady stream of steam should be maintained throughout the cooking. Mild flavourings such as herbs can be added to the water, or stock can be used instead to give a nuance of flavour to the flesh. The liquid may then be used in the making of the sauce that is served with the meat.

Sautéeing or frying

This is the method most frequently used for cooking meat, poultry and game. Make sure the meat is completely dry, at room temperature, and use a heavy based, flat bottomed pan that the meat will just fit in a single layer. Melt the butter, but do not allow it to get too hot otherwise it will burn. Add the meat, skin side down if it has a skin, and cook it quickly until set and golden brown on the underside, shaking the pan occasionally. Turn the meat over and cook the other side in a similar way. The smaller, thinner or more delicate the cut, the shorter the cooking should be and the closer it should be watched. Small, very delicate pieces, such as diced sweetbreads, kidneys and liver need constant attention.

Duck breasts

Duck breasts are cooked for longer on the skin side than they are on the other side. Magret are best cooked in a slightly different way. Place the magret, skin-side down, in a hot pan, without any additional fat, and cook it over a high heat until the skin is crisp and golden and the fat runs out. Pour the fat from the pan, turn the breast over and cook the other side more briefly. Magret may also be cooked under a hot grill.

STEAMING

Steaming is ideal for tender, delicately flavoured meat such as chicken. Herbs can be added to the water to bring out the flavour.

FISH AND SHELLFISH

Fish and shellfish need to be prepared and cooked with the utmost care to preserve their delicate texture and flavour. Cooking times are exceptionally short, especially when the fish is to be kept warm while a sauce is made, as gentle cooking will continue during this time. Keep the fish on a warm (not hot) plate over a pan of barely simmering water and cover it loosely. It should not be allowed to dry out.

Steaming and poaching are generally the best cooking methods for fish. Frying or sautéeing are also used occasionally but in a very controlled way.

Steaming
As most cuts of fish are small, a traditional fish kettle is not essential for steaming. The fish can be put in an ordinary steamer over an ordinary pan. The liquid, which must of course be boiling when the fish is put over it, can be plain water, but the careful addition of herbs, the use of wine or a court bouillon or fish stock, will give an additional subtlety of flavour. The liquid can then provide the foundation for a sauce.

Poaching
Poaching liquid should barely shudder and give no more than the occasional bubble while the fish is sitting in it. It is an integral part of the recipe and contributes towards the overall flavour of the dish. The dish may also be flavoured by vegetables, principally shallots. They are usually softened first in a little butter, then used as a bed for the fish to sit on, acting as a protective barrier between the delicate flesh and the hot pan.

To skin and fillet flat fish
The fish should be cold. Use a sharp, flexible, long bladed filleting knife. A little salt on the fingertips will stop the fish slipping when you are working on it. The skin of Dover sole is easier to remove before filleting. The fish is often served whole and filleted at the table.

Place the fish with its dark skin facing upwards. Then remove all the fins with kitchen scissors. Mark an incision in the skin just

FLAT FISH

1 *Remove the fins with scissors.*

2 *Hold the tail firmly in one hand.*

3 *Pull the skin away sharply.*

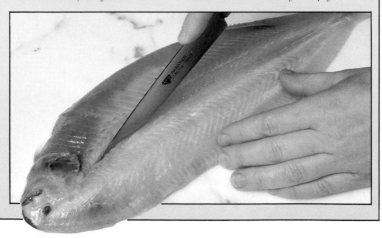

4 *To remove the fillets, cut through the flesh on top of the backbone starting from the head and working down to the tail.*

ROUND FISH

1 Slit the belly from vent to head.

2 Loosen the lateral bones.

3 Cut the backbone at the tail.

4 Pull the backbone away gently.

5 Remove any remaining bones.

6 Loosen the skin at the tail and push the flesh away.

above the tail and loosen the skin with the thumbnail, working around each side of the fish to the head.

Hold the tail firmly with one hand and pull the skin away sharply. The white skin is removed in the same way.

Remove the fillets by cutting through the flesh at the top of the backbone, allowing the knife to scrape along the bones from the head to the tail to ensure that they are all removed.

To clean, skin and fillet round fish
Slit the belly from the vent towards the head. Open up and remove the entrails. Rinse under cold running water. Use your thumbnail or a knife tip to scrape out the black blood channel down the backbone which would give the fish a bitter taste. Rinse again.

Cut off the heat just below the gills. Use a sharp, flexible knife to ease the top fillet away from the backbone. Use the blade to loosen lateral bones from the top fillet. Pull

it away and cut the skin along the belly to free it completely.

To loosen the bottom fillet, cut through the backbone at the tail end. With the help of a filleting knife, pull the backbone up and away gently. Take as many small bones as possible with the backbone. Any remaining small bones can be removed with pliers or large tweezers.

To skin, lay the fillet skin side down, loosen the skin at the tail, grip it firmly (salt helps) and 'push'

LOBSTER

1 Split the lobster in two.

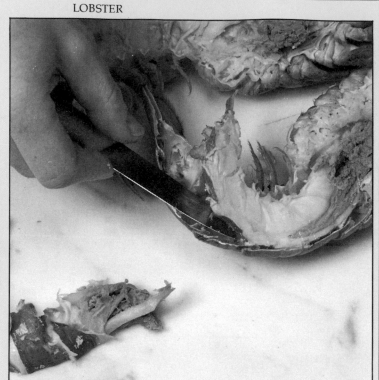

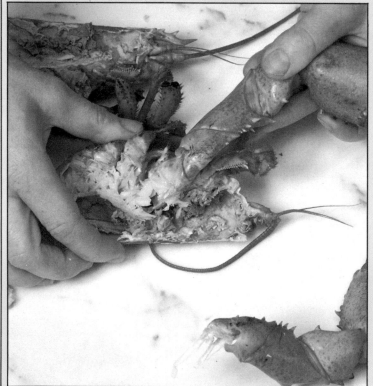

2 Remove the eye 'sac'.

3 Ease the tail flesh away with a knife.

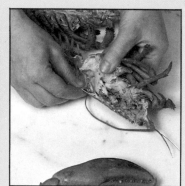

5 Discard the 'dead men's fingers'.

4 Holding the lobster firmly, remove the claws.

6 Remove the claw flesh.

the flesh away. Keep the cutting edge close to the skin and use the flat of the knife to push.

To prepare crabs

To kill a crab plunge the point of a knife through the underside behind the eyes and through the nerve centre when the tail flap is held back. If a live crab is put into boiling water it is liable to shed its claws.

To shell a crab lay it on its back and twist off the claws. Then twist off the legs — do not pull them. Prise the apron up by pulling at the pointed end near the mouth to remove the body from the shell.

Remove the 'dead men's fingers'. These are soft and spongy and are found at the sides of the body and stomach sac which lies behind the head. Strip out any cartilaginous membrane from the shell and discard it.

Remove the brown meat from the shell and put it aside. Do not mix it with the white meat from the body, legs and claws. Remove the white meat from the body, legs and claws. Crack the legs and claws with a hammer or lobster cracker.

Use a lobster pick or skewer to help you extract all the flesh

To prepare lobsters

To kill lobsters plunge them head first and upside down into a pan of heavily salted boiling water. Alternatively, plunge a trussing needle deep into the head between the eyes.

To prepare a lobster place it on a board with the tail spread out flat and push the point of a chopping knife firmly into the cross on the top of the head. Hold the side of the lobster firmly and bring the knife down to where the tail meets the head and split it in two. Remove the gritty 'sac' behind the eyes and, if it is visible, the intestine vein in the meat near the tail.

Gently insert the sharp end of the knife into the tail, and with a backwards and forwards movement remove the flesh.

Holding half of the lobster firmly on the board, pull off the claws. Discard the 'dead men's fingers'. These can be found beneath the shell with the small claws attached.

Crack the claws with a heavy weight and remove the white flesh with a skewer.

To open (shuck) an oyster

Wrap the hand in which you are to hold the oyster in a cloth. Hold the oyster flat side uppermost with the hinge facing you. Insert the end of a short sturdy knife through the seam between the two halves of the shell just beside the hinge. Give a short, sharp twist with the knife to break the hinge (or work at it until you succeed). Slide the knife from right to left, keeping the blade close to the top shell, to sever the muscle. Lift off the flat shell.

To prepare scallops and mussels

Scallops are opened in the same way as oysters. Once opened, remove and discard the fringe and black intestinal thread, then gently lift the flesh from the shell with a rounded soup spoon.

Mussels should be discarded if the shells do not close when tapped sharply. Scrape the shells with a sharp knife and then rinse in cold water.

CRAB

1 Twist off the claws.

2 Remove the body from the shell.

3 Remove the 'dead men's fingers'.

4 Remove any membrane.

5 Extract the brown meat.

6 Extract the white meat.

V E G E T A B L E S

There are two main methods of cooking vegetables — boiling and steaming. Brief boiling — blanching — is a process often used to soften a julienne for garnish. Once cooked, vegetables can be served as they are or puréed. Cuisine Vivante recipes favour small young tender vegetables and brief cooking times. The results are tender-crisp and flavoursome. If you use older vegetables, which are both larger and tougher, they will take longer to cook and will not be as satisfactory.

Whether steaming or boiling vegetables, do not cook too many at a time. The water you use will take longer to come to or return to the boil and steam will not be able to circulate properly.

To prepare vegetables, use a sharp stainless steel knife of an appropriate size. It is very difficult to cut cleanly and quickly with a knife that is either too large or too small. Vegetables that are to be cooked together, whether they are whole or cut, must be the same size to ensure they cook evenly.

Celeriac, artichokes, salsify and scorzonera discolour as soon as they are cut and so must be put immediately into water acidulated with lemon juice or white wine vinegar and cooked in acidulated water. They are often cooked unpeeled, as the skin is easier to remove after cooking.

Asparagus is also cooked in acidulated water, partly to overcome the problem of discolouration, but also for the flavour.

Beetroot must not be peeled or cut before cooking, or its juices will bleed away.

All vegetables must be drained very well after cooking, then refreshed quickly in cold running water to preserve their colour and to stop further cooking. They can then be kept warm in a warm covered dish.

Boiling
Put root vegetables, with the exception of new potatoes, into cold water, bring the water to the boil and time the cooking from boiling point. Put all other vegetables, including new potatoes, into boiling water and time cooking from the moment the water returns to the boil.

Steaming
Place the vegetables in a single layer in the steamer. They should not touch each other. Make sure the water is boiling before placing the vegetables over it. A herb that compliments a vegetable, such as summer savory with broad beans, may be added to the water.

Leafy vegetables such as spinach should not be boiled. They will cook in the few drops that cling to the leaves after they have been washed and shaken dry. Cover the pan and cook the leaves until just tender and 'fallen', shaking the pan occasionally. Uncover the pan and increase the heat to drive off as much excess water as possible. Drain extremely well. Leafy vegetables may also be steamed.

Purées
A good purée is light and delicate with a clear, fresh flavour and a good bright colour. Cook the vegetables for purées beyond the crisp stage but do not allow them to become overcooked or too soft and wet. After refreshing and draining, reduce to a purée in a food processor or blender or pass through a mouli-légumes. For extra smoothness and lightness, the purée can then be sieved.

Drive off any surplus moisture by heating the purée in a clean, preferably non-stick pan until it is dry (some very moist vegetables such as spinach and turnips may also be given a preliminary drying before puréeing).

For really dry purée, leave it to

COOKING TIMES FOR SMALL, YOUNG VEGETABLES		
Vegetables	**Boiling**	**Steaming**
Artichokes (whole)	30-40 minutes	45-55 minutes
Asparagus Tips	3-5 minutes	10-12 minutes
Beans, broad	4 minutes	6-8 minutes
French	3 minutes	7-10 minutes
Beetroot	40-90 minutes	1½-2 hours
Broccoli	4-5 minutes	6-8 minutes
Brussels Sprouts	3-5 minutes	5-10 minutes
Carrots	5-10 minutes	10-15 minutes
Cauliflower florets	2-4 minutes	5-10 minutes
Celeriac	20 minutes	
Courgettes, whole	3-6 minutes	5-9 minutes
sliced	1 minute	3-5 minutes
Cucumber, balls	30 seconds	
turned	30 seconds	
Leek, whole	4-7 minutes	10-15 minutes
sliced	2-3 minutes	5-7 minutes
Mangetouts	30 seconds	4-5 minutes
Peas	2-3 minutes	5 minutes
Potatoes, old	15-20 minutes	20-30 minutes
new	15 minutes	20 minutes
Salsify	20 minutes	25 minutes
Spinach	1-2 minutes	2-5 minutes
Turnips	10-12 minutes	15-20 minutes

drain through a sieve lined with muslin or cheesecloth then twist to remove the last vestiges of water. Over a low heat beat in warm cream and diced butter for lightness and smoothness.

Purées are delicious in themselves, and they can also form the base of other dishes. Prepare them in advance and add cream or butter at the last minute. The easiest way of doing this is to put the purée in a bowl over a saucepan of hot water to heat through gently.

Glazed vegetables
To glaze baby or 'turned' vegetables or chestnuts, melt 15 g/½ oz butter and 1 tbsp sugar in 2-3 tbsp water left over from the cooking of the vegetables. Simmer gently until slightly syrupy. Add the vegetables or nuts and cook, shaking the pan frequently, until they are an even, glossy, light golden colour.

To skin tomatoes
With the point of a sharp knife, make a small cross in the skin in the end opposite the stalk, then quickly lower the tomato into boiling water

PUREES

1 Cook and refresh with iced water.

2 Blend in a food processor.

3 Beat in the diced butter.

4 Blend in warm cream with a wire whisk for lightness and smoothness.

on a slotted spoon or skimmer or in a sieve. Remove after 10-20 seconds depending on the size and ripeness of the tomatoes. Cool the tomatoes immediately in cold water then peel back the skin from the cross.

To prepare concassé tomatoes
Skin the tomatoes and remove the seeds. Cut the flesh into strips, then cut across the strips to make diamond shapes of flesh.

To seed tomatoes
Cut tomatoes horizontally then gently press out the seeds and juice with the thumb. Shake sharply to remove any remaining seeds.

To prepare asparagus
Trim off any woody parts from the stems and cut all the spears to the same length by aligning the tips. Support the spear in the left hand (or right hand, if left handed) with the tip pointing away from you. With a vegetable peeler starting about 3-4 cm/1½ inches away from the tip, remove the little spurs and any coarse fibres.

To prepare artichoke bottoms
Snap off the stalk from the base. Pull the outer leaves outwards from the base, then pull them downwards and off the base. Continue until you reach the pale inner leaves. With a stainless steel knife trim the tops of the inner leaves by one to two thirds and rub the cut edges with lemon juice if they are to be used in a garnish. With the same knife pare away the tough, dark exterior of the base, working in a spiral from the stem. Pull out the central hairy 'choke' and remaining leaves. Rub all the cut surfaces with lemon juice.

To skin peppers
Turn the peppers under a very hot grill until the skin dries out, blackens and blisters. Allow the peppers to cool. The skin will now come away easily.

To turn vegetables
Cut off both ends of the vegetable so they are flat, then trim the sides to make a shape resembling a rectangle. With a small sharp knife trim down the corners to make a smooth oval shape.

TO SKIN TOMATOES

1 Make a small cross in the end. *2 Peel the skin from the cross.*

TO PREPARE ASPARAGUS

1 Trim off any woody parts. *2 Peel away from the tip.*

TO TURN VEGETABLES

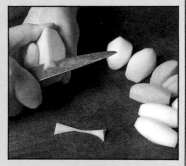

1 Square off the sides. *2 Trim the corners to make an oval.*

TO TURN MUSHROOMS

1 Make a series of cuts. *2 Remove a narrow strip.*

TO PREPARE ARTICHOKE BOTTOMS

1 Snap off the stalk.

2 Trim the inner leaves.

TO CHOP OR CUT INTO DICE

1 Slice the vegetable into strips.

2 Stack and cut across.

TO CHOP AND DICE AN ONION

1 Slice into regular widths.

2 Cut across to make small cubes.

TO SLICE VEGETABLES

1 Trim the sides and ends.

2 Slice to required thickness.

TO MAKE JULIENNE

1 Cut into slices then fine sticks.

To turn mushrooms

Choose large button mushrooms. Wipe the cap if necessary with a damp cloth. Trim the stem level with the cap. With a very sharp knife make a series of cuts, about 6 mm/$\frac{1}{2}$ inch apart following the natural shape of the cap from the top to the edge. Remove a narrow strip from each cut.

To slice vegetables

Cut the sides and ends of the vegetable so that they are flat. Hold the vegetable firmly with the fingertips. Work the knife across the vegetable moving the blade up and down just in front of the fingers and moving the fingers, closely followed by the knife, back for a distance that corresponds to the thickness of the slice required after each cut.

To make julienne

Cut the vegetable into lengthways slices the width of a matchstick. Cut through the slices to form very fine sticks.

To chop or cut into dice

Cut sliced vegetables into strips of the required thickness, as for julienne, stack the strips neatly and cut across them so they fall into small squares.

To chop and dice an onion

Cut the onion in half through to the base. Place one half cut-side downwards on a firm surface and cut down vertically to the width required, using the slicing action described above, and keeping the base intact. Then cut across the first cuts to make cubes, and continue right across the onion.

SAUCES

The foundation of the majority of Cuisine Vivante sauces is a good stock appropriate to the sauce (ie a chicken stock in a sauce to be served with chicken, a game stock for a game dish). Without this it is impossible to achieve the right depth and clarity of flavour, the bright colour, glossy appearance and light consistency. A delicate texture is achieved by boiling the sauce until it is well reduced. This makes the addition of large volumes of cream unnecessary and gives a sauce character and distinction. Reducing times and before and after quantities given in recipes can only be guidelines — there is no substitute for tasting and this must be done frequently as the sauce approaches the right consistency so that adjustments can be made.

Once a sauce has been made it should ideally be served immediately; if it is to be served within about five minutes, stand the saucepan on an asbestos mat over a very low heat. Stir the sauce occasionally and on no account allow it to boil, otherwise it will separate and become oily. The safest way to keep a sauce warm for up to half an hour is to pour it into a bowl, cover the surface closely with clingfilm and place the bowl in a pan of hot water.

ABOVE *To keep a sauce warm put it in a bowl, cover with clingfilm and stand in a pan of hot water.*

Reduction sauce

Stock or wine is usually stirred into the meat or fish cooking juices (a process known as deglazing) so their flavour can be incorporated into the sauce. Before deglazing the pan remove any burnt sediment and pour out excess fat, even if more is to be added later in the form of butter. A buttery sauce is very different from a fatty one. Always boil down wine added to deglaze a pan to concentrate its flavour. Vermouth has a more pronounced flavour and does not need to be boiled down to the same degree, so it is used in smaller quantities. Its characteristic herby note means that it needs to be used selectively.

Puréed vegetables can be incorporated into a sauce to thicken it, to give flavour and a different type of texture. Always sieve a sauce, especially if it contains a purée or small solids such as pieces of shallot, unless the recipe specifies otherwise. Herbs are usually sieved out after they have softened and given up their flavour. Fresh herbs may be scattered over the sauce when it is served to contribute added flavour and texture and for decoration.

Add butter to sauces in small amounts and gradually, to ensure that it melts without turning oily and so is completely incorporated or emulsified into the sauce. Whether the butter is added over a very high heat or, as is more common, over a very low heat, and whether it is stirred, swirled or whisked depends on the texture and appearance required. A smoother more glossy sauce can be obtained by boiling, and a light, creamy one by whisking over a very low heat.

A small amount of butter is often added at the last moment to sauces that are not ostensibly 'butter sauces', just to round off the flavour and give the sauce a sheen.

Beurre blanc

Ingredients
110 g/4 oz butter, unsalted
2 shallots, finely chopped
2 bay leaves
1½ tbsp wine vinegar
1½ tbsp water
1 tbsp double cream

Chill the butter, then cut it into meduim sized cubes. Keep cold. Put the shallot, bay leaves, vinegar and water into a thick bottomed sauté pan or shallow saucepan. Boil slowly until about 2 tbsp liquid remain.

Slowly add the cream. Using a small wire sauce whisk gradually add the butter cube by cube. When the last of the butter is beaten in, the sauce should be warm rather than hot. (As the proportion of fat to vinegar increases, the danger of separating increases if the sauce is too hot.) The process should take about 4 minutes. Sieve the sauce into a warmed bowl.

REDUCTION SAUCE

1 *Pour out excess fat.*

2 *Add the wine to the cooking juices.*

3 *Pour in the stock (appropriate to the sauce).*

4 *Sieve the sauce.*

5 *Add the butter.*

6 *Whisk to the required texture.*

BEURRE BLANC

1 *Add the shallot, bay leaves, vinegar and water.*

2 *Boil, then add the cream.*

3 *Whisk in the butter cubes.*

4 *Sieve into a warm bowl.*

MOUSSELINES

Mousselines are delicate mixtures of puréed raw meat or fish bound with egg white and lightened with cream. They are frequently used in Cuisine Vivante recipes.

Puréeing the flesh by hand is not difficult, but it does take time and effort, as it must be done in a pestle and mortar to obtain the right degree of smoothness. But with a food processor or blender it can be done in moments.

All the ingredients must be cold and it is a good idea to put the food processor bowl in the freezer for about an hour before you begin. Pass the purée through a fine sieve even after using a good processor for a really smooth mixture. This will not be necessary if a certain amount of texture is required in the dish. Salt and lemon juice helps to firm up the flesh. Egg white holds the mixture together, but too much can make it rubbery. Mixtures to be poached are in danger of disintegration and need more egg white than mixtures to be used for stuffings.

Pour the egg white slowly into the purée with the motor of the food processor or blender running. Beat the cream in very gradually by hand, with the bowl standing over ice. It is easier to incorporate the cream when the mixture is cold. Up to three times as much cream as meat or fish can be beaten into a mousseline, but usually Cuisine Vivante recipes call for much less.

Test for seasoning, texture and lightness by poaching a teaspoonful of the mixture in salted water for two minutes on each side. Cut open and taste the cooked mix-

ture. It should have a light, just-set texture and be perfectly smooth and creamy. Chill and cover the mixture for at least 30 minutes before cooking. If necessary it can be prepared a few hours ahead of time. Mousseline mixtures that are to be eaten hot or warm should be served as soon as possible after they have been cooked.

MOUSSELINE

1 Purée the fish or meat.

3 Beat in the cream.

2 Pour in the egg white.

4 Poach a teaspoonful of the mixture in salted water to test for seasoning, texture and lightness.

GARNISHES

A garnish is the final touch, the last detail that completes the picture on the plate. The right garnish adds an interesting facet to the flavour, it enlivens the colour and gives character to an uninteresting shape. It can also provide texture in an otherwise soft dish. It may be an integral part of the dish or it may be something extra; it may be formal or it may be informal, but it must always be edible and complementary. In Cuisine Vivante a garnish is not something that is picked off and put on the side of the plate before the diner begins to eat.

A garnish should never dominate a dish, be too complicated or ornate, or too abundant. It should look fresh, delicate, simple and appropriate as in salmon eggs with salmon or leaves of herbs dotted on a pool of sauce. If a dish is to be served hot, a garnish such as vegetable diamonds or julienne should be heated too, or it will cool down the food.

To prepare garnishes for Cuisine Vivante you need good sharp knives. Additional pieces of equipment that may come in handy are a potato peeler, a mandolin, a canelle knife and aspic cutters.

Don't forget before you start the number of plates to be garnished, so that you can allow enough time to do the job properly.

Garnish theory
◆ Choose a garnish that is a different shade of the colour of the sauce or main ingredient for a toning effect — such as stronger or lighter green.
◆ Blanched rings or fine julienne of a strong coloured vegetable such as red pepper, green leek or mangetout look good on a pale sauce.
◆ Strategically place a single leaf or a small sprig of herbs.
◆ Arrange a few herb leaves in a pattern.
◆ Form blanched vegetables into shapes — small balls or torpedoes.
◆ Make use of feathery leaves, such as dill, fennel or the tops of young carrots to add lightness .
◆ Add fine gratings of orange or lemon peel or stronger strips, perhaps tied into knots or bows.
◆ Knot the tops of spring onions.
◆ Make corkscrews from apple peel.
◆ Stack blanched vegetable julienne into neat piles or heap them informally. Use julienne of different coloured vegetables for greater impact, where this is required.
◆ Tie small bundles of blanched vegetable julienne together with a strip of chive or of blanched red pepper or lemon peel.
◆ Use crescents or other shapes of crisp pastry.
◆ Add small mounds of purée of toning or contrasting colours.

GARNISHES

Cucumber slices
Score the peel with a canelle knife, then cut into slices.

Cucumber rings
Score the peel with a canelle knife and cut into thick slices. Hollow out the slices, cut a slit in the ring that is left and join the rings together like links in a chain.

Cucumber boats
Cut short lengths of cucumber in half and scoop out the core of pips to make boats.

Cucumber diagonals
Canelle the cucumber skin, cut it in half lengthways, remove the seeds and cut slices on diagonal.

Cucumber circles
Canelle the cucumber, cut it into slices and cut out the centres with a small, fluted cutter. Use both the centres and the outer circles for garnishing.

Cucumber cones
Thinly slice the cucumber into rings. Cut each slice from centre to edge. Hold each side and twist to form a cone.

Cucumber knots
Quarter a short length of cucumber lengthways. Remove the seeds and make two cuts in each quarter, one going from the left not quite through to the right, the other one going the other way. Gently ease the 'Z' shape open. Twist the right hand end under the central bar and over the left hand.

SIMPLE GARNISHES

1 Cucumber cones.

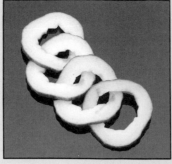

2 Cucumber rings.

3 Carrot rolls.

4 Spring onion tassels.

Cucumber butterfly

Halve the cucumber lengthways. Cut off a ¾-inch piece. Cut into 4 slices but leave a small hinge. Fold the slices back to the hinge to make wings. Repeat for the other side of the butterfly. Make the body by cutting out the seed channel. Place a length of peel on top. Finish with 2 half slices on either side and use 2 quartered slices for the antennae.

Carrot shapes

Cut decorative shapes out of carrot slices with the point of a sharp knife or aspic cutter, or canelle slim carrots before cutting into slices.

Carrot coils

Pare strips of carrot, coil them around your finger, secure with a cocktail stick. Put into iced water. Remove the cocktail stick to serve.

Carrot rolls

Peel strips from a large carrot. Roll each strip to make a curl, secure with a cocktail stick. Put into iced water. Remove the cocktail stick to serve.

CUCUMBER BUTTERFLY

1 Fold slices back making wings.

2 Cut out the seed channel.

3 Quarter a slice to make the antennae.

Carrot flowers
Peel and trim the carrot to a bluntish point at one end. Score the surface with a canelle knife. Peel off the outer layer in a circular motion from the pointed end. Remove the 'flower'.

Tomato roses
Peel the skin from a tomato in a long spiral, as you would an apple. Beginning at the end that was opposite the stem, wind the peel round and round in one continuous strip, winding the centre tightly and the rest more loosely. Secure with a cocktail stick until ready to use.

Tomato tails
Cut a tomato in half lengthways. Place the cut side downwards with a small sharp knife, make a diagonal cut just off from the middle, towards the centre. Make a similar cut in the over side to join the first in the centre to form a wedge. Continue making cuts all the way over the surface. Gently ease the wedges outwards so they are staggered.

Egg
Separate the white and yolk of a hard boiled egg and chop them separately. Arrange them in a pattern.

Spring onion tassels
To make tassels, trim the vegetable at both ends. With the point of sharp knife cut fine, lengthways slits in the green part. Place in iced water for at least 30 minutes until the strips curl. Dry well before using.

Celery sprays
Cut a long fringe at either end of a short length of celery. Cut out the centre from a slice of carrot. Thread the carrot ring into the centre of the piece of celery. Place in a bowl of iced water for about 30 minutes or until the celery curls. Dry well before using.

Courgette fans
To make fans, slice through small, young courgettes lengthways almost to the end 3 or 4 times. Ease the slices apart.

Apple tails (see tomato tails)

COURGETTE FAN	CANELLED SLICES

Slice through and ease apart.	*Score and slice.*

CELERY SPRAYS

	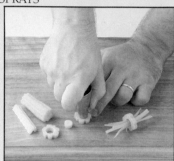
1 'Fringe' a length of celery.	*2 Slice and core the carrot.*

TOMATO TAILS

1 Make cuts from the centre.	*2 'Skin' the wing pieces.*

APPLE TAILS

1 Make cuts from the centre.	*2 Cut 'wing' sections the same way.*

TOMATO ROSES

1 Peel the skin from one end.

3 Wind up the peel into a 'rose'.

2 Continue in a spiral motion.

CARROT FLOWERS

1 Peel the outer layer from the end.

3 Remove the 'flower' from the main section.

2 Continue peeling round the tip.

BASIC RECIPES

The basic recipes contained in this section feature widely in the Cuisine Vivante recipes that follow. Many of them may be made in advance in order to cut the preparation time of the main recipes.

BROWN VEAL STOCK

INGREDIENTS
1 kg/2 lb 2 oz veal knuckle bones and
    trimmings, chopped
1 tbsp oil
1 onion, sliced
1 carrot, sliced
white of 1 leek, chopped
1 stick of celery, sliced
100 g/4 oz mushroom trimmings
150 ml/5 fl oz full-bodied dry white
    wine
450 g/1 lb tomatoes, chopped
bouquet garni of 1 bay leaf, a sprig of
    thyme, 4 parsley stalks and a sprig
    of tarragon

The bones can be browned under a preheated grill if this is more practical.

Heat the oven to 220°C/425°F/Gas 7.

Put the bones and trimmings into a roasting tin, pour the oil over and turn the bones so they are lightly coated. Put in the oven until browned, turning frequently. Stir the onion, carrot, leek and celery into the bones and return to the oven for about 10 minutes until browned. Stir in the mushroom trimmings, then tip the contents of the roasting tin into a large saucepan over a moderate heat. Stir the wine into the roasting tin to dislodge the sediment and boil until reduced by half. Pour into the saucepan. Add the tomatoes, bouquet garni and about 2 L/3½ pt water. Bring to the boil, remove the scum from the surface frequently and simmer gently for 3-4 hours, until the liquid is reduced to about 1 L/1¾ pt.

Pass the stock through a sieve lined with muslin or cheesecloth. Leave to cool, then carefully remove all the fat from the surface.

To make meat glaze
Boil brown veal stock slowly, pouring it into progressively smaller pans, until it is reduced to a thick syrupy consistency.

VEGETABLE STOCK

INGREDIENTS
25 g/1 oz butter
2 shallots, finely chopped
white of one small leek, finely chopped
1 small carrot, finely chopped
2 tbsp finely chopped fennel or 1 tsp
    fennel seeds
2 tomatoes, chopped
bouquet garni of 4 parsley stalks,
    1 bay leaf, a sprig of chervil and a
    sprig of thyme
1 tsp white peppercorns
salt

Heat the butter, add the shallots and leek, cover and cook over a low heat, shaking the pan occasionally, until the shallot is soft.

Stir in the remaining ingredients, cover with water and simmer for 1½—2 hours, removing the scum from the surface frequently.

Pass through a sieve lined with muslin or cheesecloth, leave to cool and remove the fat that comes to the surface.

FISH STOCK

INGREDIENTS
20 g/¾ oz butter
1 onion
white part of 1 leek, chopped
50 g/2 oz mushrooms, chopped
1 kg/1 lb 3 oz fish bones, heads and
*   trimmings, soaked in cold water for*
*   3 hours*
150 ml/¼ pt medium-bodied dry
*   white wine*
bouquet garni of 1 bay leaf, 3 parsley
*   stalks, a sprig of fennel*

Ask the fishmonger for bones. Do not allow the vegetables and bones to brown when they are being fried as this will colour the stock.

―――――――

Heat the butter, add the vegetables, cover and cook over a moderate heat, shaking the pan occasionally for 4-5 minutes. Stir in the fish bones and trimmings and cook, stirring, for 2-3 minutes. Stir in the wine and reduce by half. Add the bouquet garni and about 1.75 litres/3 pt water, bring to the boil, remove the scum from the surface, then simmer for 20 minutes, removing the scum from the surface occasionally.

Pass through a sieve lined with muslin or cheesecloth. Leave to cool, then remove all the fat from the surface.

To make fish glaze
Boil fish stock slowly, pouring it into progressively smaller pans, until it is reduced to a thick syrupy consistency.

CHICKEN STOCK

INGREDIENTS
1 kg/2 lb 3 oz chicken carcasses,
*   necks, wings, feet, giblets except*
*   the liver, or 1 boiling fowl, chopped*
1 pigs trotter or veal knuckle bone,
*   chopped*
1 whole onion, spiked with 2 cloves
1 carrot, sliced
1 stick of celery, sliced
white of 2 leeks, sliced
bouquet garni of 1 bayleaf, 4 parsley
*   stalks, a sprig of thyme and*
*   2 sprigs of chervil*

Pigs trotters and veal knuckles contain plenty of the gelatinous substance necessary for a good jellied stock.

―――――――

Put the chicken carcasses, bones and giblets, or the boiling fowl and the pigs trotter or veal bone into a large saucepan. Cover with cold water and bring to the boil. Carefully skim the scum from the surface, add the vegetables, bouquet garni and about 2 L/3½ pt water. Return to the boil, remove the scum from the surface, then simmer for about 3 hours, removing the scum from the surface frequently.

Pass through a sieve lined with muslin or cheesecloth. Leave to cool, then remove all the fat from the surface.

VEAL STOCK

INGREDIENTS
1 kg/2 lb 3 oz veal knuckle bones,
*   chopped*
1 onion, studded with 1 clove
1 carrot, chopped
white of 1 leek, chopped
1 stick of celery, chopped
bouquet garni of 1 bayleaf, 3 parsley
*   stalks, a sprig of thyme and a sprig*
*   of chervil*

Blanch the bones for 1 minute. Drain, then place in a large saucepan and cover with about 2 L/3½ pt water. Bring to the boil, remove the scum from the surface, add the vegetables and bouquet garni and simmer for 3—4 hours or until the liquid is reduced to about 1 L/1¾ pt.

Pass through a sieve lined with muslin or cheesecloth, leave to cool, then remove all the fat from the surface.

GAME STOCK

INGREDIENTS
1 kg/2 lb 3oz game carcasses, bones
    and trimmings, chopped
1 tbsp oil
1 onion, studded with 2 cloves
1 carrot, chopped
1 stick of celery, chopped
6 juniper berries, crushed
6 coriander seeds, crushed
bouquet garni of 1 bay leaf, 4 parsley
    stalks, a sprig of sage and a sprig of
    thyme
425 ml/¾ pt red wine
1 L/2 pt veal stock

Venison bones can also be used to make game stock, so it is worth asking the game dealer for bones. If the stock is not needed immediately, it can be frozen for future use.

Heat the oven to 220°C/425°F/Gas 7, or heat the grill.

Put the game carcasses, bones and trimmings in a roasting tin. Pour the oil over and turn the bones to coat them lightly. Place in the oven or under the grill until lightly browned.

Tip the contents of the roasting tin into a large saucepan. Over a moderate heat, stir the wine into the roasting tin to dislodge the sediment then boil until reduced by a third.

Pour into the saucepan, add the remaining ingredients, stir in the stock and about 2 L/4 pt water. Bring to the boil, remove the scum from the surface then simmer for 3—4 hours until the liquid is reduced to 1 L/1¾ pt, removing the scum from the surface frequently.

Pass through a sieve lined with muslin or cheesecloth. Leave to cool then remove all the fat from the surface.

COURT BOUILLON

INGREDIENTS
250 ml/9 fl oz medium-bodied dry
    white wine
2 tbsp white wine vinegar
2 carrots, chopped
3 shallots, thinly sliced
white of 1 leek, thinly sliced
bouquet garni of 4 parsley stalks, a
    sprig of thyme, a bay leaf, a small
    sprig of fennel
½ tsp crushed white peppercorns
2 coriander seeds, crushed
salt

Court bouillon is an aromatic, slightly acidulated liquid used for poaching fish and seafood and occasionally vegetables or meat.

Bring the wine, vinegar and 1 L/1¾ pt water to the boil. Add the remaining ingredients, bring to the boil then simmer for 15—20 minutes.

Pass through a sieve.

VINAIGRETTE

INGREDIENTS
2 tsp lemon juice
1 tsp sherry vinegar
1 tsp white wine vinegar
salt and freshly ground black pepper
1½ tbsp olive oil
1 tbsp pure vegetable oil
1 tbsp finely chopped chervil
1 tsp finely chopped parsley

The choice of herbs can be varied according to what is available or what will best compliment other flavours.

Whisk the lemon juice, vinegars and seasoning together.

Very gradually whisk in the oils to make a thick emulsion. Stir in the herbs.

CHICKEN ASPIC

INGREDIENTS (makes 1 L/1¾ pt)
175 g/6 oz chicken, finely chopped
white of 2 leeks, finely chopped
2 sticks of celery, finely chopped
2 carrots, finely chopped
2 shallots, finely chopped
2 egg whites, lightly whisked
2 egg shells, crushed
1.7L/3 pt chicken stock, brought to
* the boil*
3 tbsp gelatine

Mix the chicken, vegetables, egg whites and shells together in a large saucepan. Very gradually pour on the boiling stock, stirring with a balloon whisk. Bring to the boil very slowly, stirring constantly. As soon as boiling point is reached, stop stirring, lower the heat so the stock is gently simmering, and simmer for 1 hour without stirring.

Remove the saucepan from the heat and very carefully remove the scum from the surface. Ladle the stock into a sieve lined with muslin or cheesecloth.

Dissolve the gelatine in 4 tbsp of the liquid in a small bowl placed over a pan of hot water. Stir a little more of the liquid into the gelatine, then strain it into the bulk of the liquid. The aspic is ready to use when it has cooled to the point when it has the consistency of unbeaten egg white.

FISH ASPIC

INGREDIENTS
3 egg whites, lightly whisked
100 g/4 oz white fish, minced
2 shallots, chopped
1 carrot, finely chopped
white of 1 leek, finely chopped
4 button mushroom stalks, finely
* chopped*
10 white peppercorns
4 parsley stalks
1 bay leaf
a small sprig of thyme
¼ tsp tomato purée
juice of 1 lemon
salt
1 L/1¾ pt boiling fish stock
3 tbs gelatine

Mix the egg whites, fish, shallots, carrot, leek, mushroom stalks, peppercorns, parsley stalks, bay leaf, thyme, tomato purée, lemon juice and salt together in a large, heavy-based saucepan. Slowly pour in the boiling fish stock, stirring constantly with a wire whisk. Bring to the boil slowly, stirring.

Reduce the heat, allow the foam to rise, then simmer for 5 minutes. Remove from the heat, cover and leave for 10 minutes.

Make a hole in the surface scum. Carefully ladle out the liquid underneath, taking care to disturb the scum as little as possible, and pour it into a sieve lined with muslin or cheesecloth.

Dissolve the gelatine in 4 tbsp strained stock in a bowl over a saucepan of hot water, then strain into the remaining stock. Stir thoroughly, then leave to cool. Remove any fat that rises to the surface.

Use the aspic when it is on the point of setting and very syrupy.

RED SHELLFISH BUTTER

INGREDIENTS
100 g/4 oz red shellfish shells,
crushed
150 g/5 oz butter, softened
salt
cayenne pepper
cognac

Beat the shells and butter together, then heat very gently, stirring constantly, until a froth rises to the surface. Very carefully pour off the clear liquid beneath the froth into a sieve lined with muslin. Leave to set in a cool place then beat in a little salt, cayenne pepper and cognac.

BASIC NOODLE DOUGH

INGREDIENTS
225 g/8 oz strong plain flour
a pinch of salt
2 eggs, beaten
1 tbsp olive oil

Sieve the flour and salt onto the work surface and form a well in the centre.

Pour the eggs into the well with the oil and about 1 tbsp water. Using the fingertips of one hand draw the flour into the egg and work together to form a soft, but not sticky, pliable dough, adding more water or flour as necessary. Knead thoroughly for 5-10 minutes, until the dough is smooth and elastic and small air bubbles are visible under the surface.

Cover the dough with an inverted bowl and leave to relax at room temperature for at least an hour.

Divide the dough in half. Keep one half covered by the bowl and roll the other half out very thinly on a lightly floured surface using a lightly floured rolling pin and working from the centre to the edge.

Roll out the other half of the dough and leave both sheets to dry for about 15 minutes..

Fold each sheet into a long strip, then slice through the dough at approximately 6 mm/$\frac{1}{4}$ inch intervals along its length with a very sharp knife. Leave to dry for at least an hour draped over a clothes horse or between the backs of two kitchen chairs.

Bring a large saucepan of salted water to the boil, add the noodles, bring the water back to the boil and stir well. The addition of 1 tbsp of oil to the water prevents the noodles sticking together. (If a large amount of pasta is being cooked, add it to the water gradually and bring the water back to the boil after each addition.) Cook for about 3-4 minutes or until the noodles are tender but still resilient.

Tip into a colander, rinse with boiling water and drain.

Once dried, pasta dough can be kept for up to a week if wrapped in polythene and stored in the refrigerator.

INGREDIENTS
225 g/8 oz spinach
a pinch of salt
225 g/8 oz strong plain flour
2 eggs, beaten
1 tbsp olive oil

Green pasta

Cook the spinach for 2-3 minutes in boiling salted water. Drain thoroughly through a sieve, pressing down well on the spinach to extract as much liquid as possible. Purée, then heat in a non-stick saucepan, stirring, to drive off excess moisture.

Prepare the dough in the same way as the Basic noodle dough (above), adding the spinach with the eggs and omitting the water.

Pink pasta

Add 2 tbsp tomato purée to the Basic noodle dough (above) with the eggs and omit the water.

Red pepper pasta

Skin 200 g/7 oz red pepper, purée the flesh and add to the Basic noodle dough (above) with the eggs, omitting the water.

PUFF PASTRY

INGREDIENTS
225 g/8 oz cold butter
225 g/8 oz plain flour
a pinch of salt
1 tsp lemon juice

Puff pastry is easy to make provided everything is kept cool — if butter shows even the slightest sign of oozing through the surface of the dough or out of the sides put the dough immediately into the refrigerator or freezer to harden the fat.

Place the butter between 2 sheets of greaseproof paper or cling film and beat it with a rolling pin until it is soft and malleable. Form it into a square about 1.25 cm/$\frac{1}{2}$ inch thick. If it becomes too soft, chill it.

Sieve the flour and salt together then form into a soft, pliable but not sticky dough with about 8-10 tbsp very cold water and lemon juice. Transfer the dough to a lightly floured surface and knead lightly. Cover and chill for about 30 minutes.

Return the dough to a lightly floured surface, form into a square then roll it out to a square about 6mm/$\frac{1}{4}$ inch thick around the edges with a slightly thicker 'pad' of dough in the centre. Place the butter on the 'pad' and fold the corners of the dough around it so they meet in the centre, like an envelope, and overlap very slightly where they meet.

Gently press the block of dough with the rolling pin at 1.25 cm/$\frac{1}{2}$ inch intervals across its surface until it has grown slightly then roll it out to a rectangle, watching to make sure the butter does not break through the surface or out of the sides. Fold the two ends of the rectangle so they meet in the centre then fold the whole piece in half, like a book. Cover and chill for 30 minutes.

Repeat the rolling and folding 5 times, chilling the dough after each time. Then roll the dough once more before covering and chilling for at least 2 hours.

PUFF PASTRY CRESCENTS (FLEURONS)

Roll out pastry to about 4.5 mm/$\frac{1}{6}$inch thick. Starting at an outer edge cut semi-circles of pastry with a biscuit cutter. Carefully transfer to a baking tray with a fish slice, cover and leave in a cool place for at least 30 minutes.

Meanwhile, heat the oven to 230°C/450°F/Gas 8. Brush the tops of the crescents with beaten egg, taking care not to let any drip down the cut edges. Bake for about 10 minutes until golden brown, well-risen and crisp.

PATE BRISEE

INGREDIENTS
125 g/5 oz plain white flour
a pinch of salt
2 tsp icing sugar
75g/3oz butter
1 egg yolk, beaten

In hot weather, make pastry early in the day when the kitchen is cool. Work quickly and lightly and always leave the rolled out dough in a cool place to relax before baking to prevent shrinkage.

Sift the flour, salt and sugar onto a cold work surface and form a well in the centre.

Pound the butter with a rolling pin to soften it slightly, then chop it roughly.

Put the lumps of butter into the well with the egg yolk, then quickly and lightly blend them together with the fingertips until they are just beginning to come together and look rather like rough scrambled egg.

Sprinkle a little flour over them. Quickly and lightly draw the ingredients together by chopping through them with a cold, round bladed knife whilst at the same time drawing the flour from the edges of the pile into the centre in a smooth flowing action.

When all the flour has been incorporated, draw the mixture into a ball with the fingertips. Cover and chill for at least 30 minutes.

Roll out on a lightly floured surface with a lightly floured rolling pin to about 3mm/$\frac{1}{8}$in and cut as required.

PATE BRISEE TARTLETS

INGREDIENTS
Pastry based on 100 g/4 oz flour will make about 12 tartlets

Roll out the prepared pastry on a lightly floured surface with a lightly floured rolling pin to 3 mm/$\frac{1}{8}$inch thick. Cut out shapes with a lightly floured cutter, about 4 cm/1$\frac{1}{2}$inch. With a fish slice or palette knife carefully transfer the cut-out shapes to patty tins and ease them gently into the shape of the tins, making sure there are no air bubbles trapped underneath. Prick lightly with a fork, cover and chill for 20-30 minutes. Heat the oven to 200°C/400°F/Gas 6.

Bake the tartlet cases for about 10 minutes until crisped and a light golden brown. Leave to cool in the tins for a couple of minutes before removing carefully with a palette knife.

FILO PASTRY

INGREDIENTS (serves 4)
285g/10oz plain flour
pinch of salt
1 egg
150ml/¼pt water
1 tsp oil

Ready-made filo pastry is available from some supermarkets and Greek speciality food shops. It comes ready rolled and in convenient leaves. It can be frozen.

Sift the flour and salt into a bowl.

Beat the egg and add the water and oil. First with a knife and then with one hand mix the water and egg into the flour, adding more water if necessary to make a soft dough.

Beat the past until smooth and elastic. Put it into a clean floured bowl. Cover and leave in a warm place for 15 minutes.

The pastry is now ready for rolling and pulling.

FILO PASTRY TARTLETS

Heat the oven to 200°C/425°F/Gas 7. Brush patty tins with melted butter or oil.

Cut out shapes in sheets of filo pastry with a lightly oiled cutter, about 4 cm/1½inch. With the help of a fish slice or palette knife, carefully transfer half the pastry rounds to the patty tins, easing them gently into the shape. Brush with melted butter or oil then cover with the remaining rounds, again using a fish slice or palette knife. Bake for about 10 minutes until crisp and golden brown. Remove from the patty tins carefully with a palette knife.

CREME PATISSIERE

INGREDIENTS
250 ml/9 fl oz milk
1 vanilla pod
3 egg yolks
85 g/3½ oz sugar
40 g/1½ oz plain flour

If the sauce is not used immediately cover the surface closely with wetted greaseproof paper or cling film to prevent a skin forming.

Pour the milk into a heavy based saucepan, add the vanilla pod and bring slowly to the boil. Remove from the heat, cover and leave to infuse for 15 minutes.

Beat the egg yolks, sugar and flour together.

Remove the vanilla pod from the milk and bring the milk to the boil.

Stir the milk into the egg mixture, pour back into the saucepan then bring slowly to the boil, stirring constantly. Simmer for 2—3 minutes, still stirring.

Strain through a fine sieve.

If it is not to be used immediately, cover the surface closely with greaseproof paper or cling film to prevent a skin forming.

FIRST
COURSES

◆   *First courses serve a dual purpose in that they*
should both whet the appetite and take the edge off
the diner's hunger while not satisfying it completely.
They should flirt with the diner, proffering temptation to
the eye and palate, and they should set the tone for, and
give a preview of, the dishes to come. If so desired, two
first course dishes could, by careful selection, be served in
succession to provide a light meal perhaps ◆
more suitable for the middle of the day.

HERB TARTLETS

INGREDIENTS *(serves 6)*
FOR THE PASTRY
50 g/2 oz cold butter, diced
75 g/3 oz plain flour
a pinch of salt
a pinch of caster sugar
½ egg yolk
50 g/2 oz cream cheese

FOR THE FILLING
7 g/¼ oz butter
1 tbsp finely chopped shallot
¼ crisp lettuce, finely shredded
1½ tbsp mixed finely chopped chives,
*   parsley, tarragon, fennel and*
*   rosemary*
1 tbsp finely grated Parmesan cheese
1 egg, beaten
150 ml/¼ pt single cream
salt and freshly ground black pepper

FOR THE SAUCE
tomato and pepper sauce (see p.93)

FOR THE GARNISH
small sprigs or leaves of herbs

The tartlets can be served individually as suggested in the recipe — with a little sauce on the side — and put at each place setting for the guests when they are at table, or they can be handed round to eat with the pre-prandial drinks. In which case, omit the sauce.

For the pastry, rub the butter into the flour, salt and sugar. Add the egg yolk and cream cheese and quickly and gently bind to a soft dough. Cover and chill for at least 30 minutes.

Roll the pastry out thinly on a lightly floured board with a lightly floured rolling pin. If the dough is a little too sticky to handle roll it out between 2 sheets of cling film, separating the cling film and pastry occasionally to allow the pastry to stretch evenly.

With a lightly floured cutter, cut out circles and use to line tartlet or patty tins. Cover and chill for 30 minutes.

Heat the oven to 190°C/375°F/Gas 5.

Prick the pastry lightly with a fork and bake for 10-15 minutes until lightly coloured and crisp.

Meanwhile, heat the butter for the filling, add the shallot and cook over a moderate heat, stirring occasionally, until soft. Stir in the lettuce and cook for about 30 seconds, stirring. Purée then pass through a fine sieve and mix with the herbs.

Lightly beat the cheese, egg and cream together then stir in the herb mixture. Season.

Spoon into the baked pastry cases. Lower the oven temperature to 180°C/350°F/Gas 4 and bake for about 15 minutes.

Leave the tartlets to cool for a few minutes before removing from the tins. Spoon a little of the tomato and pepper sauce over part of 6 warmed plates. Place a tartlet to one side and garnish with herbs.

SMOKED SALMON FLOWERS

INGREDIENTS *(serves 4)*
120 ml/8 tbsp cold fish aspic (see
*   p.77)*
4 small, wafer-thin slices of smoked
*   salmon*
4 tsp caviar
4 long chives or julienne of the green
*   part of leek, blanched*
8 smaller chives or julienne of the
*   green part of leek, blanched*
8 petal shapes of lemon peel
8 small coriander or flat parsley
leaves

A 'picture on a plate' with which to welcome each guest to their place at table.

Spoon the aspic over 4 medium sized cold plates and leave until just on the point of setting.

Fold the sides of the slices of smoked salmon under and shape each slice into circles. Lightly put in position towards the edge of each plate. Make a well in the centre of each piece of salmon. Place a little caviar in each well to form the centres of the flowers.

Make a stem for the flower from the long chives or julienne

of leek and make leaves from the shorter pieces.

Place the petal shapes of lemon below the smoked salmon and the coriander or flat parsley leaves at the base of the stems. Leave in a cool place.

CHEESE POUCHES

INGREDIENTS (per pouch)
2 sheets of filo pastry, approximately
    12.5 cm/5 inches square
melted butter
1 cube of soft mild goats cheese
2 tsp chopped pecans or walnuts
oil for deep frying
thin strip of green part of leek,
    blanched

Allow one pouch per person if these tasty morsels are to be handed round with pre-prandial drinks — and do provide napkins and plates. Allow two or three per person if they are to be served as a first course.

————————

Brush one side of one piece of pastry with melted butter. Place the other sheet on top. Place the cheese and nuts in the centre.

Fold the corners of the pastry over the filling and twist them round so they are sealed and stand at right angles to the filling.

Heat a deep fat frying pan of oil to about 190°C/375°F. Lower the pouches into the oil and fry for about 3 minutes until crisp and golden brown. Serve hot with a thin strip of leek tied around the neck.

MUSHROOMS FILLED WITH TOMATO

MOUSSETTES

INGREDIENTS (serves 4)
150 g/5 oz mushroom caps
flesh of 4 large tomatoes
1 tbsp tomato purée
1 tbsp medium-bodied dry white wine
1 tsp gelatine
150 ml/¼ pt double cream, lightly
    whipped
salt and freshly ground black pepper
very small basil leaves or finely
    shredded basil

Blanch the mushroom caps in lightly acidulated, seasoned water. Drain very well then dry on absorbent paper.

Purée the tomato flesh with the tomato purée and wine in a liquidizer, then simmer gently for about 5 minutes. Leave to cool slightly.

Dissolve the gelatine in 1½ tbsp water in a small bowl placed over a pan of hot water. Remove from the heat and cool slightly.

Blend the gelatine into the tomato and leave to cool placed over a bowl of iced water. Stir occasionally.

When almost set, gently fold in the cream. Season.

Spoon tomato mixture onto individual mushroom caps. Leave in a cool place.

Place very small basil leaves or finely shredded basil on top of each moussette to serve.

OPPOSITE *Artichoke mousse in smoked salmon*
Recipe: page 88
ABOVE *Seviche of salmon*
Recipe: page 89

GINGER AND LIME SORBET

WITH MELON

INGREDIENTS (serves 4)
3—4 Ogen or Charentais melons,
*   lightly chilled*

FOR THE SORBET
200 g/7 oz sugar
finely grated rind of 1 lime
1 tbsp very finely chopped fresh root
*   ginger*
juice of 3 limes, strained

FOR THE GARNISH
small lettuce or watercress leaves
julienne of lime peel, knotted and
*   blanched*
pieces of lime

Picture: page 90

To taste the full fresh, clean glory of this sorbet do not pre-pare it more than a few hours in advance. It will then make a delicious, light refreshing first course.

For the sorbet, gently heat the sugar in 250 ml/9 fl oz water, stirring until dissolved. Add the lime rind and ginger and leave over a very low heat, covered for 15 minutes. Stir in the lime juice and leave to cool.

Pour the syrup into a shallow metal container. Chill for an hour and then cover and place in the freezer until firm, turning the mixture into a cold bowl and whisking well with a cold whisk every 45 minutes. Alternatively, freeze in a sorbetière for 10—12 minutes then transfer to a container, cover and leave in the freezer.

About 30 minutes before serving, transfer the sorbet to the refrigerator.

Cut the melons into halves; the number of melons to use depends on their size. Scoop out the seeds and cut the flesh into slices. Carefully remove the skin from the slices.

Arrange the slices of melon on 4 cold plates. Add scoops of the sorbet, the lettuce or watercress leaves, julienne of lime and pieces of lime.

ARTICHOKE MOUSSE IN

SMOKED SALMON

INGREDIENTS (serves 4)
4-6 slices of smoked salmon

FOR THE MOUSSE
2 large artichokes
a squeeze of lemon juice
1 tsp gelatine
1 tbsp dry white wine
salt and freshly ground white pepper
150 ml/¼ pt double cream

FOR THE SAUCE
2 tbsp finely chopped shallots
4 tbsp tarragon vinegar
50 g/2 oz butter, diced
1 tbsp crème fraîche
200 g/7 oz fromage blanc
salt and freshly ground white pepper

Trim the artichokes, then cook in salted, acidulated, boiling water for about 40-45 minutes until tender.

Remove the artichokes and leave upside down to drain. Pull off the leaves, (reserve some for the garnish) and scrape their flesh into a bowl. Discard the hairy choke, chop the base and add to the bowl.

Dissolve the gelatine in the wine and 2 tbsp water in a small bowl placed over a pan of hot water. Remove from the heat.

Purée the artichoke flesh with the seasoning, then mix in the gelatine. Cover and leave in a cool place until very lightly set.

Meanwhile, line 4 ramekin dishes with the slices of smoked salmon, leaving sufficient overlapping the sides of each one to fold over the tops.

Lightly whip the cream, then gently fold into the artichoke mixture. Check the seasoning and add a little lemon juice, if

FOR THE GARNISH
artichoke leaves
tarragon leaves
radicchio leaves
slices of courgette with carrot
sprigs of dill

Picture: page 86

necessary. Divide between the ramekins and fold the overlapping smoked salmon over.

Cover and leave in a cool place to set.

For the sauce, boil the shallots in the vinegar until nearly all the liquid has evaporated. Very gradually stir in the butter, making sure each piece is completely incorporated before adding the next. Stir in the crème fraîche. Remove from the heat, leave to cool slightly. Then stir in the fromage blanc. Season.

Unmould the smoked salmon parcels onto 4 cold plates, preferably oval. Arrange 4 or 5 artichoke leaves in a circle to the side of the smoked salmon and place a small spoonful of the dressing in the centre. Garnish the dressing with tarragon leaves. Add radicchio leaves, slices of courgette with carrot and sprigs of dill.

SEVICHE OF SALMON

INGREDIENTS (serves 4)
500 g/1¼ lb skinless salmon fillets, chilled
100 ml/4 fl oz lime juice
175 ml/6 fl oz lemon juice
½ red chilli, seeded
1 bunch of fresh coriander
3 avocados
3 tbsp crème fraîche
2½ tbsp thyme or tarragon vinegar
1 tbsp Dijon mustard
2 tbsp red pepper, cut into julienne
2 tbsp green pepper, cut into julienne
2 tbsp chopped shallot
salt
a squeeze of lemon juice

FOR THE GARNISH
strips of red and green peppers, blanched
slices of lemon

Picture: page 87

The origins of this dish are rooted in the traditional cuisine of South America.

Cut the salmon into 3mm/⅛ in thick slices, about 2.5cm/1 inch square, then lay them in a large shallow dish.

Mix the lime and lemon juice, chilli and the stems from the coriander together and pour over the salmon. Cover and leave in a cool place for 4—5 hours.

Drain off the marinade.

Purée the flesh from one avocado and mix with the marinade, crème fraîche, vinegar, 1½ tbsp finely chopped coriander leaves, mustard, peppers, shallot and salt. Pour over the salmon and leave for 10—15 minutes.

Peel and slice the remaining avocados. Brush with lemon juice, then arrange in fan shapes on 6 cold plates. Add the salmon slices.

Adjust the seasoning of the dressing if necessary and spoon a little over the salmon. Garnish with strips of red and green peppers and slices of lemon.

OPPOSITE
*Ginger and lime
sorbet with melon*
Recipe: page 88
ABOVE *Crab and fine julienne of
vegetables set in light aspic*
Recipe: page 93

PEAR VINAIGRETTE WITH SMOKED

SALMON MOUSSE

INGREDIENTS (serves 6)
3 ripe pears
150 ml/¼ pt white wine vinegar
50 ml/2 fl oz fruity dry white wine
10 mint leaves
10 tarragon leaves
salt and freshly ground white pepper

FOR THE MOUSSE
40 ml/1½ fl oz full-bodied dry white
    wine
½ bay leaf
65 ml/2½ fl oz fish stock
1 tsp black peppercorns, crushed
pinch of cayenne pepper
1¼ tsp lime or lemon juice
150 g/5 oz smoked salmon, skinned
    and boned
1 rounded tsp gelatine
175 ml/6 fl oz crème fraîche, lightly
    whipped

FOR THE GARNISH
radicchio lettuce
mint and tarragon leaves

Picture: page 94

Peel, core and slice the pears. Place them in a sauteuse or large frying pan, add the vinegar, wine, mint, tarragon, salt and pepper and water to cover if necessary. Poach for 5—10 minutes until just opaque. Leave to cool in the liquid, then remove with a slotted spoon and drain well. Reserve the liquor.

For the mousse, boil the wine, bay leaf, stock, peppercorns, cayenne pepper and lime or lemon juice until reduced by half. Pass through a strainer.

Purée the smoked salmon in a food processor or blender.

Dissolve the gelatine in 2 tbsp water in a bowl placed over a pan of hot water. Remove from the heat, leave to cool slightly, then stir in the reduced liquid.

Mix the gelatine mixture into the salmon, then fold in the crème fraîche. Season, then spoon into lightly oiled individual moulds. Cover and leave to set.

Unmould the mousses onto cold plates. Arrange the slices of pear around and spoon a little of the poaching liquor over them. Garnish with radicchio lettuce, mint and tarragon leaves.

FILLET DE BOEUF CRU

INGREDIENTS (serves 6)
120 ml/4¼ fl oz lemon juice
100 ml/4 fl oz olive oil
3 tbsp finely chopped shallots
2 tbsp finely chopped parsley
2 tbsp finely chopped watercress
1 tbsp finely chopped tarragon
1 tbsp finely chopped basil
1 tbsp finely chopped chervil
salt and pepper
450 g/1 lb fillet of beef, chilled in the
    freezer, wrapped in foil, for about
    an hour

FOR THE GARNISH
1 carrot, cut into julienne
6 spring onion tassels (see p.71),
    halved
7.5 cm/3 inch piece of celery, cut into
    julienne

The secret of getting really wafer-thin slices of beef lies with chilling the meat briefly in the freezer and using a long bladed, razor-sharp knife.

Mix the first 9 ingredients together in a blender. Chill.

Slice the beef as thinly as possible across the grain with a very sharp knife. Beat each slice separately between two sheets of cling film. Lay the slices on 6 cold plates.

Trickle the dressing over the slices of beef to form a pattern, then garnish with the vegetables. Serve any remaining dressing separately.

E G G S   B E H I N D   B A R S

INGREDIENTS (serves 4)
4 carrots, sliced in 5 mm/¼ in wide
    strips
65 g/2½ oz French beans, trimmed
50 g/2 oz thickly sliced smoked
    salmon, cut into 5 mm/¼ in wide
    strips
4 sprigs of chervil
butter
3 eggs, beaten
225 ml/8 fl oz double cream
finely grated rind of ½ lemon
salt and freshly ground black pepper

FOR THE SAUCE
2 tbsp olive oil
3 shallots, finely chopped
1 clove of garlic, crushed
1 large Mediterranean-type tomato,
    chopped
1 large red pepper, skinned and
    chopped
bouquet garni of a sprig of thyme,
    ½ bay leaf, 3 parsley stalks, a sprig
    of basil
salt and freshly ground black pepper
½-1 tsp tomato purée
pinch of sugar

FOR THE GARNISH
sprigs of chervil

Picture: page 95

Heat the oven to 170°C/325°F/Gas 3.

Cook the carrots and beans separately in simmering salted water until just tender. Refresh and drain very well.

Cut the carrots, beans and smoked salmon to the same height as a dariole mould. Place a sprig of chervil in the bottom of each of 4 well-buttered dariole moulds. Stand 2 strips of carrot inside each mould and press them well into the butter. Place 2 beans next to the carrots and 2 strips of smoked salmon next to the beans. Repeat until the moulds are completely lined.

Lightly beat the eggs with the cream, lemon rind and seasoning. Strain into the moulds, place the moulds in a baking or roasting tin and surround with boiling water. Cover the moulds and place in the oven for about 40 minutes until lightly set.

Heat the oil for the sauce, add the shallots and garlic and cook over a very low heat, stirring occasionally, until soft. Stir in the tomatoes, pepper and bouquet garni. Add 6-7 tbsp water to cover. Season, cover the pan and simmer for 20-30 minutes. Remove the bouquet garni and pass the tomato mixture through a sieve. If necessary, add a little tomato purée to give a good colour and adjust the flavour with a pinch of sugar. Reheat gently.

Remove the moulds from the heat and leave to stand for about 2 minutes before unmoulding towards the side of 4 warmed plates. Spoon a crescent of sauce around the moulds and garnish with sprigs of chervil.

 C R A B   A N D   F I N E   J U L I E N N E   O F

V E G E T A B L E S   S E T   I N   L I G H T   A S P I C

INGREDIENTS (serves 4)
300 ml/1½ pt fish aspic (see p.77)
150 g/5 oz cooked white crab meat,
    shredded
25 g/1 oz fine julienne of white of
    leek, blanched
25 g/1 oz fine julienne of celery,
    blanched
25 g/1 oz fine julienne of peeled,
    seeded cucumber
25 g/1 oz finely diced tomato flesh

Picture: page 91

Spoon a very thin layer of aspic over 4 cold plates then carefully arrange the garnish in the aspic. Leave to set.

Spoon a little aspic into a small decorative mould then twist and turn the mould around to coat the sides and base in aspic. Repeat with 3 more moulds.

Spoon a little of the remaining aspic into a small bowl, add the crab meat and stir it around gently until it is lightly coated. Remove, with a slotted spoon, allowing excess aspic to drain off.

Place some of the crab in the base of each mould. Coat the vegetables in aspic with the same method used for the crab, then arrange some on top of the crab. Repeat the layering until all the crab and vegetables have been used up. Fill the moulds with any remaining aspic. Leave the moulds to set.

Just before serving, unmould the moulds onto the plates.

Pear vinaigrette with smoked salmon
mousse
Recipe: page 92

Eggs behind bars
Recipe: page 93

EGGS WITH LETTUCE AND SORREL

AND CHAMPAGNE SAUCE

INGREDIENTS (serves 4)
40 g/1½ oz butter, diced
1 shallot, finely chopped
75 g/3 oz finely shredded Iceberg
    lettuce
50 g/2 oz finely shredded sorrel
25 g/1 oz finely shredded spinach
150 ml/5 fl oz dry white wine
50 ml/2 fl oz veal or chicken stock
75 ml/3 fl oz double cream
salt and freshly ground black pepper
4 eggs
champagne sauce (see p.156)

FOR THE GARNISH
individual watercress leaves
caviar
radicchio leaves

Picture: page 98

Heat half the butter, add the shallot, cover and cook over a moderate heat, shaking the pan occasionally until soft. Stir in the lettuce, sorrel and spinach, wine and stock. Cook over a moderate heat until the spinach and sorrel have nearly fallen and are almost tender but the lettuce still has some texture, then increase the heat and boil rapidly until the excess liquid has evaporated. Stir in the cream and simmer for 2—3 minutes, then lower the heat and swirl in the remaining butter. Season.

Meanwhile, poach the eggs in a large shallow pan of salted, acidulated water until the yolks are slightly set. Carefully remove with a slotted spoon and drain on a cloth. Cut to a neat shape with a plain biscuit cutter.

Gently warm the champagne sauce.

Divide the lettuce mixture between 4 warmed plates. Place the eggs on top and spoon the champagne sauce around. Garnish the egg yolks with a little caviar and arrange the watercress and radicchio leaves around the outside edge of the sauce.

SLICES OF CUCUMBER FILLED WITH

TROUT MOUSSE

INGREDIENTS (serves 4)
225g/8 oz trout fillets
a squeeze of lemon juice
1 egg, separated
salt and freshly ground white pepper
4 tbsp double cream
1 tbsp red shellfish butter, softened
    (see p.77)
1 long straight cucumber, peeled,
    trimmed and cut into 3 even
    lengths

FOR THE SAUCE
2 tbsp finely chopped shallot
flesh of 3 tomatoes, chopped
a sprig of fennel
100ml/4 fl oz medium-bodied fruity
    dry white wine
225ml/8 fl oz vegetable stock
150ml/¼pt crème fraîche
salt and freshly ground white pepper

If shellfish butter is not available, use 1-2 tsp tomato purée. Although the flavour will suffer slightly it will still be a delicious, light first course

Purée the trout in a food processor or blender until smooth, then mix in the lemon juice, egg yolk and seasoning, until smooth. Add the cream, then the egg white and shellfish butter, mixing well until smooth. Chill for about an hour.

With an apple corer, remove the seeds from the cucumber and sufficient flesh to leave a ring of cucumber about 5mm/¼ inch thick, and leave to dry on absorbent paper.

Place each piece of cucumber on a piece of foil, fill with the trout mixture then enclose in foil, securing the seams well.

Place the foil parcels in a saucepan, cover with water and simmer for 30 minutes.

Remove the parcels from the pan, open them and carefully drain off any moisture. Leave to cool completely, then chill.

For the sauce, boil the shallots with the tomatoes and fennel in the wine and stock until reduced to 150ml/¼pt.

Remove the fennel, liquidize the sauce, then pass through a sieve into a clean saucepan. Stir in the crème fraîche and simmer until slightly thickened. Season, leave to cool then chill.

About 15 minutes before serving return the cucumber to room temperature. Cut each length of cucumber into 4, making 12 rings.

Divide the sauce between 4 cold plates. Arrange 3 slices of cucumber with the diamonds of tomato and sprigs of dill in the sauce.

FOR THE GARNISH
diamond shapes of tomato flesh
sprigs of dill

MUSSEL TERRINE

INGREDIENTS (serves 6—8)
450 g/1lb mussels in their shells
75 ml/3 fl oz dry white wine
1 tsp chopped parsley
1 tsp chopped chives
450 g/1lb turbot, chopped and chilled
salt
lemon juice
2 egg whites
425 ml/15 fl oz double cream, chilled
freshly ground white pepper
1 green pepper, blanched and diced
12 spinach leaves, trimmed and
   blanched
100 g/4 oz cooked prawns, shelled

FOR THE SAUCE
flesh of 4 ripe tomatoes
1 tbsp tarragon vinegar
1½ tbsp olive oil
1 tsp tomato purée
pinch of sugar
salt and freshly ground white pepper

FOR THE GARNISH
coriander or flat parsley leaves
tomato 'roses' (see p.71)

Picture: page 99

The underrated mussel comes into its own in this terrine, at its best made in late autumn or winter, when mussels are in their prime. Use French bouchots for preference.

Cook the mussels with the wine and herbs in a covered, heavy based pan over a high heat for about 5 minutes, shaking the pan frequently, until they open. Discard any that remain closed and remove the others from their shells. Dry on absorbent paper.

Blend the turbot in a food processor, then mix in the salt and lemon juice followed by the egg whites. Pass through a sieve into a bowl placed over a bowl of ice, then gradually work in the cream. Add white pepper, cover and chill for 30 minutes.

Heat the oven to 150°C/300°F/Gas 2. Line the base of a terrine with buttered greaseproof paper.

Divide the turbot mixture into two thirds and one third. Fold the green pepper into the larger portion and spread half of this in the base of the terrine. Cover with half the spinach leaves and lay half the mussels over them. Fold the prawns into the remaining turbot mixture and carefully spread over the mussels. Place the remaining mussels on top, followed by the remaining spinach leaves. Spread the remaining green pepper mixture over the spinach leaves.

Cover with buttered greaseproof paper and stand the terrine in a roasting or baking tin. Pour in boiling water to surround the terrine and place in the oven for 1 hour.

Purée the tomatoes, vinegar and oil for the sauce, then add the tomato purée, sugar and seasoning to taste and to adjust the colour. Purée again and chill.

Leave the terrine to cool slightly before unmoulding.

Cut the terrine into slices, place one on each plate and place a spoonful of the sauce to the side. Garnish with coriander or flat parsley leaves and tomato 'roses'.

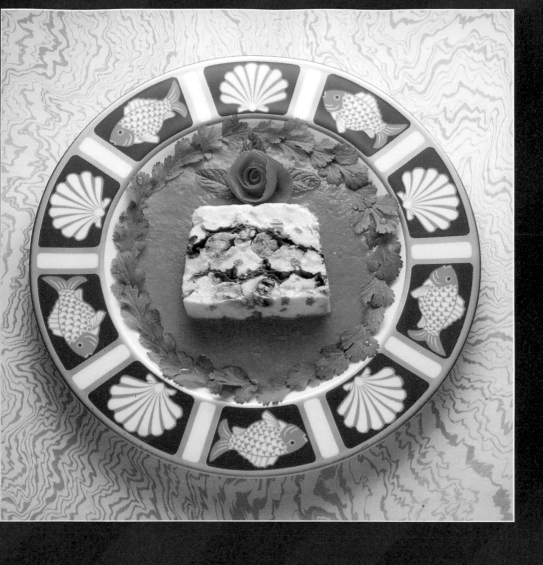

Mussel terrine
Recipe: page 97

OYSTER AND COURGETTE

CROUSTADES

INGREDIENTS (serves 4)
6 sheets of filo pastry (see p.81)
melted butter
8 oysters
100 ml/4 fl oz dry white wine
1 tbsp finely chopped shallot
200 ml/7 fl oz fish stock
25 ml/1 fl oz dry vermouth
100 ml/4 fl oz double cream
a few strands of saffron
50 g/2 oz butter, diced and softened
sea salt and freshly ground white
* pepper*
2 small courgettes, blanched and
* thinly sliced*

FOR THE GARNISH
small sprigs of thyme
finely diced concassé tomatoes
or red and black lumpfish roe and
* salmon eggs*

Picture: page 103

Scallops may be substituted for oysters and should be prepared and served in the same way — poach the bodies for 1 minute, turn them over, add the corals and poach for another minute.

Heat the oven to 220°C/420°F/Gas 7.

Fold the sheets of filo in half and cut out a circle from each piece using a plain cutter. Line 4 individual tartlet tins with 3 circles, one on top of the other, brushing with melted butter in between.

Bake for about 8 minutes until crisp and golden.

Meanwhile, open the oysters, (see p.61), reserving the liquor, and cut into halves.

Heat the wine, add the shallots and reduce by half. Lower the heat, add the oysters and poach for 15 seconds.

Carefully transfer the oysters to a warmed dish with a slotted spoon. Cover.

Add the stock and vermouth to the poaching liquor and reduce to 2 tbsp. Stir in the oyster liquor, cream and saffron and simmer until slightly thickened.

Pass through a sieve. Reheat gently without boiling and gradually whisk in 40g/1½ oz of butter, making sure each piece is completely incorporated before adding the next. Season.

Heat the remaining butter. Carefully and briefly toss in the courgette slices to warm through.

Put the oysters in the sauce for a few seconds to warm them, then place them in the centre of the croustades. Arrange the courgette slices around the sides, pour a little of the sauce over the oysters and garnish with the thyme and tomato dice or lumpfish roe and salmon eggs.

COURGETTE AND TOMATO MOUSSES

INGREDIENTS (serves 6)

FOR THE TOMATO MOUSSE
25 g/1 oz butter, diced
2 shallots, finely chopped
½ carrot, finely chopped
flesh of 3 tomatoes, chopped
bouquet garni of a sprig of parsley, a
    sprig of thyme, 1 bay leaf, a small
    sprig of rosemary
scant 2 tsp gelatine
2 tbsp finely chopped mixed herbs
salt and freshly ground black pepper
100 ml/4 fl oz whipping cream,
    lightly whipped

FOR THE COURGETTE MOUSSE
65 g/2½ oz butter, diced
25 g/1 oz courgettes, cut into
    1.2 cm/½ in dice
salt and freshly ground black pepper
1 shallot, finely chopped
2 tbsp finely chopped mixed herbs
scant 2 tsp gelatine
100 ml/4 fl oz whipping cream,
    lightly whipped
3 courgettes, finely chopped

FOR THE SALADS
1 tbsp olive oil
1 tsp red wine vinegar
1 tsp finely chopped chives
salt and freshly ground black pepper
1—2 leaves of curly endive

The salad in this recipe can be changed, and the mousse mixture made separately, perhaps to serve as a very light first course for 3 or 4 people.

Heat the butter for the tomato mousse, add the shallots and carrot and cook over a low heat, stirring frequently, until soft. Stir in the tomatoes and bouquet garni and simmer, stirring occasionally, for 25-30 minutes until reduced to 225 ml/8 fl oz.

Dissolve the gelatine in 2 tbsp water in a bowl placed over a pan of hot water. Remove from the heat and leave to cool slightly.

Remove the bouquet garni from the tomato mixture, then purée the mixture. Add the herbs and seasoning.

Blend a little of the tomato mixture with the gelatine, then mix this back into the remaining tomato mixture. Leave until just approaching setting point, stirring frequently.

Meanwhile, for the courgette mousse, heat 15 g/½ oz butter. Add the diced courgette and cook over a moderate heat, stirring occasionally for about 2 minutes. Remove with a slotted spoon, drain on absorbent paper. Season.

Heat the remaining butter, add the shallot, cover and cook over a moderate heat, shaking the pan occasionally until the shallot is soft. Add the chopped courgettes and cook until the moisture has evaporated, stirring frequently. Purée — there should be 225 ml/8 fl oz. If necessary, cook further to evaporate more moisture. Add the herbs and seasoning.

Dissolve the gelatine in 2 tbsp water in a bowl over a pan of hot water. Remove from the heat and cool slightly.

Blend a little of the courgette purée with the gelatine, then mix back into the remaining purée. Leave until approaching setting point.

Lightly fold the cream into the thickening tomato mixture and divide between 6 oiled, decorative moulds.

Lightly fold the cream and diced courgettes into the courgette mixture. Spoon into the moulds and stir through the two mixtures a few times to give a light marbled effect. Cover and leave to set.

Whisk the olive oil, vinegar, chives and seasoning together for the garnish. Arrange a little curly endive on the side of 6 cold plates. Spoon the dressing over. Unmould the mousses onto the plates.

ABOVE *Brawn of salmon*
Recipe: page 104
OPPOSITE *Oyster and courgette croustades*
Recipe: page 100

A S P A R A G U S   G A T E A U X

INGREDIENTS (serves 6)
450 g/1 lb green asparagus, trimmed
3 eggs
2 egg yolks
450 ml/¾ pt single cream
pinch of nutmeg
salt

FOR THE SAUCE
1 tbsp coriander seeds, crushed
225 ml/8 fl oz dry white wine
150 ml/4 fl oz dry vermouth
150 ml/¼ pt single cream
150 g/5 oz butter, diced
salt and freshly ground black pepper

FOR THE GARNISH
36 asparagus tips, steamed
12 strips of blanched red pepper
sprigs of chervil

Picture: page 106

Steam the asparagus for about 8 minutes, until tender.

Heat the oven to 180°C/350°F/Gas 4.

Purée the asparagus, then pass through a fine sieve. Heat the purée, gently stirring to drive off any excess moisture.

Remove from the heat. Blend the eggs, egg yolks and cream together, then stir into the asparagus. Add a pinch of nutmeg and seasoning.

Divide between 6 buttered ramekin dishes. Place the dishes in a roasting or baking tin and surround with boiling water. Cover with greaseproof paper.

Place in the oven for about 20 minutes until lightly set.

Meanwhile, lightly toast the coriander seeds in a dry non-stick pan for 2—3 minutes. Simmer with the wine and vermouth for 5 minutes, then reduce to 10ml/1½ fl oz. Stir in the cream and simmer for 2—3 minutes, then pass through a sieve. Return to the rinsed pan and reheat, then reduce the heat to low and gradually stir in the butter dice, making sure that each piece is completely incorporated before adding the next. Season and keep warm, but do not allow to boil.

Remove the gâteaux from the heat and leave for a few minutes before unmoulding onto 6 warmed plates. Spoon a circle of sauce around the gâteaux and garnish with the asparagus tips, red pepper and chervil.

B R A W N   O F   S A L M O N

INGREDIENTS (serves 4)
10 oysters
200 g/7 oz salmon fillet, cut into
    2 cm/¾ inch wide strips
150 ml/5 fl oz dry white wine
150 ml/5 fl oz fish stock
1½ tbsp chopped parsley
salt and freshly ground black pepper
scant 1½ tsp gelatine
⅓ tbsp chopped tarragon
½ tbsp chopped chervil
2 hard-boiled eggs, yolks and whites
    coarsely chopped
1½ lemons, rind cut into small squares
50 g/2 oz red pepper, blanched and
    diced
2 heaped tsp green peppercorns

FOR THE GARNISH
slices of lime
coriander leaves
red pepper sauce (see p.93), for
    serving

Picture: page 102

Remove the oysters from their shells and marinade with the salmon in the wine, stock, parsley and seasoning for 1 hour in a shallow dish covered with cling film.

Remove the salmon and oysters from the marinade with a slotted spoon and drain well. Strain the marinade.

Soften the gelatine in a little of the marinade. Gently warm the remaining marinade, then stir into the gelatine until dissolved. Cool quickly, then chill until syrupy.

Pour a thin layer of the syrupy gelatine over the base of a terrine and sprinkle some of the tarragon, chervil, egg, lemon rind, red pepper and peppercorns over. Arrange some of the salmon strips lengthways on top. Cover and chill.

Repeat the layering, adding the oysters when half the ingredients have been used.

Cover and chill for 24 hours.

Unmould onto a chilled plate and carefully cut into slices. Place the slices on cold plates and garnish with slices of lime and coriander leaves. Serve with a little red pepper sauce.

TRIPLE VEGETABLE TIMBALES

INGREDIENTS *(serves 4)*
FOR THE CARROTS
175 g/6 oz young carrots, chopped
a pinch of sugar
salt
40 ml/1½ fl oz double cream
15 g/½ oz butter
white pepper
1½ small egg whites, lightly whisked

FOR THE TURNIPS
250 g/9 oz baby turnips, peeled
salt
50 ml/2 fl oz double cream
freshly ground white pepper
a pinch of cayenne
1½ small egg whites, lightly whisked

FOR THE BROCCOLI
200 g/7 oz broccoli florets
salt
50 ml/2 fl oz double cream
freshly ground black pepper
grated nutmeg
1½ small egg whites, lightly whisked

FOR THE SAUCE
lemon sauce (see p.108)

FOR THE GARNISH
broccoli florets
julienne of carrot
baby turnips, turned

All the vegetables can be cooked and puréed in advance and all the other ingredients weighed out so that there is little to do to complete this first course.

Heat the oven to 180°C/350°F/Gas 4.

Cook the carrots with the sugar in simmering salted water until soft. Drain well, purée, then mix in the cream and butter. Add white pepper and fold in the egg whites. Spoon into 4 buttered moulds.

Cook the turnips in simmering salted water until tender. Drain well, purée, then mix in the cream, freshly ground white pepper, and a pinch of cayenne pepper. Fold in the egg whites and spoon into 4 small buttered moulds.

Cook the broccoli in simmering salted water until just tender. Drain well, purée, then mix in the cream, pepper and nutmeg. Fold in the egg whites and spoon the mixture into 4 small buttered moulds.

Place all the moulds in a roasting or baking tin. Surround with boiling water, cover the moulds with buttered greaseproof paper and place the tin in the oven for about 20 minutes until the custards are just set.

Meanwhile, prepare the lemon sauce and blanch, refresh and drain the vegetables for the garnish.

Remove the moulds from the heat and leave to cool slightly before unmoulding onto 4 warmed plates. Spoon the sauce to one side of the moulds and decorate the other side of the plates with the vegetables.

CHICKEN LIVER CUSTARDS

INGREDIENTS *(serves 6)*
300 ml/½ pt double cream
300 g/10 oz chicken livers, trimmed
3 eggs
2 egg yolks
pinch of freshly grated nutmeg
salt and freshly ground black pepper
225 g/8 oz French beans

FOR THE GARNISH
fresh tomato purée (see p.302)
broccoli florets

Picture: page 107

Heat the oven to 180°C/350°F/Gas 4.

Slowly bring the cream to simmering point.

In a food processor or blender, purée the chicken livers, eggs, egg yolks, nutmeg and seasoning, then, with the motor running, slowly pour in the cream. Pass through a fine sieve, then pour into 6 individual buttered ramekin dishes or dariole moulds. Place the dishes or moulds in a roasting or baking tin, pour boiling water around them, cover and place in the oven for 35—40 minutes.

Blanch the beans and the broccoli florets for the garnish separately. Refresh and drain well. Gently warm the purée.

Leave the custards to stand for a few minutes before turning them out onto warmed plates. Spoon a very small amount of the purée on top of each custard. Arrange the beans with a little more of the purée and serve the remaining purée separately. Garnish with broccoli florets.

ABOVE *Asparagus gâteaux*
Recipe: page 104
OPPOSITE *Chicken liver custards*
Recipe: page 105

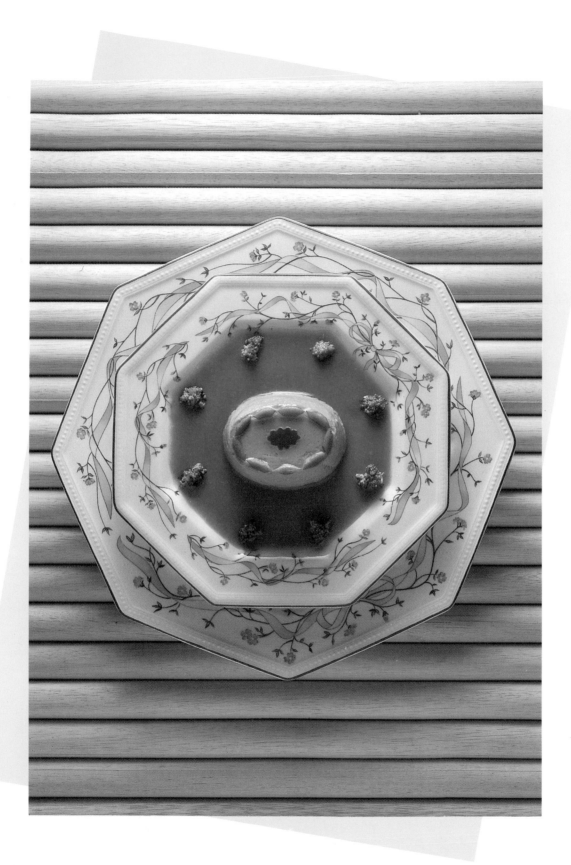

OMELETTE GATEAU

INGREDIENTS (serves 6)
2½ tbsp olive oil
flesh of 225 g/8 oz very ripe, but not
squashy, tomatoes, chopped
½ red pepper, blanched and chopped
¼ tsp chopped thyme
1 tsp tomato purée
150 g/5 oz spinach
25 g/1 oz watercress leaves
5 eggs, beaten
5½ tbsp crème fraîche
salt and freshly ground black pepper
a pinch of grated nutmeg
40 g/1½ oz Comté cheese, finely grated
a small pinch of mustard powder
red pepper sauce (see p.93)

FOR THE GARNISH
slices of cucumber, carrot and radish

Picture: page 111

Heat the oven to 130°C/265°F/Gas ½.

Heat 1 tbsp olive oil, add the tomatoes, red pepper and thyme and cook until most of the moisture from the tomatoes has evaporated. Drain through a sieve, then mix the flesh in the sieve with the tomato purée.

In a clean pan, heat 1½ tbsp oil, add the spinach and watercress leaves and cook, stirring, until the moisture has evaporated. Turn into a sieve and press out any remaining moisture, then chop the spinach mixture and leave to cool.

Divide the eggs evenly between 3 bowls. Mix the tomatoes, 1½ tbsp crème fraîche and seasoning into one bowl; the spinach, 1½ tbsp crème fraîche, nutmeg and a little salt into another and the remaining crème fraîche, cheese, mustard and seasoning into the third.

Pour the tomato mixture into an aluminium foil loaf tin, place in a roasting or baking tin and surround with boiling water. Place in the oven for 20 minutes. Cover the other two bowls.

Carefully pour the cheese mixture onto the tomato when it is set and return to the oven for about 20 minutes.

Carefully pour the spinach mixture onto the cheese when it is set and return to the oven for about 20—25 minutes.

Remove from the heat and leave in a warm place for 10—15 minutes before turning out onto a warmed plate. Cut into slices. Serve warm with the sauce and garnish with the slices of cucumber, carrot and radish.

DUO OF BROCCOLI WITH

LEMON SAUCE

INGREDIENTS (serves 6)
900 g/2 lb broccoli
1 egg, separated
salt and freshly ground white pepper
50 ml/2 fl oz crème fraîche, lightly
whipped

FOR THE SAUCE
1 tbsp lemon juice
1 tbsp double cream
225 g/8 oz cold butter, diced

This light, fresh tasting dish serves 6 for a starter but larger portions could be served as a main course for vegetarians. The purée can be prepared in advance.

———————————

Trim the florets from the stems of the broccoli. Slice the stems.

Cook, refresh and drain the stems and florets separately. Reserve some of the florets for the garnish and purée the remaining broccoli until very smooth.

Heat the oven to 180°C/350°F/Gas 4.

Gently warm the purée, stirring frequently to drive off the excess moisture. When the purée is dry, remove it from the heat and beat in the egg yolk and seasoning.

Whisk the egg white until stiff but not dry and fold into the purée with the crème fraîche.

Divide the broccoli mixture between 6 lightly oiled

decorative ovenproof moulds. Place the moulds in a roasting or baking tin, surround with boiling water, cover the moulds and place in the oven for about 20—30 minutes until just set. Remove from the heat and leave to stand for a minute or two before unmoulding.

For the sauce, boil the lemon juice until syrupy. Reduce the heat to very low, whisk in the cream then gradually whisk in the butter making sure each piece is fully incorporated before adding the next. Season.

Turn the moulds out onto 6 warmed plates and arrange the florets around. Trickle some of the sauce over and around the base of the moulds and spoon a little around the florets. Serve any remaining sauce separately.

A TRIO OF MOUSSES WITH A TRIO OF SAUCES

INGREDIENTS (serves 6)
FOR THE SCALLOP MOUSSES
9 large scallops
2 tbsp dry vermouth
salt
1 whole egg
1 egg white
300 ml/½ pt double cream, chilled
freshly ground white pepper

FOR THE SPINACH MOUSSES
750 g/1½ lb spinach
50 g/2 oz butter
2 shallots, finely chopped
salt and freshly ground black pepper
1 whole egg beaten with 1 yolk
50 ml/2 fl oz double cream

FOR THE SALMON MOUSSES
200 g/7 oz salmon fillet
salt and lemon juice
1 small egg white
225 ml/8 fl oz double cream, chilled
freshly ground white pepper
1 spinach leaf

FOR THE SAUCES
white wine sauce (see p.180)
½ quantity of red shellfish sauce (see p.176)

FOR THE GARNISH
salmon eggs
watercress leaves

For the scallop mousses, purée the scallops with the vermouth then add salt, followed by the whole egg, then the egg white. Pass through a sieve into a bowl placed over a bowl of ice. Very gradually work in the cream. Season, cover and chill for at least 30 minutes.

For the spinach mousses, blanch the spinach and drain very well, pressing down well on the leaves to extract as much liquid as possible. Heat the butter, add the shallots, cover and cook over a low heat, shaking the pan occasionally, until the shallots are soft. Stir in the spinach and seasoning then beat in the egg, egg yolk and cream. Purée, then pass through a fine sieve.

For the salmon mousses, purée the salmon then add the salt and lemon juice followed by the egg white. Pass through a sieve into a bowl over a bowl of ice. Gradually beat in the cream. Season. Cover and chill for at least 30 minutes.

Blanch the spinach leaf and drain very well. Purée with half the white wine sauce.

Warm the white wine sauce, the pale green coloured white wine sauce and the red shellfish sauce separately.

Bring a sauteuse or large frying pan of salted water to the boil. Lower the heat so the water barely moves. With the help of two spoons, form each mixture into 6 quenelle shapes. Gently lower them into the water and poach for 3 minutes each side. Remove with a slotted spoon and drain on a cloth.

Cover a third of 6 warmed plates with white wine sauce, a third with green coloured white wine sauce and the remaining third with the red shellfish sauce.

Place the spinach mousses on the white sauce, scallop mousses on the red shellfish sauce and the salmon mousses on the green sauce. Place salmon eggs in the centre and garnish with watercress leaves.

Terrine of crab and smoked salmon
Recipe: page 112

TERRINE OF CRAB AND

SMOKED SALMON

INGREDIENTS (serves 6—8)
1 kg/2 lb live crab
450 g/1 lb pike, skinned and filleted
3 egg whites
50 g/2 oz butter, diced
salt and lemon juice
3 egg yolks
300 ml/½ pt double cream, chilled
freshly ground white pepper
cayenne pepper
450 g/1 lb medium sized spinach
   leaves, trimmed
150 g/5 oz smoked salmon slices,
   chilled

FOR THE GARNISH
carrot 'roses' (see p.70)
sprigs of fresh herbs

Picture: page 110

This attractive terrine is a good choice for a meal in which the main course requires a fair amount of last minute attention, as it has to be left overnight after cooking and before unmoulding. For the choice of crab see p. 43.

Kill the crab (see p.61) and cook in boiling water for 3 minutes then refresh it in iced water.

Remove and crack the claws and remove the white meat.

Place the crab's body on a chopping board on its back and split it in half. Remove the brown meat, mix it in a liquidizer for 2 minutes, then pass it through a very fine sieve.

Combine the pike and white crab meat to make a total weight of 500 g/1¼ lb. Purée in a food processor or blender with the egg whites, butter, salt and lemon juice. Pass through a fine sieve.

Put the mixture into a bowl over a bowl of ice, then gradually beat in the egg yolks. Remove and reserve a quarter of the mixture. Gradually beat the cream into the remaining mixture while it is still on ice. Season with white pepper.

Slowly beat the brown crab meat into the reserved mixture. Check that the mixture does not become too runny by regularly dropping a teaspoonful into boiling water to see that the consistency is firm, but not rubbery. Season with a little cayenne pepper.

Blanch the spinach leaves, then refresh and drain well. Line a terrine with leaves allowing sufficient overlap to fold over the top of the terrine.

Fill a piping bag with the white mixture and pipe it to a depth of about 2.5 cm/1 inch on the bottom of the terrine and 1.25 cm/½ inch thick up the sides. Put the terrine in the refrigerator.

Cover a large tray with cling film. Form a large rectangle with the smoked salmon and spread the brown mixture over. Put the tray into the freezer for about 15 minutes, until it is very cold but not frozen.

Remove the tray from the freezer and, with the help of the cling film, roll the mixture up like a Swiss roll, then carefully place the roll in the centre of the terrine. Fill in the sides and cover the top with the white mixture.

Heat the oven to 180°C/350°F/Gas 4. Cover with the overlapping spinach leaves. Cover with well buttered foil, wrapping the edges under the rim of the terrine to seal in the steam. Place the terrine in a roasting or baking tin, surround it with boiling water and place in the oven for 1 hour.

Cool and leave overnight before unmoulding. Serve garnished with carrot 'roses' and sprigs of fresh herbs.

QUENELLES OF SWEETBREADS

INGREDIENTS (serves 4)
225 g/8 oz sweetbreads
50 ml/2 fl oz cognac
50 ml/2 fl oz dry white wine
a sprig of thyme
4 basil leaves
salt and lemon juice
1 egg white
300 ml/½ pt double cream, chilled
freshly ground white pepper
chicken stock and dry white wine for
    poaching

FOR THE SAUCE
15 g/½ oz butter
15 g/½ oz shallot, finely chopped
40 ml/2½ fl oz dry vermouth
flesh of 3 large ripe tomatoes,
    chopped
25 ml/1 fl oz tarragon vinegar
50 g/2 oz butter, diced
salt and freshly ground white pepper

FOR THE GARNISH
artichoke bottoms, sliced
tarragon leaves
coriander leaves

Picture: page 114

Lay the sweetbreads in a shallow dish. Mix the cognac, wine, thyme and basil together and pour over the sweetbreads. Cover and leave in a cool place for 4 hours.

Remove the sweetbreads, drain and dry well, then purée in a food processor or blender. Add salt and lemon juice, then the egg white. Pass through a sieve into a bowl over a bowl of ice, then gradually beat in the cream. Add the white pepper, cover and chill for at least 30 minutes.

For the sauce, heat the butter, add the shallot, cover and cook over a moderate heat, shaking the pan occasionally, until soft. Stir in half the vermouth and the tomato flesh and simmer for about 10 minutes until most of the liquid has evaporated — if necessary, boil to evaporate the liquid. Pass through a fine sieve and measure off 75ml/3 fl oz.

Boil the remaining vermouth and the vinegar until reduced to 1 tsp. Stir in the tomato mixture, bring to the boil, then reduce the heat to very low and gradually whisk in the butter, making sure that each piece is completely incorporated before adding the next. Season and keep warm, but do not allow to boil.

Heat a sauteuse or a large frying pan containing a mixture of chicken stock and dry white wine to just below simmering point. With the help of 2 spoons, form the sweetbread mixture into 8 oval shapes and gently lower them into the chicken stock/wine. Poach for about 3 minutes each side. Remove with a slotted spoon and drain on a cloth.

Arrange the quenelles on 4 warmed plates, add a little of the sauce and garnish with sliced artichoke bottoms, tarragon and coriander leaves.

SASHIMI OF TROUT

INGREDIENTS (serves 6)
3 trout, 175 g/6 oz each, chilled
juice of 1 orange
1 tsp finely grated orange rind
finely grated rind and juice of 1 lemon
1 tbsp olive oil
1 shallot, finely chopped
3 tbsp pink peppercorns
salt

FOR THE GARNISH
fine slices of orange and lemon
slices of cucumber

Picture: page 115

Do make sure the trout have a good true flavour. Chilling them well makes them easier to skin and slice thinly and neatly. Adjust the garnish according to your own degree of skill.

––––––––––––––

Skin the trout, then, with an extremely sharp, flexible knife, cut the flesh into wafer-thin slices.

Lay the slices in a shallow dish, sprinkle the fruit juices and rinds, the oil, shallot, peppercorns and salt over and leave for 1 hour.

Carefully lift the trout slices from the marinade and arrange on 6 cold plates. Spoon a little of the marinade, including the peppercorns, over. Garnish with the orange, lemon and cucumber slices.

ABOVE *Quenelles of sweetbreads*
Recipe: page 113
OPPOSITE *Sashimi of trout*
Recipe: page 113

SEAFOOD SAUSAGE 'EN L'AIR'

INGREDIENTS (serves 6)
*Use apples with skin that has a
positive colour, whether red or green,
to add brightness to the dish.*

400 g/14 oz monkfish, skinned and
  boned
salt and lemon juice
2 egg whites
½ tbsp chopped parsley
½ tbsp chopped chives
freshly ground white pepper
600 ml/1 pt double cream, chilled
6 Iceberg lettuce leaves
35 g/1¼ oz smoked salmon, diced
court bouillon, for poaching
150 ml/¼ pt fish stock
150 ml/¼ pt dry cider
300 ml/½ pt double cream, lightly
  whipped
lemon juice
50 g/2 oz clarified butter
2 crisp apples

FOR THE GARNISH
sprigs of chervil

Picture: page 118

The inspiration for this dish comes from the traditional French way of serving boudins blancs (white sausages).

Purée the monkfish in a food processor or blender, then mix in the salt and lemon juice followed by the egg whites, herbs and pepper. Transfer to a bowl placed over a bowl of ice and very gradually beat in the cream. Cover and chill for at least 30 minutes.

Blanch the lettuce leaves, refresh and dry very well. Spread out.

Fold the smoked salmon into the monkfish mixture, divide it into 6 and place almost along the length of the base of the lettuce leaves. Fold the sides of the lettuce leaves over the mixture and roll each one up into a neat sausage shape.

Bring the court bouillon just to simmering point and poach the 'sausages', with the loose end on the bottom of the pan, for 7—10 minutes. Drain well and keep warm.

Reduce the stock and cider by a half, then stir in the cream and reduce by one third. Season and add a little lemon juice to taste. Keep warm, but do not allow to boil.

Meanwhile, heat the clarified butter. Core and slice, but do not peel the apples, and cook in the clarified butter for 1—2 minutes each side.

Slice the sausages, re-form, cover and keep warm.

Spoon the sauce over 6 warmed plates. Arrange the sausage slices almost completely overlapping on the sauce and add the apple slices. Garnish with sprigs of chervil.

OYSTERS WITH WATERCRESS

INGREDIENTS (serves 2)
12 oysters
lemon juice
3 shallots, very finely chopped
1 tsp white wine vinegar
150 g/5 oz butter, diced
freshly ground white pepper and sea
  salt
7 g/¼ oz butter
50 g/2 oz spinach, sliced
25 g/1 oz watercress leaves
12 small spinach leaves

FOR THE GARNISH
julienne of cucumber
chopped chives
radicchio leaves
mint leaves

Picture: page 119

Six oysters per person is quite a generous portion. For 4 people you may find it more practical to reduce the number to 4 for each serving, making a total of 16. The other ingredients can then be increased by half as much again.

Open the oysters (see p.61) and strain the juices into a pan. Add a squeeze of lemon juice and bring to just below simmering point. Add the oysters and heat for about 45 seconds. Transfer to a lightly warmed plate with a slotted spoon. Cover. Wash the oyster shells and put in a low oven.

Simmer the shallots in the vinegar and half the oyster cooking juices until nearly all the liquid has evaporated. Reduce the heat to very low and gradually whisk in 150g/5 oz butter, making sure each piece is fully incorporated before adding the next. Season with white pepper and a little juice if necessary.

Meanwhile heat the 7g/¼ oz butter in a small pan, add the spinach and watercress and cook until soft. Increase the heat to drive off the excess moisture. Purée, then season, adding a squeeze of lemon juice if necessary. Keep warm over a low heat.

Place the small spinach leaves and cucumber julienne in the top half of a steamer or a colander. Bring a pan of salted water to the boil. Cover with the top half of the steamer or the colander, cover and steam for 30 seconds.

Line the oyster shells with the spinach leaves, add the watercress and spinach purée, then the sauce and finally the oysters. Garnish with cucumber julienne and chives. Arrange the radicchio and mint leaves around.

SASHIMI OF SCALLOPS

INGREDIENTS (serves 4)
8 scallops
4 tbsp lime juice
a few strands of saffron
sea salt
4 tbsp dry white wine
6 tbsp mayonnaise
2 tbsp finely chopped chives
4 wakame (seaweed) soaked in
    cold water for 10 minutes

FOR THE GARNISH
sprigs of chervil

The technique of 'cooking' delicate flesh by the action of an acid, in this case lime juice, has been borrowed from the Japanese.

Remove the scallops from their shells (see p.61). Remove and reserve the corals. Carefully cut the scallop bodies into slices horizontally.

Mix the lime juice, saffron and a little sea salt together and lightly toss with the scallop slices. Cover and chill for 30—40 minutes.

Bring the wine to the boil with 4 tbsp water, pour over the corals, drain immediately, cover and chill the corals.

Remove the scallop slices from the marinade with a slotted spoon and dry on absorbent paper. Strain the marinade into the mayonnaise and add the chives.

Strain the seaweed and divide between the centres of 4 plates, spreading it out to form a circle. Place the slices of scallop and the corals on the circles of seaweed so that some of the seaweed shows.

Spoon a very small amount of the mayonnaise on to the slices of scallops and serve the rest separately. Garnish with sprigs of chervil.

OPPOSITE *Seafood sausage 'en l'air'*
Recipe: page 116
ABOVE *Oysters with watercress*
Recipe: page 116

VEGETABLE TERRINE

INGREDIENTS (serves 8)
6 long, slim leeks
4 young carrots
10 French beans, trimmed
3 artichoke bottoms
2 mint leaves
juice of 1 lemon
250 g/9 oz smoked chicken breast,
    diced
1 egg white
175 ml/6 fl oz olive oil
salt and freshly ground white pepper

FOR THE DRESSING
75 ml/3 fl oz walnut oil
75 ml/3 fl oz olive oil
40 ml/1½ fl oz lemon juice
40 ml/1½ fl oz sherry vinegar
salt and freshly ground white pepper

FOR THE GARNISH
slices of cucumber
concassé tomatoes
sprigs of parsley

Picture: page 122

The vegetables can be varied as long as the appearance and flavour of the dish are always considered. Strips of blanched red pepper could replace the carrot, and petits pois the French beans. Remember that the vegetables will receive further cooking in the oven.

Heat the oven to 180°C/350°F/Gas 4.

Cook the leeks, carrots, beans and artichoke bottoms separately in simmering, salted water, adding the mint leaves to the carrots and half the lemon juice to the artichokes, until just tender. Drain, refresh and dry well separately. Thinly slice the leeks, carrots and artichoke bottoms then wrap the vegetables separately in a cloth to make sure they are completely dry, especially the leeks.

Purée the chicken in a food processor then add the remaining lemon juice followed by the egg white. With the motor running slowly, pour in the oil in a thin stream. Season.

Line the bottom and sides of a terrine with a layer of the smoked chicken mixture. Lay one third of the leeks over the mixture. Mix the carrots, beans and artichoke bottoms with three quarters of the remaining smoked chicken mixture, then cover the leeks with half of this mixture. Cover with one third of the leeks, the remaining vegetable/smoked chicken mixture followed by the last of the leeks. Finish with the remaining plain smoked chicken mixture.

Place the terrine in a roasting tin and surround with boiling water. Cover the terrine with buttered greaseproof paper and place in the oven for about 40 minutes.

Remove from the heat and leave to cool completely, then cut into slices and place a slice on each of 8 cold plates. Shake all the ingredients for the dressing together and trickle over the terrine. Garnish with slices of cucumber, concassé tomatoes and sprigs of parsley.

TROUT MOUSSE IN LEEK PARCELS

INGREDIENTS (serves 6)
3-4 very large leeks
salt
700 g/1½ lb boneless, skinless trout
    fillets, chopped
2 egg whites
225 ml/8 fl oz crème fraîche, chilled
150 ml/¼ pt fish stock (see p.75)
olive oil for brushing the leeks

FOR THE SAUCE
2 tbsp finely chopped shallots
2 tbsp dry vermouth

If 3 'parcels' are served per person, this dish would provide a light luncheon main course for 4 people. The mousseline mixture can be prepared in advance. The remaining parts of the leeks can be used for Turbot with leek and mushroom mélange or Rack of lamb with leek purée.

Cut the roots and green parts from the leeks and make a lengthways split in each one as deep as the centre. Separate off 12 outer leaves about 22.5 cm/9 inches long. Rinse well, if necessary. Use the remaining leeks in another dish.

2 tbsp white wine vinegar
225 g/8 oz cold butter, diced
salt and freshly ground white pepper

FOR THE GARNISH
12 strips of red pepper, blanched
sprigs of parsley
strips of tomato

Picture: page 123

Cook the 12 leaves in boiling salted water for 2 minutes. Refresh, drain and dry well.

Purée the trout with a little salt in a food processor, then add the egg whites and mix until the mixture stiffens. Pass through a sieve.

Transfer the trout mixture to a bowl placed over ice and very gradually beat in the crème fraîche, beating the mixture well after each addition. Cover and chill for at least 30 minutes.

Heat the oven to 200°C/400°F/Gas 6.

Spread out the leek leaves and place about 3 tbsp of the trout mixture on the base of each. Roll up across the grain to make a neat parcel.

Place the parcels, seam-side down, in a baking tin. Boil the stock and pour around the leeks. Place in the oven for 10-15 minutes.

Remove the parcels with a slotted spoon (reserve the liquid) and brush with a little olive oil to make them shiny. Cover and keep warm.

For the sauce, boil the shallot in the reserved cooking liquid, the vermouth, vinegar and 2 tbsp water until nearly all the liquid has evaporated. Reduce the heat to very low and gradually whisk in the butter, whisking well after each addition, to make a smooth, creamy sauce. Season.

Spoon the sauce onto 6 warmed plates, arrange 2 parcels on each plate and lay a strip of red pepper across the centre of each one. Garnish with parsley and tomato.

PARCELS OF SMOKED SALMON

INGREDIENTS (serves 4)
350 g/12 oz smoked salmon, very
*   thinly sliced*
2 tsp fresh tomato purée (see p.302)
a pinch of cayenne pepper
1 tbsp salmon eggs, optional
175 ml/6 fl oz crème fraîche, chilled
*   and whipped*
flesh of 450g/1lb tomatoes
2 tbsp olive oil
1 tbsp tarragon vinegar
salt and pepper
a pinch of caster sugar

FOR THE GARNISH
salmon eggs
sprigs of chervil

Line 4 lightly oiled ramekin dishes with about half the smoked salmon.

Pass the remaining smoked salmon through a sieve into a bowl over a bowl of ice. Beat in half the fresh tomato purée, cayenne pepper and salmon eggs, then gradually beat in three quarters of the crème fraîche. Fold in the remaining crème fraîche. Spoon the mixture into the ramekin dishes. Cover and chill for 2—3 hours.

Purée the tomatoes, then pass through a fine sieve. Gradually beat in the oil, then the vinegar and remaining fresh tomato purée. Season, adding a pinch of caster sugar if necessary, then cover and chill.

Invert the moulds onto 4 plates. Spoon the sauce around and garnish with salmon eggs and sprigs of chervil.

ABOVE *Vegetable terrine*
Recipe: page 120
OPPOSITE *Trout mousse in leek parcels*
Recipe: page 120

CAULIFLOWER AND BROCCOLI FEUILLETE

INGREDIENTS (serves 4)
175 g/6 oz puff pastry (see p.79)
beaten egg
100 g/4 oz even sized cauliflower
  florets
100 g/4 oz even sized broccoli
  florets
50 ml/2 fl oz vegetable stock
50 ml/2 fl oz full-bodied dry white
  wine
a sprig of fennel
25 ml/1 fl oz double cream
100 g/4 oz butter, diced
1 tbsp lemon juice
1 tsp chopped parsley
salt and freshly ground white pepper

FOR THE GARNISH
lemon julienne

This is an attractive first course ideal for vegetarians. The feuilleté can be made from filo pastry with each layer comprised of 2 small sheets stacked together with melted butter or oil brushed between them.

Roll the pastry out to a circle about 5 mm/¼ inch thick and, with a 7.5 cm/3 inch fluted cutter, cut 4 circles. With the point of a sharp knife score a line about 5 mm/¼ inch all the way round from the edge. Transfer to a baking tray, cover and leave in a cool place for at least 30 minutes.

Heat the oven to 220°C/425°F/Gas 7.

Brush the tops of the pastries with beaten egg, taking care not to let any drip over the cut edges, then bake for about 8 minutes until golden brown and well risen.

Meanwhile, steam the cauliflower and broccoli florets until just tender.

Bring the stock, wine and fennel to the boil and reduce to 25 ml/1 fl oz. Add the cream and boil for 1 minute. Gradually add the butter, making sure each piece is fully incorporated before adding the next. Remove the fennel, add the lemon juice, parsley and seasoning. Keep warm but do not allow to boil.

Leave the pastries to cool very slightly on a wire rack, then carefully ease off the inner 'lids'. With the point of a sharp knife, carefully scoop out any soft pastry from the centres.

Reserve a few of the florets for the garnish and divide the remainder between the pastry cases. Spoon the sauce over and place the 'lids' on top. Garnish with the reserved florets and lemon julienne.

INDIVIDUAL SALMON, SOLE AND WATERCRESS TERRINES

INGREDIENTS (serves 4)
225 g/8 oz salmon fillets
salt and freshly ground white pepper
65 ml/2½ fl oz full-bodied dry white
  wine
150 g/5 oz butter, softened
1 tbsp finely chopped shallot
225 g/8 oz sole fillets, chopped
a squeeze of lemon juice
2 small egg whites
1 small bunch watercress, trimmed
  and chopped

This would be a good choice for a first course when the main course requires some last minute preparation.

Lightly season the salmon, pour the wine over, cover and leave in a cool place for about an hour.

Heat 1 tbsp butter, add the shallot, cover and cook over a moderate heat, shaking the pan occasionally until softened.

Mix the shallot with the sole in a food processor or blender until very smooth, then add salt and lemon juice, followed by the egg whites, then the remaining butter.

Blanch the watercress for 1 minute. Refresh and drain well.

Remove two thirds of the sole mixture, then put the watercress into the food processor and blend with the remaining sole mixture. Cover both mixtures and chill for 1 hour.

Heat the oven to 170°C/325°F/Gas 3.

Trim the salmon fillets so that they will fit into 4 individual dishes.

Lightly oil the dishes and cover the bases with the white sole mixture. Cover with the salmon, then add the green mixture.

Place the dishes in a roasting or baking tin, surround with boiling water, cover and place in the oven for 30—40 minutes until the terrines are lightly set.

Allow to cool slightly, then chill overnight. Unmould about half an hour before serving and leave at room temperature.

CHICKEN BREAST TERRINE

INGREDIENTS (serves 8)
450 g/1lb chicken breasts, skinned
150 ml/¼ pt dry white wine
salt and freshly ground white pepper

FOR THE TOMATO ASPIC
2½ tsp gelatine
350 ml/12 fl oz clarified chicken stock
75 ml/3 fl oz dry white wine
1 tbsp lemon juice
120 ml/4½ fl oz tomato juice
2 tbsp finely chopped chives
2 tbsp finely chopped tarragon
2 tbsp finely chopped chervil
40 g/1½ oz pistachio nuts, chopped
300 ml/½ pt aspic, made with the
   strained chicken liquor

Poach the chicken breasts in the wine with salt and pepper for about 10 minutes until tender.

Remove the breasts with a slotted spoon. Strain the liquor and use in the making of the aspic. Allow the breasts to cool and then cut into slices. Leave to cool completely.

Dissolve the gelatine for the tomato aspic in a little of the clarified stock in a bowl placed over a pan of hot water. Leave to cool slightly.

Warm the remaining stock, the wine, lemon juice and tomato juice and season lightly. Stir in the dissolved gelatine.

Pour half into a cold loaf tin to form a layer over the base. Chill until set. Keep the remaining liquor just off setting point.

Sprinkle some of the herbs over the bottom of the terrine then add layers of chicken slices and pistachio nuts.

Have the aspic just on the point of setting and spoon it over the chicken, moving the meat slightly with the point of a knife to make sure the aspic flows right through. Leave in a cool place until just on the point of setting.

Sprinkle the remaining herbs over the top of the terrine and leave to set completely.

Cover with the remaining tomato aspic and leave for 3—4 hours.

Serve in slices on cold plates.

SOUPS

♦ The soups of Cuisine Vivante have little in common with the thick and chunky varieties that are often more than an adequate meal in themselves. Cuisine Vivante soups are more appetite refreshers, providing a relaxing respite between courses. Delicately flavoured servings of light liquids, often with a supplementary ingredient suspended as if by magic in the centre, giving off tantalizing and titillating aromas provide an enticing prelude to the dishes to come and create an air of anticipation in the diner. ♦

MUSHROOM SOUP

INGREDIENTS (serves 4)
15 g/½ oz butter
2 tbsp olive oil
2 shallots, sliced
225 g/8 oz wild mushrooms, sliced
1 heaped tsp mixed finely chopped
    sage, rosemary and thyme
salt and freshly ground black pepper
a squeeze of lemon juice

FOR THE GARNISH
4 pieces of chanterelle
7 g/¼ oz butter
finely chopped chervil

Heat the butter with the oil, add the shallots, cover and cook over a very low heat, shaking the pan occasionally, until they are soft. Stir in the mushrooms and herbs, cover and cook gently for about 5 minutes.

Stir in 600 ml/1 pt water and simmer very gently for about 20 minutes. Season, adding a squeeze of lemon juice to taste. Pass through a sieve lined with muslin or cheesecloth then reheat in a clean saucepan.

Heat the butter for the garnish, add the chanterelles and cook for 2 minutes. Remove with a slotted spoon and drain on absorbent paper.

Pour the soup into 4 warmed bowls. Garnish with the chanterelles and sprinkle over the chervil.

 # SEAFOOD AND SAFFRON CONSOMME

INGREDIENTS (serves 4)
4 mussels
60 ml/4 tbsp full-bodied dry white
    wine
a few strands of saffron
1 fillet of brill, cut into 4 strips
4 clams
8 crescent shapes of thinly sliced
    carrot
8 cooked prawns, shelled
chervil leaves

FOR THE CONSOMME
1.1 L/2 pt fish stock (see p.75)
100 g/4oz lemon sole, finely chopped
2 shallots, finely chopped
1 carrot, finely chopped
1 leek, finely chopped
4 mushroom stalks, finely chopped
4 stalks of parsley
1 bay leaf
4 sprigs of chervil
8 white peppercorns, crushed
¼ tsp tomato purée
3 tbsp lemon juice
a long strip of lemon peel
2 egg whites
2 egg shells, crushed
sea salt

For the consommé, bring the stock to the boil. Mix all the remaining ingredients together in a large pan, then gradually whisk in the stock. Return to the boil, whisking continuously. Stop whisking, reduce the heat to very low and simmer for 5 minutes.

Remove the pan from the heat, cover and leave for 10 minutes.

Carefully skim the scum from the surface and ladle the stock into a muslin-lined sieve. Leave to cool, then remove any fat from the surface.

Poach the mussels in a little water in a coverd pan over a moderate heat, shaking the pan frequently until the mussels open. Remove them from their shells. Discard any closed mussels.

Gradually bring the wine and saffron to just below simmering point. Add the brill and poach for 1—2 minutes until opaque. Remove with a slotted spoon.

Open the clams (see p.43) and poach them in the wine until just opaque. Remove with a slotted spoon.

Blanch the carrot crescents. Refresh and drain well.

Add the wine to the consommé and bring to the boil.

Meanwhile, divide the fish and carrot crescents between 4 warmed bowls. Pour the consommé over and garnish with sprigs of chervil.

CHILLED BEETROOT CONSOMME

INGREDIENTS (serves 6)
1.7 L/3 pt jellied chicken stock
2 beetroot, each approximately
    175 g/6 oz
3 shallots, finely chopped
2 leeks, chopped
2 sticks of celery, chopped
2 carrots, chopped
2 egg whites
shells of 2 eggs, crushed
4 tbsp fresh orange juice, strained

FOR THE GARNISH
6 tbsp crème fraîche or soured cream
orange peel julienne
sprigs of chervil

Picture: page 131

There is a flavour of Russian Borscht here but this recipe is more delicate than the traditional version, the good jellied chicken stock replacing the beef stock of the original.

Bring the stock to the boil in a large pan, add the beetroot, shallot, leek, celery and carrot, then stir in the egg whites and shells and return to the boil, whisking continuously. Simmer gently for 1 hour.

Very carefully remove the scum from the surface of the liquid, then strain the liquid through a muslin-lined sieve. Leave to cool completely and remove all the fat from the surface. Stir in the orange juice and chill in the refrigerator.

Spoon into 6 cold bowls and garnish with a spoonful of crème fraîche or soured cream, orange and chervil.

 # GREEN PEA SOUP

INGREDIENTS (serves 6)
1.5 kg/3 lb peas in the
    pod or 450 g/1 lb shelled peas
1 tbsp butter
4 spring onions, chopped
½ head of round lettuce
2 tbsp mixed chopped chervil, parsley
    and tarragon
100 ml/4 fl oz chicken stock
100 ml/4 fl oz double cream
salt and freshly ground white pepper

FOR THE GARNISH
julienne of cucumber
flower shapes cut from very thin slices
    of carrot and turnip

Shell the peas, reserving a few of the best looking pods and setting some peas aside for the garnish.

Heat the butter and add the spring onions, lettuce and herbs. Cover and cook over a moderate heat, shaking the pan occasionally, until the onions are soft. Stir in the peas, reserved pods and chicken stock, then simmer until the peas are just tender.

Strain off and reserve the liquor. Pass the peas through a sieve.

Blend the purée with the liquor and heat through gently. Stir in the cream and heat just long enough to warm it. Season.

Meanwhile, blanch, refresh and drain the cucumber, carrot, turnip and reserved peas for the garnish.

Divide the soup between 6 warmed soup bowls then very carefully slide the garnish on to the surface of the soup so that it floats. Serve immediately.

ABOVE *Quail
consommé*
Recipe: page 132

LEFT *Mussel soup*
Recipe: page 132

◆
ABOVE
*Clear vegetable
and scallop soup*
Recipe: page 133

◆
LEFT
*Chilled beetroot
consommé*
Recipe: page 129

QUAIL CONSOMME

INGREDIENTS *(serves 4)*
2 quails
15 g/½ oz butter
½ veal knuckle bone, chopped
½ small onion
1 clove
½ bay leaf
1 young carrot
½ small leek
1 stick of celery
75 g/3 oz chicken breast meat
2 egg whites
2 egg shells, crushed
1 small tomato, chopped
6 parsley stalks
4 tarragon stalks
100 ml/4 fl oz full-bodied dry white
    wine
salt and pepper

FOR THE GARNISH
4 quails eggs
julienne of celery
julienne of leek
julienne of carrot
sprigs of watercress

Picture: page 130

Carefully skin the quails and remove the flesh from the carcasses.

Heat the butter, add the quail skin and carcasses and the knuckle bone and cook, stirring occasionally, until lightly browned. Pour out the excess fat, add 1 L/2 pt water and bring to the boil. Remove the scum from the surface and simmer for 45 minutes.

Stud the onion with the clove and add to the pan with the bay leaf, carrot, leek and celery and simmer for 30 minutes. Pass through a conical sieve, pressing down well on the bones and vegetables to extract as much liquid as possible. Leave to cool then remove the fat from the surface.

Chop the quail flesh and chicken breast coarsely and put into a pan with the egg whites, shells, tomato, herbs, wine and the prepared stock. Bring to the boil, stirring constantly, then simmer for 20 minutes. Season.

Boil the quails eggs for 2½ minutes, then carefully remove the shells.

Blanch, refresh and drain the vegetables.

Pass the soup through a muslin or cheesecloth-lined sieve and remove the fat from the surface. Reheat gently then pour into 4 warmed soup bowls. Garnish with the quails eggs, vegetables julienne and sprigs of watercress.

MUSSEL SOUP

INGREDIENTS *(serves 4)*
2 kg/2 lb 3 oz mussels, cleaned
175 ml/6 fl oz full-bodied dry white
    wine
20 g/¾ oz butter
l shallot, finely chopped
50 g/2 oz celery, chopped
50 g/2 oz carrot, chopped
600 ml/1 pt fish stock (p.75)
a sprig of thyme
l small bay leaf
65 ml/2½ fl oz double cream
salt and freshly ground white pepper
a pinch of saffron threads soaked in a
    little dry vermouth

FOR THE QUENELLES
100 g/4 oz skinned fillet of sole
a very small pinch of grated nutmeg
salt and lemon juice
½ egg white
65 ml/2½ fl oz double cream, chilled
freshly ground white pepper

Cook the mussels in the wine in a covered, heavy based pan over a high heat for about 5 minutes, shaking the pan frequently, until they open. Discard any mussels that remain closed and remove the rest from their shells. Place the mussels in a covered bowl and strain the cooking liquor.

Heat the butter, add the shallot, celery and carrot, cover the pan and cook over a low heat, shaking the pan frequently until the vegetables have softened. Stir in the cooking liquor, stock and herbs, bring to the boil then reduce the heat and simmer for 40 minutes.

Meanwhile, purée the sole in a food processor or blender with the nutmeg. Add the salt and lemon juice followed by the egg white. Pass through a fine sieve into a bowl placed over a bowl of ice, then gradually work in the cream. Add the white pepper, cover and chill for at least 30 minutes.

Pour the soup through a sieve lined with muslin or cheesecloth, return to the rinsed pan and bring to the boil. Stir in the cream and saffron with its soaking liquor, return to the boil then reduce the heat to very low. Adjust the seasoning.

Bring a wide shallow pan of salted, acidulated water to simmering point. Using 2 teaspoons, shape the sole mixture into 8 quenelles. Carefully lower them into the water and

FOR THE GARNISH
julienne of carrot and celery
sprigs of dill

Picture: page 130

poach for about 2 minutes until just firm. Remove with a slotted spoon and drain on a cloth. Blanch the carrot and celery for the garnish.

Divide the mussels between 4 warmed soup bowls, pour the soup over, add the carrot and celery and carefully float the quenelles on the surface. Finish with a sprig of dill on each plate.

CLEAR VEGETABLE AND

SCALLOP SOUP

INGREDIENTS (serves 5)
25 g/1 oz very fine julienne of carrot
25 g/1 oz very fine julienne of celery
25 g/1 oz button mushroom caps,
  finely sliced
150 ml/5 fl oz dry white wine
salt and freshly ground white pepper
9 scallops
2 tbsp gin

FOR THE STOCK
2 egg whites, lightly whisked
1.4 kg/3 lb white fish bones and
  heads, cleaned and chopped
2 leeks, sliced
stick of celery, chopped
9 parsley stalks
4 sprigs of chervil
4 tbsp lemon juice
300 ml/½ pt dry white wine

FOR THE GARNISH
1 small red pepper, blanched, skinned
  and cut into julienne strips
sprigs of chervil

Picture: page 131

This is a very light, elegant soup. The stock can be prepared in advance up to the point of reheating.

———————————

For the stock, put all the ingredients except the wine into a large saucepan, cover with about 1.5 L/2½ pt water and gradually bring to the boil, whisking. Lower the heat and simmer without whisking for 30 minutes. Remove the scum from the surface.

Pass through a sieve lined with a double thickness of muslin and leave to cool.

Carefully ladle off 1.25 L/2¼ pt of the stock, taking care to avoid the sediment and heat gently with the carrot, celery and mushrooms to just below simmering point.

Gently heat the wine with the seasoning.

Open the scallops (see p.61) and slice into three, leaving the corals whole. Poach the scallops for 30 seconds in the wine until just opaque.

Remove with a slotted spoon. Add the gin to the poaching wine and reduce to 1½ tbsp. Strain into the stock. Add to the scallops and season.

Ladle the vegetables, scallops and the liquor into 5 warmed bowls and garnish with red pepper and sprigs of chervil.

SALADS

◆ Cuisine Vivante salads can be served either as a first course or as a light main course. In the latter case it may be necessary to increase the quantity of one or two of the main ingredients. However, it is important that the overall balance of the ingredients is not disturbed — striking the correct balance between the various ingredients is part of the art of creating a successful salad. Always select ingredients that complement each other in terms of taste, texture and colour, and remember that the dressing should be treated as ◆ one of the integral ingredients.

CHICORY, TOMATO AND QUAILS

EGGS SALAD

INGREDIENTS (serves 4)
flesh from 450 g/1lb tomatoes, diced
salt
4 quails eggs
2 tbsp sherry vinegar
1½ tsp Dijon mustard
6 tbsp olive oil
*20 g/¾ oz finely chopped watercress
   leaves*
freshly ground black pepper
12 chicory leaves

To serve individual portions choose small plates and use enough chicory leaves to give a balanced appearance.

———————

Place the tomatoes in a sieve, sprinkle with salt and leave to drain for 30 minutes.

Cook the quails eggs in gently boiling water for 2 minutes. Cool under running water, then peel.

Blend the vinegar, mustard and a pinch of salt together, then gradually whisk in the oil. Mix in the watercress and the pepper.

Dry the tomatoes on absorbent paper and mix into the dressing.

Arrange 6 chicory leaves in a circle around 2 cold plates. With a slotted spoon, lift some of the tomatoes and watercress from the dressing and place a little in the bases of the chicory leaves. Quarter the quails eggs and arrange in front of the chicory. Lift the remaining tomato and watercress from the dressing and place in the centre of the plates. Trickle a little of the dressing over the tomatoes and watercress and the chicory. Serve any remaining dressing separately. Serve 1 plate of salad between 2 people.

SMOKED CHICKEN SALAD

WITH FIGS

INGREDIENTS (serves 4)
½ ripe avocado
lemon juice
curly endive
sprigs of watercress
*350 g/12 oz smoked chicken breast,
   thinly sliced*
4 fresh figs, sliced
40 g/1½ oz hazelnuts, chopped
julienne of orange rind

FOR THE DRESSING
3 tbsp olive oil
1 tbsp lemon juice
salt and freshly ground black pepper
a pinch of caster sugar

Picture: page 138

Peel the avocado, remove the stone and cut the flesh into slices. Brush with lemon juice.

Arrange the curly endive, watercress, chicken, figs and avocado on 4 cold plates. Sprinkle with hazelnuts. Shake the ingredients for the dressing together and spoon a little over each salad. Finish with julienne of orange peel.

SALAD TAHITIENNE

INGREDIENTS (serves 4)
450 g/1 lb mixed fish and shellfish
juice of 2 limes
1 small shallot, finely chopped
1 small coconut
1 small pink grapefruit
1 orange
1 tomato, peeled and chopped
½ green pepper, blanched, skinned
    and diced
1 small shallot, finely diced

FOR THE GARNISH
slices of lime
capers
cubes of pineapple
salmon eggs

Picture: page 139

Mix the fish with the lime juice and shallot. Cover and leave in a cool place for 2-4 hours, turning occasionally.

Pierce 2 of the 3 eyes in the coconut and strain out and reserve the milk. Crack the shell open, prize out the flesh and remove any dark skin with a small sharp knife. Chop the flesh finely in a blender or food processor. Remove half the flesh. Add the coconut milk to the blender or food processor and mix briefly. Turn into a muslin-lined sieve and leave to drain. Press down firmly to extract as much liquid as possible.

Strain the liquid from the fish and mix with the coconut liquor. Season.

Peel the grapefruit and orange, adding any juice that comes out to the coconut liquid. Divide into segments, making sure that all the pith and membrane are removed.

Lightly toss the fish, reserved coconut flesh, grapefruit, orange and tomato together with the coconut liquor.

Spoon into 4 halves of coconut shell, if available.

Garnish with the slices of lime, capers, pineapple and salmon eggs.

WARM SALAD OF BROCCOLI, AVOCADO AND SOLE WITH ORANGE DRESSING

INGREDIENTS (serves 4)
1 shallot, finely chopped
1 tbsp orange peel julienne
75 ml/3 fl oz orange juice
salt and freshly ground white pepper
3 sole fillets, skinned and cut into
    strips
50 ml/2 fl oz fish stock
50 ml/2 fl oz dry white wine
a sprig of thyme
225 g/8 oz broccoli florets
100 g/4 oz butter, diced
1 avocado
a squeeze of lemon juice
finely chopped chives

Simmer the shallot and orange rind in the orange juice until the liquid is reduced to 1 tbsp.

Season the sole.

Heat the stock and wine with the thyme to simmering point. Add the sole, cover with buttered paper and poach for about 2 minutes until the flesh is just opaque. Remove with a slotted spoon. Cover and keep warm.

Meanwhile, cook the broccoli in boiling salted water for about 5 minutes until just tender. Refresh, drain and dry well.

Gradually whisk the butter into the reduced orange juice over a very low heat to make a thickened, fluffy sauce. Season.

Peel then thinly slice the avocado. Cut the slices in half and brush with lemon juice.

Arrange the broccoli florets, avocado and sole on 4 warm plates, then spoon the dressing over. Sprinkle chopped chives over the dressing on the sole and avocado.

WARM BUNDLES OF FRENCH BEANS
WITH SHRIMPS

INGREDIENTS (serves 4)
350 g/12 oz slim French beans,
    trimmed to equal lengths
salt
225 g/8 oz cooked, peeled shrimps
court bouillon (see p.76)
1 small red pepper, skinned and cut
    into fine julienne

FOR THE DRESSING
2 tbsp softened butter
2 tbsp hazelnut oil
2 tbsp tarragon vinegar
a pinch of cayenne pepper
salt and freshly ground white pepper

FOR THE GARNISH
small sprigs of chervil
peeled shrimps
concassé tomatoes

This very neat salad makes a light first course — for a more substantial portion, serve the beans and shrimps on a bed of lettuce.

———————

Cook the beans in simmering salted water until just tender. Refresh and drain well. Cut the beans in half if they are long.

Place the shrimps in a single layer in the top half of a steamer and place over the bottom half of a steamer containing a little simmering court bouillon for 2-3 minutes, to warm through gently.

Divide the beans into 20 small bundles and tie a strip of red pepper around each bundle leaving the ends of the pepper loose. Keep the bundles just warm.

Gently heat the ingredients for the dressing, whisking them together.

Arrange the bundles of beans on 4 plates, then arrange the shrimps in the centres. Spoon a little of the warm dressing over the shrimps and trickle a small amount on the beans. Garnish with sprigs of chervil, peeled shrimps and concassé tomatoes.

NEW POTATO, PEA AND SOFT
CHEESE SALAD

INGREDIENTS (serves 4)
16 small new potatoes
salt
¾ quantity pea and mint purée
    (see p.300)
150 g/5 oz soft cheese, chilled
vinaigrette dressing, lightly warmed
    (see p.76)
1 head of radicchio
finely chopped chervil

In the summer months a good quality soft goats cheese is an excellent choice, because at that time of the year, when the goats are feeding on young grass, the flavour of the cheese is at its best.

———————

Put the potatoes into a pan of boiling salted water and boil gently for 12-15 minutes until tender.

Prepare and warm the pea and mint purée.

Form the cheese into small balls using a melon baller or teaspoon. Keep them cool.

Drain the potatoes very well. Cut them in half horizontally and carefully scoop out the centres with a teaspoon, taking care not to pierce the sides, to make potato cups. If necessary cut a small slice from the bottom of the cups so that they will stand straight.

Spoon or pipe pea and mint purée into the cups. Keep warm.

Gently warm the dressing in a bowl over a pan of hot water, whisking. Arrange the radicchio on 4 plates. Place the potatoes in the centre, spoon the dressing over the radicchio then place the balls of cheese on top. Sprinkle the cheese with chervil.

LOBSTER SALAD WITH RED PEPPER MOUSSE

INGREDIENTS (serves 6)
flesh from 2 cooked lobsters
concassé tomatoes
julienne of courgettes
lamb's lettuce

FOR THE MOUSSE
75 ml/3 fl oz red wine vinegar
25 ml/1 fl oz raspberry vinegar
300 g/10 oz red peppers, skinned and diced
1 red pimento
salt and freshly ground white pepper
1 tsp gelatine
100 ml/4 fl oz whipping cream, lightly whipped

FOR THE DRESSING
¼ tsp Dijon mustard
4 tbsp olive oil
2 tbsp white wine vinegar
salt and freshly ground white pepper
a squeeze of lemon juice
finely chopped chives

FOR THE GARNISH
basil leaves
strips of cucumber
ends of lobster tails

Picture: page 142

For choosing lobster see p.43. The mousse should not be prepared more than 2 or 3 hours in advance. It also goes very well with crayfish, Dublin Bay prawns and sole.

Reduce the vinegars for the mousse by two thirds, then add the red pepper and simmer until thick. Purée with the pimento and seasoning, then pass through a fine sieve. Dissolve the gelatine in 2 tbsp water in a small bowl placed over a pan of hot water. Remove from the heat, leave to cool, then blend in the red pepper mixture. Gently fold in the cream, cover and chill until set.

Use 2 spoons to form 12 oval shapes from the mousse and place 2 on 6 cold plates. Arrange the lobster, tomatoes, courgettes and lettuce attractively.

Mix the mustard, oil and vinegar together, then season with salt, pepper, lemon juice and chives. Spoon a little over the salad. Garnish with basil leaves, strips of cucumber and ends of lobster tails.

WARM CHICKEN LIVER AND PISTACHIO SALAD

INGREDIENTS (serves 4)
350 g/12 oz whole chicken livers,
    trimmed
4 tbsp olive oil
4 tbsp raspberry vinegar
3 tbsp pistachio nuts, skinned and
    roughly chopped
salt and freshly ground black pepper
1 head radicchio lettuce
1 small head curly endive

FOR THE GARNISH
4 tbsp raspberries
a little white wine

Picture: page 143

Serve this salad as a first course or a light main course — to increase the size of each portion add about 100 g/4 oz lightly cooked mushrooms. Raspberry vinegar makes a delightful complementary dressing.

Heat the oil, add the livers and cook over a moderate heat for 2-3 minutes — they should remain pink inside.

Remove the livers with a slotted spoon and stir the vinegar, nuts and seasoning into the pan. Bring to the boil and remove from the heat.

Arrange the radicchio and curly endive on 4 plates.

Gently heat the raspberries for the garnish in the wine.

Cut the livers into lengthways strips, place on the salad leaves and spoon the vinegar and nuts over the liver. Remove the raspberries from the wine with a slotted spoon and arrange around the livers.

SALAD OF QUAIL WITH GRAPES

INGREDIENTS (serves 4)
4 plump quail
salt and freshly ground black pepper
8 juniper berries, crushed
4 slices of smoked bacon
1 heart of Cos lettuce
1 head of oak leaf lettuce
20 g/¾ oz butter
175 g/6 oz seedless green grapes,
    peeled and halved
50 g/2 oz walnut halves
3 tbsp red wine vinegar
75 ml/3 fl oz walnut oil
50 ml/2 fl oz olive oil
1 tsp Dijon mustard
2 tbsp finely chopped chervil

Heat the oven to 230°C/450°F/Gas 8.

Season the quail inside and out. Place 2 juniper berries in the cavity of each bird and tie a slice of bacon over the breasts. Place on a rack in a roasting tin and roast for 8 minutes. Remove the bacon and return the quail to the oven for 5 minutes.

Just before the quail are cooked divide the lettuces between 4 plates.

Heat the butter, add the grapes and nuts and cook, stirring occasionally, for 2 - 3 minutes until warmed through. Remove the quails from the roasting tin, stir the vinegar into the cooking juices and simmer briefly, stirring up the sediment. Pour into a bowl and immediately whisk in the oils and mustard. Cover to keep warm.

Remove the grapes and nuts with a slotted spoon and keep warm.

Skin the quails and quickly remove the flesh from the breasts. Divide the quail meat, grapes and nuts between the plates of lettuce. Stir the dressing, adjust the seasoning and spoon over the salads. Finish with the chervil.

CRAB-PASTA SALAD

INGREDIENTS (serves 6)
7 g/¼ oz butter
l tbsp finely chopped shallot
100 g/4 oz crab meat
salt and lemon juice
½ egg white
100 ml/4 fl oz double cream, chilled
freshly ground white pepper
½ quantity red pepper pasta (see p.78)

FOR THE SAUCE
150 ml/¼ pint fish stock (see p.75)
65 ml/2½fl oz double cream
65 ml/2½ fl oz hazelnut oil
salt and freshly ground white pepper
lemon juice

FOR THE SALAD
2 heads of radicchio lettuce
2 tbsp finely chopped basil

Heat the butter in a small saucepan, add the shallot, cover and cook over a moderate heat, shaking the pan occasionally, until the shallot is soft.

Purée the crab in a food processor or blender with the shallot, then add salt and a squeeze of lemon juice. Mix in the egg white, then, with the motor still running, gradually pour in the cream. Season, cover and chill for an hour.

Prepare the red pepper pasta and leave to relax under an inverted bowl for 1 hour.

Divide the pasta dough in half. Keep one half covered by the bowl and roll the other half out very thinly. Cut out .18 circles with a plain cutter. Divide the crab mixture between the circles, placing a small mound on each one. Roll out the other piece of pasta dough very thinly and cut out another 18 circles. Dampen the edges of the first set of circles and carefully cover each one with a circle from the second set. Line up the top and bottom edges and press them together.

Bring a pan of salted water to boiling point, add the pasta in batches and cook for 5 - 7 minutes. Remove with a slotted spoon and drain on a cloth.

Meanwhile, reserve a little of the stock for the sauce and boil the remainder until reduced to a slightly syrupy glaze. Stir in the cream and bring just to the boil. Pour into a blender, then, with the motor still running, slowly pour in the oil. Season with salt, pepper and a squeeze of lemon juice. If the sauce is too thick add a little of the reserved stock.

Divide the radicchio between 6 plates. Place 3 pasta parcels on each plate, pour the sauce over and sprinkle with basil.

FENNEL AND FRENCH BEAN SALAD

INGREDIENTS (serves 4)
2 tsp tarragon vinegar
100 g/4 oz fromage blanc
1 tbsp green peppercorns, crushed
salt
75 g/3 oz French beans, cut into strips
1 head of fennel, cut into julienne
1 small courgette, cut into julienne
leaves from ½ bunch of watercress
½ green pepper, blanched, peeled and
*   cut into diamond shapes*
1½ tbsp finely chopped tarragon

FOR THE GARNISH
fennel leaves

A green salad with a difference. Serve it as a first course or to accompany simply cooked meats or fish. Fromage blanc is a soft, low-fat cheese that is available from good delicatessens and supermarkets. If it is not available German quark would make a suitable alternative.

———————

Beat the vinegar into the fromage blanc, then stir in the peppercorns and salt. Chill lightly.

Cut the strips of French beans in half, lightly toss together with the fennel, courgette, watercress, green pepper and tarragon.

Arrange the vegetables to make 4 salads. Pour the green peppercorn dressing to one side. Garnish the dressing with fennel leaves.

FISH AND SHELLFISH

Fish and shellfish feature strongly in Cuisine Vivante recipes, and for obvious reasons. Largely delicate creatures they demand a great deal of precision and careful judgement when cooking if the most is to be made of their subtle flesh and absolute freshness. The abundant variety of flavours, textures and styles provides immense scope for innovative sauce combinations that exentuate the nuances and subtleties of the flesh, be it sole, scallops, turbot or lobster.

SALMON TROUT WITH CHAMPAGNE

SAUCE

INGREDIENTS (serves 4—6)
1 salmon trout, approximately
    1 kg/2¼lb, with head, cleaned
400 ml/14 fl oz champagne or good
    quality sparkling dry white wine
200 ml/7 fl oz fish stock
1 sprig of tarragon
1 sprig of dill
5 green peppercorns
sea salt
300 ml/10 fl oz double cream

FOR THE GARNISH
salmon eggs
sprigs of dill

Picture: page 150

The cucumber and tomato for the garnish can be prepared by any of the methods described on p.70-73.

———————

Heat the oven to 190°C/375°F/Gas 5.

Place the fish in a fish kettle or a large casserole, pour the champagne or sparkling wine and fish stock over, add the herbs, peppercorns and sea salt, cover closely with buttered greaseproof paper, then bring just to the boil over a low heat. Transfer to the oven and cook for 20 minutes or until the flesh flakes easily.

Carefully transfer the fish to a warmed plate, cover and keep warm.

Boil the champagne liquor until reduced by about three quarters.

Strain the liquor and reheat, stirring in the cream. Simmer until thick enough to coat the back of a spoon. Season.

Carefully remove the fillets from the fish, discard the skin and place on 4 warmed plates. Spoon a very little of the sauce over the fish. Spoon the rest around the fish. Scatter the salmon eggs over the salmon trout and lay the sprigs of dill on the sauce.

SALMON WITH LEMON

BUTTER SAUCE

INGREDIENTS (serves 4)
16 slim asparagus spears, trimmed
salt and freshly ground white pepper
4 salmon escalopes
1 tbsp finely chopped shallot
150 ml/5 fl oz dry white wine
150 ml/5 fl oz fish stock
2 tbsp lemon juice
225 g/8 oz butter, diced

FOR THE GARNISH
salmon eggs
strips of lemon peel

Picture: page 151

Steam the asparagus for 12 — 15 minutes until tender. Blanch the strips of lemon peel for the garnish, refresh and drain and dry well.

Meanwhile, season the salmon and poach with the shallots in the wine and stock in a large, buttered frying pan for about 8-10 minutes, until the flesh flakes easily.

Transfer the salmon to a warmed plate using a fish slice. Cover and keep warm.

Reduce the poaching liquor with the lemon juice to 1 tbsp. Reduce the heat to very low and gradually whisk in the butter, making sure that each piece is completely incorporated before adding the next. Season.

Divide the sauce between 4 warmed plates. Place the salmon on top and place the salmon eggs on the salmon. Arrange the asparagus spears attractively on the sauce and garnish with lemon.

SLICES OF SALMON WITH DILL

INGREDIENTS (serves 6)
450 g/1 lb salmon fillet, chilled
3 tbsp lemon juice
salt and freshly ground white pepper
40 g/1½ oz butter
2 shallots, finely chopped
175 ml/6 fl oz fish stock
1 tbsp finely chopped celery leaves
3 stalks of parsley, chopped
4 tbsp finely chopped dill
250 ml/9 fl oz full-bodied dry white
   wine
2 egg yolks
50 ml/2 fl oz double cream

FOR THE GARNISH
diamond shapes of red and green
   pepper
julienne of lemon rind

At least 8 hours before serving, slice the salmon very thinly, lay the slices in a large shallow, non-metal dish, sprinkle with lemon juice and seasoning, cover and leave in a cool place.

Heat the butter and add the shallots. Cover and cook over a moderate heat, shaking the pan occasionally, until the shallots are soft. Stir in the stock and reduce to a syrupy glaze. Stir in the celery leaves, parsley stalks, 3 tbsp dill and the wine, cover and simmer for 15 minutes. Reduce to 175ml/6 fl oz. Pass through a sieve. Leave to cool, then remove the fat from the surface.

Just before serving, dry the salmon slices on absorbent paper. Place 6 plates in a very low oven to warm.

Bring the reduced liquid to the boil.

Blend the egg yolks and cream together. Stir in a little of the hot liquid then stir this mixture into the remaining liquid and cook over a very low heat, stirring constantly, until the sauce coats the back of a spoon. Remove from the heat, season and stir in the remaining dill.

Spoon most of the sauce over the plates. Place the salmon slices on top and trickle the remaining sauce over it. Garnish with the red and green pepper diamonds and lemon julienne.

SMALL SALMON LOAVES

INGREDIENTS (serves 4)
300 g/10 oz fillet of salmon, skinned,
   chilled
2 eggs, separated
2 tbsp double cream, chilled and
   lightly whipped
salt and freshly ground white
   pepper
100 g/4 oz Swiss chard leaves, green
   part only
4 pigs caul
white wine sauce (see p.180)

Chop half the salmon, then mix in a food processor with the egg yolks to make a smooth purée. With the motor running, add the cream and seasoning and mix to a smooth light mixture. Chill for at least 30 minutes.

Heat the oven to 180°C/350°F/Gas 4.

Blanch the chard leaves, refresh, drain and dry on absorbent paper.

Slice the remaining salmon into 8 small thin circles.

Place 4 of the salmon circles on the work surface. Use half the chard to cover the salmon, add a layer of the salmon mousse and cover with the remaining chard. Finally, top with the remaining circles of salmon.

Wrap each pile in caul. Beat the egg whites lightly and use to seal the caul.

Place the loaves in the oven for about 10 minutes.

Prepare the sauce.

Remove the loaves from the oven and leave to stand for a few minutes.

Spoon the sauce over 4 warmed plates. Cut the loaves in half and place on the sauce.

Salmon trout with champagne sauce
Recipe: page 148

Salmon with lemon butter sauce
Recipe: page 148

PLAITED CROWN OF SALMON AND BRILL

INGREDIENTS (serves 6)
450 g/1 lb brill fillets, cut lengthways
  into 9 thin strips
450 g/1 lb salmon fillets, cut
  lengthways into 9 thin strips
salt and freshly ground white pepper
225 g/8 oz cold butter, diced
1 red pepper, skinned and chopped
2 tbsp white wine vinegar
1 tbsp lemon juice
3 tbsp medium-bodied, fruity dry
  white wine
3 tbsp finely chopped shallot

FOR THE GARNISH
cucumber, turned, with the skin on
diamond shapes of skinned red pepper
sprigs of fennel

Make 3 plaits of 1 strip of brill and 2 strips of salmon and 3 plaits of 2 strips of brill and 1 of salmon. Form the plaits into rings and hold in place with wooden cocktail sticks. Season.

Heat 15 g/½ oz butter in a large non-stick frying pan over a low heat. Add the fish, cover closely with buttered greaseproof paper and cook for 5-8 minutes, turning carefully once, until the flesh is just opaque.

Steam the cucumber for the garnish for 3-4 minutes until just tender.

Meanwhile purée the red pepper. Boil the vinegar, lemon juice, wine and shallot until nearly all the liquid has evaporated. Remove from the heat and whisk in 15 g/½ oz butter. Place over a very low heat and very gradually whisk in the remaining butter, making sure each piece is fully incorporated before adding the next. When all the butter has been incorporated, whisk in the red pepper purée. Season.

Divide the sauce between 6 plates. Place the rings on the sauce. Place the cucumber in the centre of the rings. Arrange the red pepper in the cucumber. Place sprigs of fennel on the sauce.

SALMON AND SCALLOPS WITH SEAWEED AND CHAMPAGNE SAUCE

INGREDIENTS (serves 4)
4 scallops
600 ml/1 pt fish stock
450 g/1lb salmon, cut into strips
1 tbsp finely chopped parsley
1 tbsp finely chopped chives
1 stick of celery, cut into julienne
1 leek, cut into julienne
7.5 cm/3 inch piece of cucumber,
  seeded and cut into julienne
150 ml/5 fl oz champagne or other
  good quality sparkling dry white
  wine
6 tbsp double cream
salt and freshly ground white pepper
1 sheet of nori (Japanese dried
  seaweed)
4 tbsp concassé tomato

Picture: page 154

Nori is available in Oriental food shops and some health food shops. If it is not available, another type of Japanese seaweed could be substituted — prepare it according to the instructions on the packet or ask the advice of the shop assistant.

Remove the scallops from their shells (see p.61). Reserve the liquor. Cut the scallop bodies in half. Season.

Boil the stock and reduce by one third. Add the scallop liquor and reduce the heat so the stock just simmers.

Add the salmon, parsley and chives and poach for about 5 minutes. Add the scallop slices and corals and cook for 2—3 minutes, turning them once, until just opaque.

Meanwhile, steam the celery and leek for about 3 minutes, then add the cucumber and steam for 30 seconds.

Remove the fish with a slotted spoon and keep warm.

Stir the champagne or sparkling wine into the poaching liquor, then stir in the cream and simmer until slightly thickened. Season and keep warm without boiling.

Place the nori under a hot grill for a few moments, then cut into julienne.

Spoon the sauce over 4 warmed plates. Arrange the fish, then arrange the vegetable julienne, nori and tomato concassé around.

STRIPS OF SALMON WITH

MUSHROOMS AND QUAILS EGGS

INGREDIENTS (serves 4)
50 g/2 oz butter, diced
550 g/1¼ lb wild salmon, cut into strips
salt and freshly ground white pepper
225 g/8 oz wild mushrooms
4 quails eggs
2 tbsp finely chopped chervil, tarragon, chives, and parsley, mixed

FOR THE SAUCE
375 ml/13 fl oz light, fruity red wine, eg red Loire or Beaujolais Villages
3 tbsp chopped shallots
a sprig of thyme
1 bay leaf
1 tbsp fish glaze (see p.75)
25 ml/1 fl oz double cream
175 g/6 oz butter, diced

The superior flavour and texture of wild salmon give the best results in this recipe.

For the sauce, simmer the wine, shallots, thyme and bay leaf until syrupy, then stir in the fish glaze and cream. Pass through a sieve, return to the rinsed pan and reheat gently over a very low heat. Gradually stir in the butter, making sure that each piece is fully incorporated before adding the next. Season and keep warm but do not allow to boil.

Heat 20 g/¾ oz butter. Season the salmon lightly, add to the pan for 2—3 minutes, turning the strips so they cook evenly. Remove with a slotted spoon and drain on absorbent paper.

Add the remaining butter to the pan, then add the mushrooms and cook for 2—3 minutes, depending on the type. Remove with a slotted spoon and drain on absorbent paper. Sprinkle with seasoning.

Meanwhile, cook the quails eggs in gently boiling water for 2 minutes. Peel then cut into quarters.

Arrange the salmon and mushrooms in the centre of 4 warmed plates. Pour the sauce over and arrange the eggs. Sprinkle with the herbs.

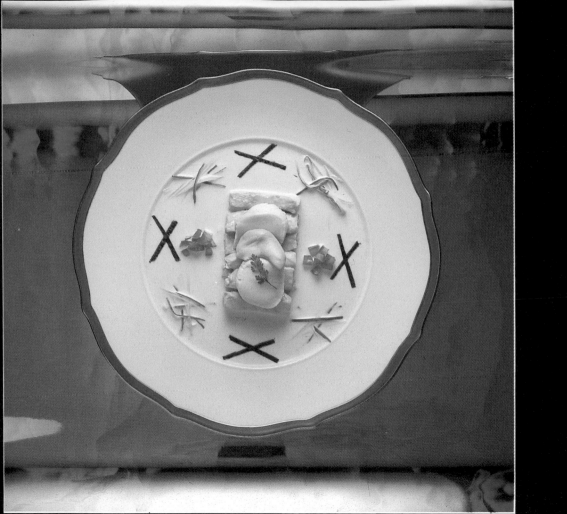

T U R B O T   A N D   P R A W N   T I M B A L E S

INGREDIENTS (serves 4—6)
225 g/8 oz skinless turbot fillets
salt and lemon juice
1 egg white
300 ml/½ pt double cream, chilled
a few strands of saffron
freshly ground white pepper
100 g/4 oz peeled cooked prawns
1½ tbsp chopped pistachio nuts

FOR THE SAUCE
1 shallot, finely chopped
a small pinch of finely chopped
    tarragon
½ tbsp butter, diced
90 ml/6 tbsp dry white wine
90 ml/6 tbsp champagne or good
    quality sparkling dry white wine
300 ml/½ pt double cream

FOR THE GARNISH
cooked prawns, some in their shells,
    some shelled
sprigs of fennel
slices of cucumber

Picture: page 158

Purée the turbot in a food processor or blender, then mix in the salt and lemon juice followed by the egg white.

Pass through a sieve into a bowl placed over a bowl of ice. Reserve 25 ml/1 fl oz of the cream and very gradually beat the remainder into the fish with the saffron and pepper. Cover and chill for at least 30 minutes.

Heat the oven to 170°C/325°F/Gas 3. Line the bottom of 4 or 6 dariole moulds with buttered greaseproof paper.

Mix the prawns with the reserved cream, pistachio nuts and seasoning.

Line the base and sides of the moulds with most of the turbot mixture, then spoon the prawn mixture into the centres and cover with the remaining turbot mixture. Tap the moulds firmly to get rid of the air bubbles, then place them in a roasting or baking tin and surround with boiling water. Cover the tops of the moulds with buttered greaseproof paper and place in the oven for about 20 minutes.

For the sauce, add the shallot and tarragon to the butter, cover and cook over a moderate heat, shaking the pan occasionally until soft. Stir in the wines and reduce to 2 tbsp. Stir in the cream and simmer until the sauce coats the back of a spoon. Pass through a fine sieve, season and keep warm.

Remove the timbales from the heat and allow to stand for a few minutes before unmoulding onto warm plates. Spoon the sauce around and garnish with the prawns, fennel and slices of cucumber.

P A R C E L S   O F   T U R B O T   W I T H

S C A L L O P S

INGREDIENTS (serves 4)
4 fillets of turbot, thinly sliced, each
    approximately 100 g/4 oz
salt and freshly ground white pepper
4 scallops
4 large spinach leaves
300 ml/½ pt medium-bodied dry white
    wine
200 ml/7 fl oz double cream
a few strands of saffron soaked in
    2 tbsp medium-bodied dry white
    wine
2 egg yolks

Season the turbot fillets.

Open the scallops and separate the bodies from the corals (see p.61). Slice the bodies into 3 horizontally, then place along half the length of the fillets. Put the corals in the centre. Fold the remaining lengths of the fillets over the filling.

Blanch, refresh, drain and dry the spinach leaves then wrap around the turbot fillets to form neat parcels. Place in the top part of a steamer and cover with buttered greaseproof paper.

Bring some seasoned water to simmering point in the bottom part of the steamer. Put the top part in place and cover. Cook the fish for 5—6 minutes until the fish is just opaque throughout.

Meanwhile, boil the wine until reduced to 90 ml/3½ fl oz. Stir in the cream and reduce again to 100 ml/4 fl oz. Stir in the saffron liquor.

Blend the egg yolks together in a small bowl then whisk in

the hot liquid. Place the bowl over a pan of hot water and whisk until the mixture coats the back of the spoon. Remove from the heat and season.

Carefully cut each parcel from end to end, about two thirds of the way down.

Spoon the sauce over 4 warmed plates and place the parcels, partially opened to show the fish, in the centre of the plates.

TURBOT WITH LEEKS AND MUSHROOM MELANGE

INGREDIENTS (serves 6)
12 young leeks, white parts only
salt and freshly ground white pepper
6 turbot fillets, each approximately
*   150 g/5 oz*
3 tbsp lemon juice
215 g/7½ oz butter, diced
2 shallots, finely chopped
300 ml/½ pt fruity dry white wine
100 g/4 oz button mushrooms, finely
*   chopped*
300 g/10 oz chanterelles, morels or
*   mousserons*
2 tbsp truffle juice (optional)
2 tbsp sercial madeira (or 4 tbsp if
*   truffle juice is not used)*
2 tbsp whipping cream
175 g/6 oz butter, diced
1 tbsp finely chopped chives

Picture: page 155

Choose dishes that do not require much last minute preparation to serve before and after this dish. Just a simple vegetable is all that is needed to accompany it.

Heat the oven to 200°C/400°F/Gas 6.

Blanch the leeks for 3—4 minutes. Refresh, drain well, then cut into 1.5 cm/½inch slices.

Season the turbot and sprinkle with some of the lemon juice.

Heat 15 g/½ oz butter in a sauteuse or frying pan large enough to hold the turbot fillets in one layer. Add the shallots and cook over a moderate heat until soft. Stir in the wine and boil for 1 minute. Add the button mushrooms and place the turbot on top. Place a piece of buttered greaseproof paper on the fish, put on the lid and put in the oven for 3 minutes.

Meanwhile, melt 15 g/½ oz butter, add the wild mushrooms and cook for 2—3 minutes. Add a squeeze of lemon juice and the truffle juice (if using), and cook for 1 minute. Remove the mushrooms with a slotted spoon, cover and keep warm.

Stir the madeira into the mushroom juices and reduce until syrupy. Reduce the heat to very low and gradually whisk in 15 g/½ oz butter.

Gently warm the slices of leek in 15 g/½ oz butter and a very little water in a small covered pan.

Lift the turbot from the sauteuse, cover and keep warm. Pass the juices through a fine sieve, pressing hard to extract as much flavour as possible, then boil until reduced by one third. Stir in the cream, bring to the boil and gradually whisk in the remaining butter at a full boil. Add the chives, seasoning and lemon juice to taste. Keep warm, but do not boil.

Place a turbot fillet in the centre of each warmed plate and arrange small mounds of leeks and small circles of dark sauce alternately around the fish. Place small mounds of mushrooms on the sauce. Pour the white wine sauce over the fish.

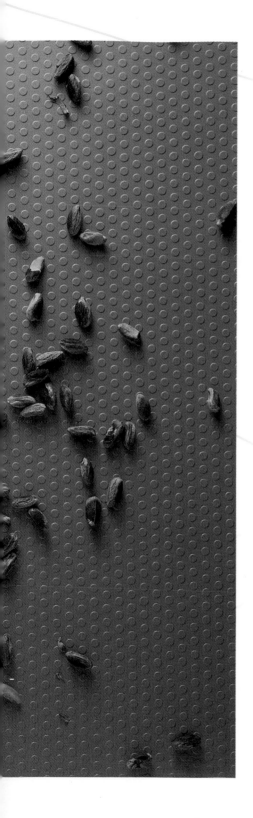

LEFT *Turbot and prawn timbales*
Recipe: page 156
ABOVE *Pike quenelles with white wine*
sauce
Recipe: page 180

TURBOT WITH TOMATOES AND MUSHROOMS

INGREDIENTS (serves 4)
150 ml/¼ pt good quality sparkling dry
    white wine
150 ml/¼ pt sercial madeira
200 ml/7 fl oz fish stock
2 tbsp very finely chopped shallots
flesh of 3 tomatoes, chopped
225 g/8 oz button mushrooms, sliced
4 fillets of turbot, each approximately
    175 g/6 oz
salt and freshly ground black pepper
225 ml/8 fl oz double cream
2 tbsp finely chopped parsley

Heat the sparkling wine, madeira and stock in a saucepan or flameproof dish that is large enough to hold the fish in a single layer, to simmering point. Add the shallots, tomatoes and mushrooms, reduce the heat so the liquid is just moving, then lay the fillets on the vegetables. Season, cover the fish with buttered greaseproof paper and poach for 4 minutes.

Carefully transfer the fish to a warmed plate, cover and keep warm.

Boil the liquor until reduced to about 75 ml/3 fl oz. Stir in the cream and any juices that have come out of the fish and boil until the sauce is slightly thickened, stirring frequently.

Divide the sauce between 4 warmed plates and arrange a bed of vegetables on one half of each plate. Sprinkle the parsley over the borders of the 'beds' and the surrounding sauce then place the fillets on the 'beds'.

FILLETS OF TURBOT WITH CUCUMBERS

INGREDIENTS (serves 4)
1½ tbsp finely chopped shallot
salt and freshly ground white pepper
4 turbot fillets, approximately
    175 g/6 oz, each cut into 3
150 ml/¼ pt dry white wine
75 ml/3 fl oz fish stock
½ large firm straight cucumber
50 ml/2 fl oz dry vermouth
150 ml/¼ pt double cream
40 g/1½ oz butter, diced
a squeeze of lemon juice
½ tsp finely chopped tarragon

FOR THE GARNISH
small sprigs of tarragon
lemon

Scatter the shallots over a large buttered flameproof dish. Season the turbot and lay the slices side by side on the shallots. Heat the wine and stock and pour over the turbot. Cover with buttered foil. Bring just to the boil, lower the heat and poach for 5 minutes.

Cut the cucumber in half lengthways, scoop out the seeds and 'turn' the flesh (see p.65) so that each piece is backed by green skin. Blanch, refresh and drain well.

Carefully transfer the fish to a warmed plate, cover and keep warm.

Add the vermouth to the poaching liquor and reduce by a quarter. Stir in the cream and boil until slightly thickened. Pass through a sieve and reheat gently. Gradually swirl in 25 g/1 oz butter, making sure each piece is fully incorporated before adding the next. Season and add a squeeze of lemon juice. Keep warm but do not boil.

Heat the remaining 15 g/½ oz butter, stir in the tarragon, add the cucumber and heat through gently, shaking the pan frequently. Carefully remove with a slotted spoon.

Spoon the sauce over 4 warmed plates, carefully arrange the fish on top, add the cucumber and garnish with the sprigs of tarragon and lemon.

TROUT WITH GREEN SAUCE

INGREDIENTS (serves 4)
100 ml/4 fl oz medium-bodied dry
     white wine
1 shallot, chopped
1 small stick of celery, with leaves,
     chopped
½ carrot, chopped
1 small bay leaf
a sprig of thyme
salt and freshly ground black pepper
4 trout
65 g/2½ oz lettuce leaves
2 egg yolks
1 tsp lime juice
100 g/4 oz clarified butter, melted
½ spring onion, very finely chopped

FOR THE GARNISH
turned cucumber
sprigs of dill
salmon eggs

Heat the oven to 180°C/350°F/Gas 4.

Put the wine, vegetables, herbs and seasoning into a greased flameproof dish large enough to hold the fish. Bring to the boil, add the trout, cover with buttered greaseproof paper and put in the oven for about 15 minutes until the flesh is just opaque.

Blanch the lettuce leaves for 2 minutes. Refresh, drain well and dry on absorbent paper.

Carefully remove the skin from the trout, then gently lift the fillets off the bones. Place on a warmed plate, cover and keep warm.

Steam the cucumber for 2 minutes.

Boil the cooking juices until reduced to 1 tbsp.

Combine the lettuce, egg yolks, lime juice and cooking juices in a food processor. With the motor still running, pour in the hot butter in a slow stream. Add the spring onion and taste for seasoning.

Place the trout on 4 warmed plates. Spoon the sauce to the side. Garnish with cucumber, sprigs of dill and a few salmon eggs.

TROUT WITH CUCUMBER SAUCE

INGREDIENTS (serves 4)
40 g/1½ oz butter, chopped
1 shallot, finely chopped
4 trout, filleted and skinned
salt and freshly ground white pepper
100 ml/4 fl oz dry white vermouth
300 ml/½ pt fish stock
½ large, firm cucumber, peeled, seeded
     and chopped
a sprig of thyme
75 ml/3 fl oz good quality sparkling
     dry white wine
100 ml/4 fl oz double cream

FOR THE GARNISH
baby new potatoes
small balls of pea or pea and mint
     purée (see p.300)
concassé tomatoes

This light main course fish dish, which needs no other accompaniment except wine, is an ideal choice for a summer luncheon.

Heat 15 g/½ oz butter, add the shallot and cook gently for 2-3 minutes.

Cut each trout fillet into 3 strips lengthways. Lay them on top of the shallots. Season. Pour the vermouth over. Cover with buttered greaseproof paper and cook over a low heat for about 2 minutes until the flesh is just opaque. Transfer to a warmed dish, cover and keep warm.

Add the stock, cucumber and thyme and reduce by three quarters. Remove the thyme, purée the sauce then pass through a sieve. Add the sparkling wine and cream and simmer for about 3 minutes. Gradually swirl in the remaining butter over a low heat.

Meanwhile, cook the baby new potatoes in a steamer and warm the balls of purée on a piece of foil on top of it.

Coat 4 warmed plates with the sauce. Arrange the strips of trout on the sauce and arrange the potatoes and purée around. Finish with the tomato.

Scallops with saffron sauce
Recipe: page 165

SCALLOPS WITH MUSSEL PARCELS

INGREDIENTS (serves 4)
100 ml/4 fl oz dry white wine
16 mussels
16 spinach leaves
spinach mousseline (see p.308)
    (optional)
salt and freshly ground white pepper
28 small scallops

FOR THE SAUCE
75 g/3 oz butter, diced
900 g/2 lb shells from cooked prawns,
    crushed
225 g/8 oz mixed chopped carrots and
    leeks and diced celery
1 tsp tomato purée
2 tbsp cognac
225 ml/8 fl oz dry white wine
450 ml/15 fl oz fish stock
150 ml/5 fl oz double cream
salt and freshly ground white pepper

Picture: page 166

For the sauce, heat the butter and add the prawn shells and vegetables and cook over a low heat for about 5 minutes, stirring occasionally. Stir in the purée and cognac and ignite with a taper. Stir in the wine and boil until nearly all the liquid has evaporated. Stir in the stock and reduce until syrupy. Stir in the cream and seasoning and simmer for about 3 minutes. Pass through a conical strainer, pressing down well to extract as much liquid as possible. Keep warm over a low heat.

Heat the wine, add the mussels and steam for a few seconds until they have only just opened. Remove them from their shells and drain well.

Blanch and refresh the spinach leaves and drain well, then spread them out and place a mussel and a spoonful of spinach mousseline in the centre of each. Fold the leaves over to make neat parcels, but leave one end open so part of the mussel shows. Place over a steamer to keep warm.

Reheat the wine with a little seasoning to just below simmering point. Remove the scallops from their shells (see p.61), add to the wine and poach for about 45 seconds each side.

Coat 4 warmed plates with sauce, arrange 4 spinach-wrapped mussels in the centre of each one and arrange 7 scallops around.

SCALLOPS WITH DILL

INGREDIENTS (serves 4)
12 scallops
50 g/2 oz butter
2 small leeks, cut into julienne
2 small carrots, cut into julienne
1 courgette, cut into fine batons
150 ml/$\frac{1}{4}$ pt fish stock
150 ml/$\frac{1}{4}$ pt dry white wine
65 ml/$2\frac{1}{2}$ fl oz double cream
sea salt and freshly ground white
    pepper
2 tbsp chopped dill

FOR THE GARNISH
mangetouts, cut into julienne, or
    sprigs of dill

Picture: page 162

Remove the scallops from their shells. Reserve their liquor. Separate the corals and cut the bodies in half horizontally.

Heat half the butter in a large heavy pan, add the vegetables and cook, covered, over a low heat for about 4 minutes, shaking the pan occasionally. Do not allow them to brown. Stir in the stock, scallop liquor, and wine and bring to the boil. Reduce to about 65 ml/$2\frac{1}{2}$ fl oz, then stir in the cream and simmer for a few minutes until the sauce thickens slightly. Season lightly.

Heat the remaining butter, add the scallops, a little salt and most of the dill. Cook gently for 1 minute, turn them over, add the corals and cook for a further minute — do not allow them to brown or toughen.

Tip a little of the scallop cooking liquor into the sauce and stir briefly to mix.

Meanwhile, blanch, refresh and drain the julienne of mangetouts, if using.

Divide the sauce and vegetables between 4 warmed dishes and arrange the scallops and corals on top. Sprinkle with the remaining dill and garnish with julienne of mangetouts or sprigs of dill.

SCALLOPS WITH SMOKED SALMON

AND BASIL

INGREDIENTS (serves 4)
16 scallops
25 g/1 oz butter
2 shallots, finely chopped
4 thin slices of smoked salmon, cut
 into thin strips
2½ tbsp finely chopped basil
50 ml/2 fl oz full-bodied dry white
 wine
175 ml/6 fl oz double cream
salt and freshly ground black pepper
175 g/6 oz noodles (see p.78)
1 tbsp oil
50 g/2 oz hazelnuts, toasted and
 coarsely chopped

FOR THE GARNISH
asparagus tips

Use 2 or 3 different colours of noodles to produce a delight-ful harlequin effect.

Open the scallops (see p.61), separate the corals from the bodies and slice the bodies horizontally into 3.

Heat the butter, add the shallots, cover and cook over a moderate heat, shaking the pan occasionally until the shallots are soft. Stir in half the smoked salmon and the basil and cook for 2 minutes. Stir in the wine and cream and reduce by a quarter. Season.

Cook the noodles with the oil in plenty of salted water until just tender. Steam the asparagus tips for the garnish.

Meanwhile, add the scallops to the sauce and cook with the sauce just below simmering point for about 1 minute. Add the corals and cook for a further minute until the scallops are just opaque. Season.

Drain the noodles well and toss with freshly ground black pepper and the hazelnuts.

Spoon the scallops and sauce onto 4 warmed plates and arrange the noodles around in small mounds. Garnish with asparagus tips.

SCALLOPS WITH SAFFRON SAUCE

INGREDIENTS (serves 4)
16 large scallops
20 g/¾ oz butter
2 tbsp finely chopped shallots
salt and freshly ground pepper
150 ml/5 fl oz medium-bodied
 fruity dry white wine
225 ml/8 fl oz fish stock
200 ml/7fl oz double cream
several strands of saffron dissolved
 in a little of the white wine

FOR THE GARNISH
sprigs of dill
concassé tomatoes

Picture: page 163

Open the scallops (see p.61). Separate the corals from the bodies and cut the bodies in half horizontally. Place on a cloth.

Heat the butter, add the shallots, cover and cook over a low heat, shaking the pan occasionally, until soft.

Season the scallops, add the bodies to the pan, then cook over a low heat for 1 minute. Add the corals and cook for a further minute.

Remove the scallops with a slotted spoon, cover and keep warm.

Stir the wine into the pan and reduce to 25 ml/1fl oz. Stir in the stock and reduce to 50 ml/2 fl oz. Stir in the cream and dissolved saffron, and simmer until slightly thickened. Season.

Divide the sauce between the warmed plates. Arrange the scallop bodies and corals on top. Garnish with sprigs of dill and concassé tomatoes.

LEFT *Scallops with mussel parcels*
Recipe: page 164
ABOVE *Lobster medallions with chive sauce*
Recipe: page 177

167

ROLLS OF SOLE WITH SORREL SAUCE

INGREDIENTS (serves 4)
225 g/8 oz turbot
salt and lemon juice
1 large egg white
225 ml/8 fl oz double cream, chilled
1 tbsp cognac
approximately 2 tbsp well-drained
    puréed watercress
freshly ground white pepper
8 sole fillets, skinned
court bouillon

FOR THE SAUCE
200 ml/7 fl oz fish stock
175 ml/6 fl oz dry white wine
175 ml/6 fl oz dry vermouth
1 shallot, finely chopped
225 ml/8 fl oz crème fraîche
50 g/2 oz sorrel, thinly sliced
salt
lemon juice

FOR THE GARNISH
carrot shapes (see p.70)
long lozenges of tomato
sprigs of dill

Picture: page 171

Purée the turbot in a food processor or blender. Mix in the salt and lemon juice, followed by the egg white. Pass through a sieve into a bowl in a bowl of ice. Gradually beat in the cream. Add the cognac and enough puréed watercress to give a good green colour. Add the pepper. Cover and chill for at least 30 minutes.

Lightly score the skinned side of the sole fillets. Season lightly, then spread the turbot mixture over. Roll up the fillets.

Pack the fillets into a well-buttered sauteuse or frying pan which they should just fit. Gently pour in sufficient court bouillon to come almost up the sides of the sole. Cover the rolls with buttered greaseproof paper and poach for about 12 minutes.

For the sauce, boil the stock, wine, vermouth and shallot until reduced to 50 ml/2 fl oz. Whisk in the crème fraîche and simmer until slightly thickened. Add the sorrel and simmer for 30 seconds. Season and add lemon juice to taste.

Remove the fish rolls with a slotted spoon and place on 4 warmed plates. Spoon the sauce around and garnish with carrot, tomato and dill.

SOLE WITH OYSTER PARCELS

INGREDIENTS (serves 4)
1 tbsp finely chopped shallot
150 ml/5 fl oz fish stock
65 ml/2½ fl oz dry vermouth
6 fillets of sole, skinned and cut into
    strips
salt and freshly ground pepper
12 oysters
12 lettuce leaves
a small sprig of fresh thyme
150 ml/5 fl oz double cream
1½ tsp white wine vinegar
15 g/½ oz butter, diced
1 tsp finely chopped chervil

FOR THE GARNISH
12 diamond shapes of tomato flesh

Simmer the shallot in the stock and vermouth for 3-4 minutes in a small covered pan. Pour into a sauteuse or frying pan that will hold the sole in a single layer. Lay the sole strips in the pan, season, cover with greaseproof paper and poach for about 1½ minutes until just opaque.

Carefully transfer to a warmed dish with a slotted spoon, cover and keep warm.

Meanwhile open the oysters. Blanch the lettuce leaves, drain well and dry on absorbent paper.

Add the oysters to the poaching liquor and poach for 30 seconds. Remove with a slotted spoon and wrap each oyster into a lettuce leaf, folding the leaf over to make a neat parcel.

Meanwhile, add the thyme to the liquor and reduce to 50 ml/2 fl oz. Pour into a small saucepan, stir in the cream and simmer for 5 minutes. Pass through a sieve. Return to the heat, stir in the vinegar and reheat gently then, over a low heat, gradually whisk in the butter, making sure each piece is fully incorporated before adding the next. Stir in the chervil.

Spoon the sauce over 4 warmed plates. Arrange the strips of sole and the oyster parcels in the sauce. Place a diamond of tomato on each parcel.

ROULADE OF SOLE

INGREDIENTS (serves 4)
6 poached crayfish, shelled
40 ml/1½ fl oz double cream
salt and freshly ground white pepper
4 fillets of sole, skinned
court bouillon

FOR THE WHITE SAUCE
50 ml/2 fl oz fish stock
300 ml/7 fl oz full-bodied dry white
    wine
75 g/3 oz butter, diced
salt and freshly ground white
    pepper

FOR THE RED SAUCE
75 ml/3 fl oz red shellfish glaze (see
    Lobster gâteaux with lobster sauce
    p.176)
75 g/3 oz butter, diced

Peel the crayfish and remove the veins running down the back. Chop the flesh coarsely, then process briefly in a food processor. Add the cream and seasoning and mix briefly. Pass through a fine sieve.

Lightly season the skinned side of the sole then spread the crayfish mixture in a line down the centre. Fold the sides of the sole over the filling. Place with the join underneath in the top half of a steamer. Put the lid on.

Heat some court bouillon in the bottom half of the steamer to simmering point. Put the top half in place and cook the fish for about 5 minutes until just opaque.

Meanwhile, reduce the fish stock and wine for the white sauce to 50 ml/2 fl oz. Reduce the heat to very low, then gradually stir in the butter, making sure that each piece is fully incorporated before adding the next. Season and keep warm but do not allow to boil.

Remove the fish from the heat but keep warm.

Heat the shellfish glaze to simmering point, then reduce the heat to very low and gradually stir in the butter, making sure each piece is fully incorporated before adding the next. Season and keep warm but do not allow to boil.

Trim the ends from the fillets, then cut each fillet into 6 slices and arrange around the centre of 4 warmed plates.

Spoon some of the red sauce into the centres of the plates. Spoon the white sauce around the edge and streak the remaining red sauce from the centre onto the white sauce.

 ## SOLE WITH MANGETOUTS

INGREDIENTS (serves 4)
225 g/8 oz mangetouts
2 small carrots, cut into julienne
salt and freshly ground white pepper
8 fillets of sole, cut in half lengthways
16 very thin slices of fresh ginger
    root, cut into strips
8 spring onions, cut in half
    lengthways
2 tsp olive oil
rind of 2 oranges, cut into short
    julienne
1 tbsp very finely chopped ginger root
2 tbsp soy sauce
6 tbsp fino sherry
a squeeze of lemon juice

Picture: page 170

Arrange the mangetouts and carrots in a large steamer or 2 small ones. Sprinkle with salt and freshly ground white pepper. Season the skin-side of the pieces of sole, then roll them up loosely, seasoned side innermost, starting from the narrow end. Place a little way apart on the vegetables. Place a piece of ginger and a spring onion half on each piece of fish.

Place the steamer over a pan of simmering water and steam for about 8 minutes until the sole is just opaque all the way through.

Meanwhile, heat the oil, add the orange julienne and cook until just beginning to curl. Stir in the chopped ginger and cook for about 30 seconds, then stir in the soy sauce, sherry, lemon juice and 4 tbsp water. Bring to the boil, then reduce the heat and simmer for 5 minutes.

Spoon the sauce onto parts of 4 warmed plates. Carefully place the rolls of sole on the sauce. Scatter the orange julienne on the rolls and garnish the plates with the vegetables.

ABOVE *Sole with mangetouts*
Recipe: page 169
OPPOSITE *Rolls of sole with sorrel sauce*
Recipe: page 168

SOLE AND DUBLIN BAY PRAWNS

WITH RED PEPPER CREAM

INGREDIENTS (serves 4)
50 g/2 oz butter, diced
450 g/1 lb red peppers, diced
1 tbsp sugar
1 tbsp cider vinegar
½ tsp paprika pepper
salt
4 scallops
1 tbsp finely chopped shallot
freshly ground white pepper
225 ml/8 fl oz medium-bodied dry
    white wine
3 fillets of sole, cut into cubes
12-16 large cooked Dublin Bay
    prawns, peeled
50 ml/2 fl oz medium dry sherry
225 ml/8 fl oz whipping cream

FOR THE GARNISH
½ large cucumber, peeled, cut into 12
    slices, 1.25 cm/½ inch thick,
    centres removed, sprinkled with
    salt, left to drain for 30
    minutes, drained and blanched for
    3 minutes
flesh of 1 tomato, finely diced
sprigs of dill

Heat half the butter in a small heavy saucepan, stir in the peppers, sugar, vinegar, paprika and salt, cover and cook for about 5 minutes or until the peppers are very soft, stirring occasionally. Uncover, increase the heat to medium and cook to a thick purée and until all the liquid has evaporated, stirring frequently. Pass through a sieve.

Open the scallops, reserve the liquor and separate the bodies from the corals (see p.61).

Heat the remaining butter in a sauteuse or large frying pan, stir in the shallots, seasoning and half the wine and simmer for 2-3 minutes. Add the sole, reduce the heat and poach the sole for 1¼ minutes. Turn it over, add the prawns and cook for a further minute until the sole is just opaque. Transfer to a warmed dish with a slotted spoon and cover.

Add the remaining wine and the sherry to the pan and reduce to 50 ml/2 fl oz. Whisk in the cream and boil until the sauce is slightly thickened, stirring occasionally.

Whisk the red pepper purée into the sauce and warm through but do not allow to boil. Season.

Place a sheet of foil on the bottom of the top part of a steamer. Place the cucumber rings on the foil. Divide the tomato amongst the cucumber rings, then steam for 2 minutes. Divide the sauce between 4 warmed plates. Arrange the sole, prawns, scallop bodies and corals, then garnish with 3 tomato-topped cucumber rings per plate and sprigs of dill.

FILLETS OF SOLE WITH LIGHT

TOMATO FILLING

INGREDIENTS (serves 4)
flesh of 4 tomatoes, chopped
salt and pepper
3 small egg whites, lightly whisked
4 large fillets of sole, skinned
2 tbsp finely chopped shallot
2 tbsp chopped basil
175 ml/6 fl oz fish stock
150 ml/5 fl oz full-bodied dry white
    wine
75 ml/3 fl oz double cream
25 g/1 oz butter, diced

FOR THE GARNISH
4 diamond shapes of puff pastry
caviar

Cook the tomatoes over a very low heat, stirring frequently until nearly all the moisture has evaporated and the mixture is very thick. Season, leave to cool then turn into a bowl over a bowl of crushed ice and leave to chill.

Gradually beat the egg whites into the tomato pulp.

Season the skinned side of the sole then spread the tomato mixture over the widest half of the length of each fillet. Fold the other half over the mousse and place in the top half of a steamer. Cover with buttered greaseproof paper.

Heat the shallots and basil in the stock and wine in the bottom half of the steamer to simmering point. Put the top half of the steamer in place and cook the sole for about 10 minutes until the flesh is opaque.

Warm the puff pastry diamonds.

Transfer the sole to a warmed plate, cover and keep warm.

Reduce the cooking liquor to 100 ml/4 fl oz then stir in the cream and reduce until thick enough to coat the back of a spoon. Pass through a sieve then reheat in a clean saucepan. Over a very low heat, gradually stir in the butter, making sure each piece is completely incorporated before adding the next. Season.

Spoon the sauce over 4 warmed plates. Place the sole on the sauce. Split the puff pastry diamonds in half lengthways, place some caviar on the bottom half and replace the top at an angle. Place on the plates.

CROWN OF LOBSTER AND SCALLOPS WITH ASPARAGUS

INGREDIENTS (serves 4)
a sprig of thyme
1 shallot, chopped
175 ml/6 fl oz pink champagne or other good quality dry sparkling rosé wine
300 ml/½ pt fish stock
100 ml/4 fl oz double cream
50 g/2 oz butter, diced
1 tbsp champagne vinegar
salt and freshly ground white pepper
12 scallops
100 ml/4 fl oz fruity dry white wine
flesh from 2 cooked lobster tails, sliced
12 green asparagus spears, sliced on the diagonal

FOR THE GARNISH
crayfish tails
slices of truffle

This is a very elegant looking and tasting dish that is not at all complicated. It is ideal for a summer dinner.

Bring the thyme, shallot, champagne and stock to the boil and reduce by three quarters. Pass through a fine sieve, return to the rinsed pan, stir in the cream and simmer for 5 minutes. Reduce the heat to very low and gradually whisk in 25 g/1 oz butter, making sure that each piece is completely incorporated before adding the next. Stir in the vinegar. Season and keep warm, but do not allow to boil.

Remove the scallops from their shells (see p.61) and separate the corals from the bodies. Slice the bodies in half horizontally.

Heat the wine, season lightly, add the scallop bodies and slices of lobster tail and poach for about 1 minute. Turn them over, add the corals and poach for a further minute.

Meanwhile, steam the slices of asparagus for about 5 minutes.

Spoon the sauce over 4 warmed plates. Remove the fish from the wine with a slotted spoon and arrange on the sauce in a circle like a crown. Arrange the asparagus in the centres and garnish with crayfish tails and slices of truffle.

LOBSTER GATEAUX WITH
LOBSTER SAUCE

INGREDIENTS (serves 4)
2 tbsp olive oil
½ lobster shell, crushed and pounded
2 shallots, finely chopped
1 carrot, finely chopped
2 parsley stalks
10 red peppercorns
1 bay leaf, broken
2 tbsp cognac
200 ml/7 fl oz fish stock
115 ml/4½ fl oz dry white wine
salt and white pepper
225 g/8 oz butter, diced

FOR THE GATEAUX
200 g/7 oz turbot fillets
50 g/2 oz lobster tail meat
50 g/2 oz lobster coral, sieved
salt and lemon juice
1 large egg white
300 ml/½ pt double cream, chilled
a small pinch of cayenne pepper

FOR THE GARNISH
sprigs of chervil
crayfish claws

Picture: page 174

The base for the sauce and the lobster gâteaux mixture can be prepared in advance. Other ways of glazing apart from the cobweb pattern in the photograph, include a halo around the gâteaux or tear-drop shapes in the sauce.

Heat the oil, add the lobster shell and cook for 5 minutes, stirring occasionally. Stir in the shallots, carrot, parsley, peppercorns and bayleaf and cook, stirring occasionally, until the shallots are transparent. Pour the cognac over and ignite with a taper. When the flames have subsided, stir in the stock, wine, and seasoning. Cover and simmer for 10 minutes.

Pass through a conical strainer, pressing down well onto the vegetables and shell to extract as much liquid as possible. There should be about 175 ml/6 fl oz — if it is not reduced sufficiently, boil down further.

For the gâteaux, mix the turbot, lobster meat and coral in a food processor, then add the salt and lemon juice, followed by the egg white. Pass through a sieve into a bowl placed over a bowl of ice, then gradually beat in the cream. Season with cayenne pepper. Cover and chill for at least 30 minutes.

Heat the oven to 190°C/370°F/Gas 5.

Divide the lobster mixture between 4 ramekin dishes or dariole moulds, place in a roasting or baking tin, surround with boiling water and cover the tops of the moulds with buttered greaseproof paper. Place in the oven for 20 minutes.

Bring 100 ml/4 fl oz of the lobster liquor to the boil, reduce the heat to very low, then gradually whisk in the butter, making sure each piece is completely incorporated before adding the next. Season and keep warm but do not allow to boil.

Meanwhile, boil the remaining liquor to a light syrupy glaze.

Remove the gâteaux from the heat and allow to stand for a few minutes before turning out onto 4 warmed plates. Place a sprig of chervil on each one. Spoon the sauce around. Make a pattern in the sauce with the lobster glaze and garnish with chervil and crayfish claws.

LOBSTER MEDALLIONS WITH CHIVE SAUCE

INGREDIENTS *(serves 4)*
*8 slices blanched lobster meat from
    the tail*
*8 slices of blanched lobster meat from
    the large claw*
25 g/1 oz unsalted butter

FOR THE SAUCE
1 shallot, finely chopped
100 ml/4 fl oz dry white wine
100 ml/4 fl oz fish stock (see p.75)
100 ml/4 fl oz double cream
75 g/3 oz cold unsalted butter, diced
5 g/¼ oz puréed chives
salt and freshly ground black pepper

FOR THE GARNISH
cucumber shapes (see p.70)
tomato shapes

Picture: page 167

The cucumber and tomato for the garnish can be prepared in advance, or a less complicated garnish can be prepared at the last minute.

———————

Gently cook the lobster slices in the butter for 30 seconds each side. Remove with a slotted spoon, cover with cling film and keep warm.

For the sauce, cook the shallot in the pan in which the lobster was cooked over a moderate heat until soft. Stir in the wine, stock and cream and boil until slightly syrupy.

Gradually whisk in the butter a piece at a time, making sure that each piece is incorporated before adding the next. Add the chives and seasoning.

Pour the sauce over 4 warmed plates and arrange 2 slices of lobster tail meat and 2 slices of lobster claw meat on each one. Garnish with cucumber and tomato.

CRAYFISH AND MUSHROOM RAGOUT

INGREDIENTS *(serves 4)*
16 fresh crayfish
court bouillon (see p.76)
15 g/½ oz butter, diced
50 g/2 oz ceps, sliced
½ tbsp finely chopped shallots
¼ tsp finely chopped thyme
½ clove of garlic, finely chopped
salt and freshly ground white pepper
1 tbsp Pernod
75 ml/3 fl oz dry white wine
150 ml/¼ pt double cream

FOR THE GARNISH
sprigs of chervil
slices of truffle
crayfish

Picture: page 175

Poach the crayfish in the court bouillon for about 10 minutes until bright red. Remove and keep warm. Keep the court bouillon warm.

Heat the butter, add the shallots, thyme, garlic and seasoning and cook for 2—3 minutes. Stir in the Pernod and wine and reduce by half. Stir in the cream. Season.

Remove the crayfish from their shells. Bring the court bouillon to just below simmering point. Add the crayfish and heat for 30 seconds.

Transfer the crayfish to 4 warmed plates with a slotted spoon and pour the sauce over. Garnish with sprigs of chervil and slices of truffle. Arrange the crayfish around the edge of the plates.

ABOVE *Fillets of brill with tomatoes and
vermouth sauce*
Recipe: page 180
OPPOSITE *Goujons of brill with
redcurrant dressing*
Recipe: page 181

FILLETS OF BRILL WITH TOMATOES

AND VERMOUTH SAUCE

INGREDIENTS (serves 4)
25 g/1 oz butter, diced
6 fillets of brill, each
 150—175 g/5—6 oz
salt and freshly ground black pepper
2 shallots, sliced
2 tbsp chopped chives
flesh of 4 tomatoes, chopped
150 ml/5 fl oz dry vermouth
500 ml/18 fl oz fish stock
250 ml/9 fl oz double cream

FOR THE GARNISH
saffron rice timbales (see p.301)
tomato concassé
sprigs of chervil

Picture: page 178

Prepare the saffron rice timbales.

Heat the butter. Season the brill and the butter and cook gently until the flesh is just opaque — do not allow it to colour. Remove carefully, cover and keep warm.

Add the shallots to the pan, cover and cook over a moderate heat, shaking the pan occasionally, until soft. Stir in the chives, tomatoes, vermouth and stock and simmer until reduced to 150 ml/5 fl oz. Stir in the cream and simmer until slightly thickened. Purée, season and reheat gently.

Spoon the sauce over 4 warmed plates. Unmould the saffron rice timbales, place the fish on the sauce and garnish with tomato concassé and chervil.

PIKE QUENELLES WITH

WHITE WINE SAUCE

INGREDIENTS (serves 4)
250 g/9 oz skinless pike, chopped and
 chilled
salt and white pepper
a squeeze of lemon juice
1 egg white
225 ml/8 fl oz double cream, chilled
$\frac{1}{2}$ tsp tomato purée
1 L/1$\frac{3}{4}$ pt fish stock (see p.75), for
 · poaching
15 g/$\frac{1}{2}$ oz butter
1 tbsp finely chopped shallot
200 g/ 7 oz blanched spinach, well
 drained

FOR THE SAUCE
65 g/2$\frac{1}{2}$ oz butter
1$\frac{1}{2}$ tbsp finely chopped shallot
200 ml/7 fl oz fish stock
100 ml/4 fl oz full-bodied dry white
 wine
25 ml/1 fl oz dry vermouth
100 ml/4 fl oz double cream
salt and freshly ground white pepper

Mix the pike in a food processor until it is puréed , add the salt and lemon juice then mix in the egg white until smooth.

Pass through a fine sieve into a bowl placed over a bowl of ice, then gradually beat in the cream. Add the pepper, then divide the mixture in half and add sufficient tomato purée to one half to colour it a delicate pink. Cover both mixtures and chill for at least 30 minutes.

Fill a sauteuse or large frying pan with fish stock and bring to just simmering point.

Using 2 spoons, form each of the pike mixtures into 4 quenelles, gently lower them into the stock and poach for about 3 minutes each side.

For the sauce, heat 15g/$\frac{1}{2}$ oz butter, add the shallot and cook over a moderate heat in a covered pan, shaking the pan occasionally, until soft. Stir in the stock, wine and vermouth and reduce to 1 tbsp. Stir in the cream and simmer for 2 minutes. Pass through a sieve, place over a very low heat and whisk in the remaining butter. Do not allow it to boil. Season and keep warm.

Heat the butter, add the shallot and cook over a moderate heat in a covered pan, shaking the pan occasionally until soft. Stir in the spinach and cook for about 3 minutes, stirring frequently.

Remove the quenelles from the poaching liquor with a

FOR THE GARNISH
8 slices of truffle (or strips of blanched yellow and red pepper)

Picture: page 159

slotted spoon and drain on a cloth. With a sharp knife, cut each quenelle diagonally across to form halves.

Divide the spinach between 4 warmed plates. Place half a pink quenelle and half a white one on each plate with the edges touching so that they form one complete quenelle. Spoon the sauce around. Place a strip of truffle or yellow and red pepper on the join in each quenelle.

MONKFISH WITH BASIL

INGREDIENTS (serves 6)
200 ml/7 fl oz fish stock
250 ml/8 fl oz full-bodied dry white wine
2 tbsp finely chopped shallots
3 tbsp finely chopped basil
salt and pepper
700 g/1½ lb piece of filleted monkfish, cut into 16 slices
50 ml/2 fl oz champagne vinegar or white wine vinegar
100 g/4 oz butter, chopped

FOR THE GARNISH
concassé tomatoes

In a sauteuse or frying pan large enough to hold the fish in a single layer, heat the stock, wine, shallots, 1 tbsp basil and salt and pepper to simmering point. Add the fish and poach until the flesh is just opaque.

Transfer the fish to a warmed plate, cover and keep warm.

Boil the poaching liquor until reduced to 175 ml/6 fl oz. Pass through a sieve into a clean saucepan, stir in the vinegar and simmer for a minute or two, then reduce the heat to very low and gradually whisk in the butter, making sure each piece is fully incorporated before adding the next. Season. Add the remaining basil, season and spoon over 4 warmed plates.

Arrange the slices of monkfish on the sauce and garnish with concassé tomatoes.

GOUJONS OF BRILL WITH
REDCURRANT DRESSING

INGREDIENTS (serves 4)
4 fillets of brill, each approximately 175 g/6 oz, skinned and cut into strips
oak leaf lettuce

FOR THE DRESSING
3 tbsp champagne vinegar
9 tbsp olive oil
3 tbsp redcurrant juice
1½ tbsp finely chopped shallot
½ tbsp finely chopped chives
200 g/7 oz redcurrants
salt and freshly ground black pepper

FOR THE GARNISH
redcurrants
sprigs of chervil

Picture: page 179

Shake all the ingredients together for the dressing.

Steam the brill for about 5 minutes until just opaque — take care not to overcook. Remove the brill from the heat, cover and keep warm.

Gently warm the dressing.

Meanwhile, arrange the lettuce on 4 large cold plates.

Arrange the brill in the centre of the plates and spoon the dressing over. Garnish with redcurrants and sprigs of chervil.

Mediterranean bream with lemon and
fennel sauce
Recipe: page 184

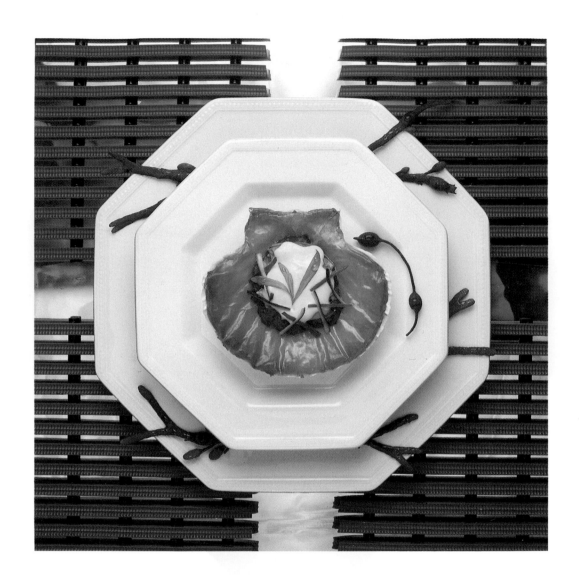

Mussels on a spinach bed
Recipe: page 185

MEDITERRANEAN BREAM WITH LEMON AND FENNEL SAUCE

INGREDIENTS (serves 4)
1½ lemons
3 tbsp white wine vinegar
1 tsp fennel seeds
25 g/1 oz butter, diced
1 tbsp olive oil
4 fillets of bream approximately
   175 g/6 oz, skinned and cut into 3
   strips
225 ml/8 fl oz fish stock
100 ml/ 4 fl oz full-bodied dry white
   wine
2 tbsp dry vermouth
1 tbsp crème fraîche
1—2 tbsp finely chopped dill
salt and freshly ground white pepper

FOR THE GARNISH
sprigs of broccoli
slices of lemon
sprigs of chervil

Picture: page 182

The day before the dish is required, pare the rind of half a lemon finely, squeeze 1 tsp of juice, and strain. Mix the rind and juice with the vinegar and fennel seeds, cover and leave in a cool place.

The next day thinly pare the rind from the remaining lemon, cut into a fine julienne, then blanch for 2 minutes. Refresh and drain well.

Heat the butter and oil, add the bream and cook gently for 2-3 minutes until just opaque. Remove with a slotted spoon, drain on absorbent paper, then cover and keep warm.

Meanwhile, boil the stock until reduced by half.

Tip the excess fat and oil from the pan. Stir in the wine, vermouth and stock. Remove the lemon rind from the vinegar and add the vinegar to the pan. Boil until slightly thickened.

Meanwhile, blanch the broccoli for the garnish, refresh and drain well.

Reduce the heat beneath the pan with the sauce and stir in the crème fraîche, dill and lemon julienne. Season.

Arrange the fish on 4 warmed plates. Spoon the sauce over and garnish with sprigs of broccoli, lemon slices and chervil.

MUSSELS WITH SAFFRON AND GINGER SAUCE AND POTATO BASKETS OF VEGETABLES

INGREDIENTS (serves 4)
1 shallot, finely chopped
3 parsley stalks
100 ml/4 fl oz dry white wine
1.75 L/3 pt mussels
3 tsp finely chopped fresh root ginger
a pinch of freshly grated nutmeg
300 ml/½ pt fish stock
150 ml/5 fl oz double cream
several strands of saffron soaked in a
   little warm dry white vermouth
butter
salt and freshly ground white pepper
a squeeze of lemon juice
4 potato baskets (see p.302)
macédoine of colourful vegetables —
   petit pois, fine dice of carrots,
   turnips, courgettes, small
   cauliflower florets or asparagus
sprigs of dill

Put the shallot, parsley and wine into a pan. Add the mussels, cover and put over a moderately high heat for about 5 minutes, shaking the pan frequently, until the shells open. Remove them as they are ready. Remove the mussels from their shells and keep warm. Discard any that remain closed.

Add 2 tsp ginger, the nutmeg and stock to the pan and reduce by three quarters. Pass through a sieve. Simmer with the cream and saffron in a clean saucepan for about 3 minutes. Add the remaining ginger. Reduce the heat to very low and gradually swirl in the butter. Season with salt and pepper and a squeeze of lemon juice.

In the meantime, prepare and cook the potato baskets and steam the vegetables.

Divide the vegetables between the baskets and place either in the centre or to one side of 4 warmed plates. Spoon the sauce around. Arrange the mussels in the sauce. Finish with sprigs of dill.

MUSSELS ON A SPINACH BED

INGREDIENTS (Serves 4)
8 sheets of filo pastry
melted butter
600 ml/1 pt fish stock
225 ml/8 fl oz dry white wine
16 mussels
35 g/1¼ oz courgettes, cut into julienne
35 g/1¼ oz red pepper, skinned, and cut into julienne
35 g/1¼ oz celery, cut into julienne
225 g/8 oz butter, diced
salt and freshly ground white pepper
225 g/8 oz spinach purée, well drained (see p.62)
5 ml/2 fl oz double cream

Picture: page 183

Very thinly rolled puff pastry (see p.79) could be used instead of filo pastry. The scallop shells should be lined in advance, covered and kept in a cool place.

Heat the oven to 220°C/425°F/Gas 7.

Fold the sheets of filo in half and use half of them to line 4 buttered scallop shells. Brush with melted butter and cover with the remaining sheets. Brush the edges with melted butter. Bake for about 8-10 minutes until crisp and a light golden brown.

Gently heat the fish stock and wine, add the mussels and cook until they open. Reserve the liquor. Remove the mussels from their shells.

Blanch the vegetables in the liquor until they are just tender. Remove them with a slotted spoon, drain well and keep warm.

Reduce the liquor to 115 ml/4½ fl oz. Reduce the heat to very low, then gradually whisk in the butter, making sure that each piece is completely incorporated before adding the next. Season and keep warm, but do not allow to boil.

Gently heat the spinach purée, then beat in the cream and seasoning. Divide between the pastry cases. Arrange the mussels on top. Spoon a little of the sauce over and scatter the vegetables over.

LEFT *Seafood cassolette*
Recipe: page 188
ABOVE *Seafood with a rainbow of noodles*
Recipe: page 188

LEFT *Panaché of seafood*
Recipe: page 189

SEAFOOD CASSOLETTE

INGREDIENTS (serves 4)
25 g/1 oz butter
25 g/1 oz shallots, finely chopped
4 cooked crayfish, shelled
4 scallops
100 g/4 oz sole fillets, cut into strips
100 g/4 oz cooked prawns, shelled
12 fresh basil leaves, thinly sliced
175 ml/6 fl oz dry white wine
175 ml/6 fl oz fish stock
100 ml/4 fl oz double cream
25 g/1 oz red shellfish butter (see
* p.77), diced*
salt and freshly ground white pepper

FOR THE GARNISH
tomato concassé
crayfish
sprigs of dill

Picture: page 186

Cuisine Vivante transforms a traditional cassoulet, with its long slow cooking and hearty ingredients, into a light quickly cooked cassolette.

––––––––––––––––

Heat the butter, add the shallots, cover and cook over a moderate heat, shaking the pan occasionally, until soft. Add the crayfish and cook for 2 minutes.

Remove the scallops from their shells (see p.61), separate the bodies from the corals and cut the bodies in half. Add to the pan with the sole, prawns, basil, wine and stock and cook gently for 2 minutes. Remove the fish with a slotted spoon and keep warm.

Reduce the liquor by three quarters, then stir in the cream and simmer until slightly thickened. Reduce the heat to very low and gradually whisk in the red shellfish butter, making sure that each piece is completely incorporated before adding the next. Season.

Divide the fish between 4 warmed plates, arranging them attractively, then spoon the sauce over. Garnish with the concassé tomatoes, crayfish and sprigs of dill.

SEAFOOD WITH A RAINBOW OF NOODLES

INGREDIENTS (serves 4)
100 g/4 oz salmon fillets, cut into
* strips*
4 peeled Dublin Bay prawns
8 clams out of their shells
8 mussels out of their shells
2 tbsp lemon juice
salt and freshly ground white pepper
1 tbsp each of chopped parsley, basil
* and thyme*
75 g/3 oz fresh pink noodles (see p.78)
75 g/3 oz fresh green noodles
* (see p.78)*
75 g/3 oz fresh white noodles
* (see p.78)*
1 tbsp oil
15 g/½ oz butter, diced
1 tbsp finely chopped shallot
1 tbsp cognac
200 ml/7 fl oz full-bodied dry white
* wine*
300 ml/½ pt double cream
40 g/1½ oz red shellfish butter
* (see p.77), diced*

Providing the amounts are kept fairly constant, and bearing in mind the appearance of the dish, the type of fish can be altered. Eight scallops, their bodies separated from the corals, could be used instead of mussels and clams, and crayfish in place of Dublin Bay prawns.

––––––––––––––––

Put the fish and shellfish into a shallow dish, keeping the varieties separate. Spoon the lemon juice over and sprinkle with seasoning and herbs. Cover and leave in a cool place for 30 minutes.

Cook the noodles together with the oil, in boiling salted water until just tender.

Meanwhile, heat the butter, add the shallot, cover and cook over a moderate heat, shaking the pan occasionally until soft.

Remove the fish from the marinade with a slotted spoon, strain the marinade and reserve. Add the salmon and Dublin Bay prawns to the shallots, pour in the cognac and ignite with a taper. Cook gently for 2 minutes.

Add the clams, mussels and the wine and cook for 2 minutes.

FOR THE GARNISH
Dublin Bay prawns
sprigs of parsley
julienne of truffle

Picture: page 187

Remove the fish with a slotted spoon and keep warm. Reduce the liquor by two thirds, then stir in the cream and simmer until slightly thickened. Reduce the heat to very low and gradually stir in the red shellfish butter, making sure that each piece is completely incorporated before adding the next. Add the fish to the sauce. Season and add a little of the marinade.

Drain the noodles (if necessary, they can be kept warm in a steamer) and arrange them on 4 warmed plates, forming a slight well in the centre. Divide the fish and sauce between them and garnish with the Dublin Bay prawns, the sprigs of parsley and the truffle.

PANACHE OF SEAFOOD

INGREDIENTS (serves 4)
100 g/4 oz skinned, boned salmon
salt
½ tsp egg white
150 ml/¼ pt double cream, chilled
cayenne pepper
a few strands of saffron
200 ml/7 fl oz fish stock
100 ml/4 fl oz dry white wine
1½ tsp lemon juice
freshly ground white pepper
4 scallops
350 g/12 oz John Dory fillet
225 g/8 oz sea bass fillets
225 g/8 oz monkfish fillets

FOR THE GARNISH
sprigs of coriander and chervil

Picture: page 187

Start to cook the sea bass and monkfish before adding the John Dory and then the scallops to the steamer, as the more delicate fish will become too tough if cooked for the same length of time as the firmer ones.

———————————

Purée the salmon in a food processor or blender, add the salt then the egg white. Pass through a sieve into a bowl over a bowl of ice, then gradually beat in the chilled cream. Add a little cayenne pepper, cover and chill for 30 minutes.

Pipe the salmon mixture into 4 small decorative moulds, pushing it well into the sides. Place the moulds in a shallow pan, surround with hot water, place over a low heat and poach for 10 minutes. Leave to stand off the heat for 2 minutes.

Meanwhile, stir the saffron into a little of the stock. Bring the remaining stock, the wine and lemon juice to the boil and reduce by three quarters. Stir in the cream and saffron liquor and simmer for 2 minutes. Season and add a little more lemon juice if necessary.

Open the scallops (see p.61) and cut the other fish into 4 pieces each. Season all the fish lightly and steam for 3-5 minutes until just opaque.

Unmould the salmon moulds onto the centre of 4 warmed plates. Spoon the sauce around and arrange the fish on top. Garnish with sprigs of coriander and chervil.

190

MEAT

DISHES

The portions of meat in Cuisine Vivante recipes are generally kept to a size that will not defeat the appetite, overload the stomach or overwhelm the digestive system but they can, of course, be adjusted to accommodate individual requirements. In a meal of five, six or even seven courses just 75-100g/3-4oz of meat per person should provide the right balance, whereas 175-200g/6-7oz would be more acceptable for a hearty eater of a short menu. Recommendations for quantities in the following recipes are intended as guidelines only and amounts can easily be changed.

VEAL WITH SALSIFY

INGREDIENTS (serves 4)
425 ml/15 fl oz veal stock
25 g/1 oz piece white of leek, sliced in
    half lengthways
a long strip of lemon peel
4 parsley stalks
550 g/1¼ lbs salsify
lemon juice
50 g/2 oz butter, diced
salt and freshly ground black pepper
4 tournedos of veal, approximately
    150-175 g/5-6 oz
225 ml/8 fl oz dry white wine
100 ml/4 fl oz dry vermouth
100 ml/4 fl oz double cream
freshly ground white pepper

FOR THE GARNISH
French beans cut into 4 cm/1½ inch
    lengths
diamond shapes of blanched red
    pepper

Picture: page 194

Either salsify or scorzonera can be used — see p.31. The base for the sauce can be prepared in advance.

Simmer the stock with the leek, lemon peel and parsley for 30 minutes, then boil until reduced to 200 ml/7 fl oz. Strain.

Meanwhile, peel the salsify with a potato peeler and cut into 4 cm/1½ inch pieces — as each one is prepared, put it into water acidulated with lemon juice to prevent discoloration.

Simmer the salsify in acidulated water for about 45 minutes until tender. Drain well.

Meanwhile, heat half the butter. Season the veal and cook in the butter for 3—4 minutes each side. Transfer to a warmed plate with a slotted spoon, cover and keep warm.

Stir the wine and the vermouth into the pan and reduce to 3 tbsp. Stir in the stock and simmer for 2—3 minutes. Stir in the cream and simmer until slightly thickened. Reduce the heat to very low and swirl in the remaining butter. Season and keep warm, but do not boil.

Blanch the beans for the garnish, refresh and drain.

Place the tournedos on 4 warmed plates and spoon the sauce around. Arrange the diamonds of red pepper around the plate and place the French beans on the tournedos.

ROLLED ESCALOPES OF VEAL WITH LIGHT PISTACHIO SAUCE

INGREDIENTS (serves 4)
4 escalopes of veal
225 g/8 oz spinach
    leaves
salt and freshly ground black pepper
150 ml/5 fl oz medium-bodied dry
    white wine
225 ml/8 fl oz veal stock
a sprig of marjoram
65 g/2½ oz pistachio nuts
50 ml/2 fl oz armagnac or cognac
150 ml/4 fl oz double cream

FOR THE GARNISH
white wine sauce (see p.180)
skinned pistachio nuts

The pistachios can be prepared in advance. Put the escalopes of veal between 2 sheets of cling film to flatten them but take care not to break holes in the flesh.

Prepare the white wine sauce for the garnish. Cover the surface with greaseproof paper or cling film and keep warm in a bowl over a pan of hot water.

Blanch the spinach leaves, refresh, drain and dry very well on absorbent paper. Lay the spinach leaves over the veal and roll each escalope up like a Swiss roll. Season and place seam-side down in the top part of a steamer. Put the lid on.

Bring the wine, 50 ml/2 fl oz stock and the marjoram to the boil in the bottom part of the steamer. Cover with the top part. Reduce the heat to simmering and cook the veal for about 3 minutes.

Meanwhile, bring a saucepan of water to the boil, add the pistachios and return to the boil. Drain the pistachios and remove the skins. Place the nuts in a food processor or blender and mix to a smooth paste.

Transfer the veal to a warmed plate, cover and keep warm.

Ignite the armagnac or cognac, pour into the wine and remaining stock then reduce to 50 ml/2 fl oz.

Remove the marjoram, stir in the cream and simmer for 2—3 minutes. Reduce the heat to very low and gradually whisk in the pistachio paste, making sure each piece is incorporated before adding the next. Season and keep warm but do not allow to boil.

Trim the ends from the veal rolls then cut the rolls into thin slices. Re-form and keep warm.

Divide the pistachio sauce between 4 warmed plates. Arrange the veal slices on top. Carefully pour on some of the white wine sauce around the edge of the pistachio sauce then swirl the rest of the white wine sauce at intervals into the pistachio sauce. Garnish with pistachio nuts.

POACHED VEAL WITH TOMATO

SAUCE

INGREDIENTS (serves 4)
600 ml/1 pt veal stock
12 parsley stalks, chopped
a strip of lemon peel
6 black peppercorns, crushed
4 medallions of veal about 150—
  175 g/5—6 oz each
25 g/1 oz butter, diced
2 tbsp finely chopped shallot
450 g/1 lb tomatoes, diced
150 ml/¼ pt double cream
2 tbsp sweet vermouth
salt and freshly ground black pepper

FOR THE GARNISH
15 g/½ oz butter, diced
a squeeze of lemon juice
chervil leaves
8 button mushrooms
baby carrots

Picture: page 198

Be sure to use fleshy, sun-ripened tomatoes for this delicate, light and fresh-tasting dish.

Bring the stock, parsley stalks, lemon peel and peppercorns to the boil, add the veal, reduce the heat to just simmering and poach the veal for about 6 minutes.

Meanwhile, heat the butter, add the shallots, cover and cook over a moderate heat, shaking the pan occasionally, until just soft. Stir in the tomatoes and simmer for 10 minutes, then pass through a sieve. Return to the rinsed pan and boil rapidly to thicken, if necessary. Stir in the cream and vermouth and boil for 2 minutes. Season and keep warm without boiling.

Heat the butter for the garnish, add the lemon juice and mushrooms and cook for 3—4 minutes. Remove with a slotted spoon and drain on absorbent paper. Slice into fans. Meanwhile, blanch, refresh and drain the carrots for the garnish and keep warm in a steamer.

Remove the veal and dry on absorbent paper. Season lightly.

Spoon the sauce over 4 warmed plates, place the veal on top and sprinkle the chervil over the sauce. Garnish with the mushrooms and baby carrots.

◆

ABOVE *Veal with salsify*
Recipe: page 192
OPPOSITE *Croustade of a mélange of veal*
Recipe: page 197

194

VEAL WITH COURGETTES AND GRAPEFRUIT

INGREDIENTS (serves 4)
450 g/1 lb loin of veal, very thinly
    sliced
salt and freshly ground black pepper
50 g/2 oz butter
450 g/1 lb courgettes, thinly sliced
100 ml/4 fl oz veal stock
juice of 1 grapefruit
1 grapefruit, peeled, all skin and pith
    removed, thinly sliced
a few strands of saffron dissolved in
    150 ml/5 fl oz dry vermouth

FOR THE GARNISH
sprigs of chervil

Season the veal.

Heat 40 g/1½ oz butter in a sauteuse or large frying pan, add the veal and cook for 1 minute each side.

Meanwhile, place the slices of courgette in the top half of a steamer or a colander. Heat some salted water in the bottom half of the steamer to simmering point, cover with the top half or the colander, cover and cook for about 2 minutes until just tender.

Transfer the veal to a warmed plate, cover and keep warm. Pour nearly all the fat from the pan.

Stir the stock, grapefruit juice and the saffron/vermouth liquid into the pan and reduce to 6 tbsp. Reduce the heat to very low and gradually swirl in the remaining butter, making sure each piece is fully incorporated before adding the next. Add the slices of grapefruit and heat through gently and briefly. Season, then spoon over 4 warmed plates.

Arrange the slices of veal and slices of grapefruit and courgettes on the sauce and garnish with sprigs of chervil.

POCKET OF VEAL WITH VEGETABLES AND LEMON SAUCE

INGREDIENTS (serves 4)
60 g/2¼ oz butter, diced
35 g/1¼ oz leek, diced
35 g/1¼ oz courgettes, diced
35 g/1¼ oz button mushroom caps,
    diced
35 g/1¼ oz skinned red pepper, diced
a pinch of chopped thyme
salt and freshly ground black pepper
approximately 640 g/1 lb 6 oz loin of
    veal, trimmed

FOR THE SAUCE
1 tbsp finely chopped shallot
100 ml/4 fl oz dry white wine
25 ml/1 fl oz dry vermouth
150 ml/5 fl oz veal stock
2 tbsp lemon juice
225 g/8 oz butter, diced
salt and freshly ground black pepper

Picture: page 199

Heat 20 g/¾ oz butter, add the leeks, cover and cook over a low heat for about 3 minutes, stirring occasionally, until softened. Stir in the courgettes and cook for 2 minutes, then add the mushrooms and red pepper and cook for 2 minutes. Stir in the thyme and seasoning and leave to cool.

Cut the veal into 4 tournedos and partially cut through each one horizontally to form a pocket. Season the pocket.

Divide the vegetables between the pockets, then season the outside of the tournedos.

Heat the remaining butter in a flameproof casserole that the veal will just fit. Add the veal and cook for 3—4 minutes each side. Transfer to a warmed plate, cover and keep warm.

For the sauce, reduce the shallots, wine, vermouth, stock and lemon juice to 1 tbsp. Reduce the heat to very low and gradually whisk in the butter, making sure each piece is completely incorporated before adding the next. Season.

Transfer the veal pockets to warmed plates, spoon the sauce around.

CROUSTADE OF A MELANGE

OF VEAL

INGREDIENTS (serves 4)
450 g/1 lb calves sweetbreads, soaked
in several changes of cold water
until the water is clear
salt
12 sheets of filo pastry
melted butter
450 g/1 lb fillet of veal, trimmed
450 g/1 lb calves kidneys, trimmed
freshly ground black pepper
40 g/1½ oz butter, diced
100 ml/4 fl oz veal stock
75 ml/3 fl oz full-bodied dry white
wine
75 g/3 oz butter, diced
1 tbsp Meaux mustard
1 tbsp green peppercorns
25 ml/1 fl oz double cream, whipped

FOR THE GARNISH
concassé tomatoes

Picture: page 195

If you wish to prepare some of the dish in advance you can bake the croustade cases and warm them through about 4 minutes before required. Or use very thinly rolled puff pastry, cover with cling film and chill ready to put in a pre-heated oven about 6 minutes before serving.

Heat the oven to 220°C/420°F/Gas 6.

Cook the sweetbreads in simmering, salted, acidulated water for 5 minutes. Drain well, then trim and remove the skin. Place in a cloth and press under a lightly weighted board.

Line 4 individual well buttered ovenproof dishes with 4 of the sheets of filo pastry. Brush with melted butter, cover with another sheet, brush with melted butter and cover with the remaining sheets. Brush once more with butter and bake for about 12 minutes.

Cut the sweetbreads, veal and kidneys into 1.25cm/½ inch cubes. Season.

Heat 25 g/1 oz butter, add the sweetbreads and cook over a low heat for 5—6 minutes. In a separate pan, heat 15 g/½ oz butter, add the veal and cook for 2 minutes, stirring occasionally. Remove with a slotted spoon, drain on absorbent paper, cover and keep warm.

Add the kidneys to the pan in which the veal was cooked and cook, stirring occasionally, for 2—3 minutes. Remove with a slotted spoon, drain on absorbent paper, cover and keep warm.

Stir the stock and wine into the pan, dislodging any sediment and reduce by half. Reduce the heat to very low, then gradually whisk in the 75 g/3 oz diced butter and the mustard, making sure that each piece is completely incorporated before adding the next. Lightly stir in the peppercorns and cream. Season.

Drain the sweetbreads on absorbent paper when they are cooked. Cover and keep warm.

Lightly mix the veal, kidneys and sweetbreads into the sauce and divide between the croustades. Garnish with concassé tomatoes.

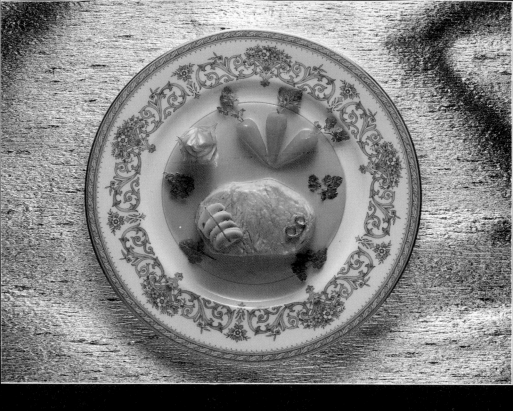

ABOVE *Poached veal with tomato sauce*
Recipe: page 193
OPPOSITE *Pocket of veal with vegetables*
and lemon sauce

FILLET OF VEAL WITH SHELLFISH AND SHERRY SAUCES

INGREDIENTS (serves 4)
1 fillet of veal
1 whole, cooked lobster tail
salt and freshly ground black pepper
25 g/1 oz butter, diced

FOR THE SHERRY SAUCE
25 g/1 oz shallots, finely chopped
1 tsp meat glaze (see p.74)
150 ml/5 fl oz fino sherry
2 tbsp double cream
225 g/8 oz butter, diced
salt and freshly ground black pepper

FOR THE SHELLFISH SAUCE
25 g/1 oz butter, diced
25 g/1 oz shallots, finely chopped
25 g/1 oz celery, finely chopped
25 g/1 oz leeks, finely chopped
25 g/1 oz fennel bulb, finely chopped
450 g/1 lb lobster or shellfish shells,
    crushed
2 tbsp cognac
1 tsp finely chopped mixed herbs
150 ml/5 fl oz dry vermouth
1 tsp tomato purée
2 tbsp double cream
salt and freshly ground white pepper

FOR THE GARNISH
Sprigs of chervil

Picture: page 202

For a well-balanced meal serve simple, light dishes before and after this luxurious main course.

Heat the oven to 220°C/425°F/Gas 7.

For the sherry sauce, boil the shallots, meat glaze and 100 ml/4 fl oz sherry until reduced to 1 tbsp. Stir in the cream. Reduce the heat to very low and gradually whisk in the butter, making sure that each piece is completely incorporated before adding the next. Pass through a fine sieve then stir in a little more sherry to give a smooth sauce. Season and keep warm but do not boil.

Trim the veal to a neat shape, then cut a slit along the fillet and carefully insert the lobster tail. Tie the veal into a good shape and season lightly.

Heat the butter in a flameproof casserole that the veal will just fit, add the veal and sear evenly all over. Place in the oven for about 15 minutes. The veal will be pink and moist inside. Transfer to a warmed plate, cover and keep warm.

For the shellfish sauce, heat the butter, add the vegetables, lobster or shellfish shells and cook for 2—3 minutes, stirring frequently. Stir in the cognac and ignite with a taper. When the flames have died down stir in the herbs, vermouth, tomato purée and cream and simmer, still stirring, until slightly thickened. Pass through a conical sieve, pressing down well to extract as much flavour as possible. Season and heat very gently but do not allow to boil.

Slice the veal, re-form into one piece, cover and keep warm.

Spoon some of the shellfish sauce onto the centre of 4 warmed plates. Arrange the veal slices on top and spoon the sherry sauce around. Streak the shellfish sauce into the sherry sauce. Garnish with sprigs of chervil.

MEDALLIONS OF VEAL WITH

RHUBARB

INGREDIENTS (serves 4)
450 g/1 lb tender, young pink
  rhubarb
approximately 50 g/2 oz sugar
75 g/3 oz butter, diced
225 ml/8 fl oz full-bodied, fruity dry
  white wine
150 ml/¼ pt double cream
4 medallions of veal about 150 g/5 oz
  each
salt and freshly ground white pepper

FOR THE GARNISH
4 redcurrants (or cranberries)
2 apples
approximately 50 ml/2 fl oz full-
  bodied fruity dry white wine
4 sprigs of mint

Picture: page 203

Gently cook the rhubarb with the sugar and half the butter in a covered pan until it softens. Reduce to a very smooth pureé, then pass through a sieve.

Boil the wine until reduced to 50 ml/2 fl oz. Stir in the rhubarb juice and simmer together for 2-3 minutes.

Stir in the cream and bring to the boil.

Meanwhile, heat 25 g/1 oz butter, add the veal and cook for about 3 minutes each side.

As soon as the sauce comes to the boil, reduce the heat and swirl in the remaining butter. Season. Keep the sauce warm over a low heat.

Poach the redcurrants or cranberries in the wine until tender. Remove with a slotted spoon and keep warm.

Peel and core the apples then slice very thinly. Gently poach in the wine until just tender. Carefully remove with a slotted spoon.

Spoon the sauce over 4 warmed plates. Place a veal medallion in the centre of each. Arrange the slices of apple around the veal and place a redcurrant or cranberry on top. Add a sprig of mint.

Fillet of veal with shellfish and sherry
sauces
Recipe: page 200

Medallions of veal with rhubarb
Recipe: page 201

MEDALLIONS OF VEAL WITH
COURGETTES AND LEMONS

INGREDIENTS (serves 4)
rind of 3 lemons, cut into julienne
1 tbsp sugar
800 g/1¾ lb veal fillet, trimmed
salt and freshly ground white pepper
350 g/12 oz cold unsalted butter,
*   diced*
400 ml/6 fl oz dry white wine
4—6 medium courgettes, thinly sliced
*   lengthways*

FOR THE GARNISH
mint leaves

Picture: page 207

The lemon julienne for this light summery dish can be prepared in advance.

Blanch and refresh the lemon julienne.

Dissolve the sugar in 120 ml/6 tbsp water, add the lemon
julienne and boil until the water has just evaporated. Remove
from the heat immediately, as the lemon must not brown.

Slice the veal into 12 equal medallions, flatten slightly and
season on both sides.

Heat 100 g/4 oz butter and cook the medallions for 3—4
minutes each side. Remove with a slotted spoon, cover and
keep warm.

Pour the butter out of the pan, then place the pan over a
high heat and stir in the wine, dislodging the sediment from
the bottom. Boil until reduced to 120 ml/6 tbsp. Remove from
the heat.

Briefly cook the courgette slices in 25 g/1 oz butter until
only just tender. Remove from the pan carefully with a slotted
spoon and keep warm.

Reheat the reduced wine, then gradually whisk in the
remaining butter, making sure that each piece is completely
incorporated before adding the next, to make a smooth sauce.
Season.

Arrange 3 medallions on each of 4 warmed plates, spoon
the sauce around and add the courgette slices. Sprinkle the
lemon julienne on the medallions and garnish the courgette
slices with mint leaves.

LAMB PROVENCAL

INGREDIENTS (serves 4)
8 slices of aubergine, about 6 mm/¼
*   inch thick and 6 cm/2½ inches wide*
salt
65 g/2½ oz butter
2 tbsp shallot, finely chopped
3 ripe tomatoes, peeled, seeded and
*   finely chopped*
½ red pepper, skinned and finely
*   chopped*
1 small sprig of thyme
¼ bay leaf
8 oz spinach, washed and trimmed
2 fillets of lamb
2 sprigs of thyme
1 small sprig of rosemary
425 ml/¾ pt veal stock (see p.75)
freshly ground black pepper
2 tsp parsley, finely chopped
4 tbsp meat glaze (see p.74)

FOR THE GARNISH
3 tbsp concassé tomatoes (see p.64)
4 small basil leaves

This recipe is not as complicated as it may seem at first sight — it is merely a series of simple steps. The vegetable moulds (tians) may be prepared in advance and heated in a warm oven whilst the lamb is 'resting'.

———————

Heat the oven to 220°C/425°F/Gas 7.

Place the aubergine slices in a colander, sprinkle with salt and leave to drain for 30 minutes. Rinse in cold water then dry well with absorbent paper.

Heat 15 g/½ oz butter, add the shallot, cover and cook over a low heat, shaking the pan occasionally, until softened. Stir in the tomatoes, red pepper, small sprig of thyme and the bay leaf and simmer for about 15 minutes until the excess moisture has evaporated.

Cook the spinach over a moderately high heat, stirring constantly until the excess moisture has evaporated. Season.

Remove the thyme and bay leaf from the tomato mixture. Season. Heat 25 g/1 oz butter in a sauteuse or large frying pan, add the lamb and cook for about 2 minutes, turning each fillet so that it is evenly browned. Place in the oven for 6-8 minutes until pink and still moist in the centre.

Transfer the fillets to a warmed plate, cover and keep warm. Turn the oven off. Add the 2 sprigs of thyme and the rosemary to the stock and reduce to 150 ml/¼ pt.

Meanwhile, heat 25 g/1 oz butter in a large sauteuse or frying pan, add the aubergine slices in a single layer and cook for 1 minute on each side. Remove with a slotted spoon and drain on absorbent paper. Sprinkle with pepper and parsley. Place a slice of aubergine in the bottom of 4 lightly oiled individual ramekin dishes of a slightly larger diameter than the aubergines. Cover with a layer of spinach and then the tomato mixture. Finish with a slice of aubergine. Place in the oven to warm. Place the concassé tomatoes for the garnish in the oven as well.

Remove the herbs from the stock and stir in the meat glaze. Keep warm over a low heat.

Cut the lamb into thick slices. Cover and keep warm. Unmould the vegetables onto 4 warmed plates and place a little concassé tomato and a basil leaf on each mound. Divide the sauce between the plates then place the slices of lamb around the vegetable mounds.

*Medallions of veal with courgettes and
lemons
Recipe: page 204*

NOISETTES OF LAMB WITH

TARRAGON

INGREDIENTS (serves 4)
3 tbsp walnut oil
50 g/2 oz butter
12 noisettes of lamb, seasoned
6 tbsp sercial madeira
2 tbsp coarsely chopped tarragon
4 tbsp double cream
salt and freshly ground black pepper

FOR THE GARNISH
tarragon leaves

Picture: page 210

In a sauteuse or large frying pan, heat the oil and half the butter. Add the noisettes and cook for about 3 minutes on each side until they are pink in the centre and still moist.

Remove with a slotted spoon, cover and keep warm.

Tip off the excess oil from the pan then melt the remaining butter in it. Stir in the madeira, dislodging the sediment, then stir in the tarragon and cream. Boil until slightly thickened then pass through a sieve. Season and divide between 4 warmed plates. Place 3 noisettes on each plate and garnish with tarragon leaves.

RACK OF LAMB

WITH MANGOS AND MINT

INGREDIENTS (serves 4)
2 racks of lamb with 6 bones each,
    trimmed
1 clove of garlic
salt and freshly ground black pepper
1 large ripe mango, peeled, puréed
    and sieved
150 ml/¼ pt full-bodied dry white wine
100 g/4 oz butter, diced
a squeeze of lime juice
150 ml/¼ pt red wine
600 ml/1 pt brown veal stock (see
    p.74)
1 tsp finely chopped fresh mint

FOR THE GARNISH
slices of lime
or slices of mango
strips of red pepper, blanched
slices of cucumber

Picture: page 211

Heat the oven to 220°C/425°F/Gas 7.

Rub the racks with garlic then season with salt and pepper. Cover the tips of the bones with foil and place in the oven for about 30 minutes — the meat should remain pink and moist. Cover the racks loosely and leave in a warm place.

Boil the mango flesh with the white wine until reduced to a fairly thick consistency. Reduce the heat to very low and gradually whisk in the butter — do not allow the sauce to boil. Add the lime juice and season. Keep warm but do not allow to boil.

Boil the red wine and stock until reduced by half, then stir in the mint. Keep warm.

Divide the lamb into cutlets and arrange on 4 warmed plates. Add the mango purée and spoon the sauce around. Garnish with slices of lime, or mango, red pepper and cucumber.

LAMB WITH BROAD BEANS

INGREDIENTS (serves 4)
325 g/11 oz shelled broad beans
salt and freshly ground black pepper
4 sprigs of summer savory
40 g/1½ oz butter
600 g/1¼ lb loin of lamb, cut into 12
* slices*
1 shallot, finely chopped
190 ml/6½ fl oz full-bodied dry white
* wine*
240 ml/8½ fl oz chicken stock
207 ml/7¼ fl oz double cream

To get the very best out of broad beans, you should remove the outer skin — inside there lies a heart of almost unbelievable tenderness and flavour.

———————————

Cook the broad beans in simmering salted water with the savory until tender. Drain well then squeeze the beans between a finger and thumb so that the tender centres pop out of the outer skin. Reserve some of the beans and purée the remainder. Season.

Heat 25 g/1 oz butter, season the slices of lamb and cook in the butter for 1-2 minutes. Remove with a slotted spoon, cover and keep warm.

Stir the shallot into the butter, cover and cook over a moderate heat, shaking the pan occasionally. Pour off the surplus fat then stir in 100 ml/4 fl oz of the wine and reduce to 1 tbsp. Stir in 175 ml/6 fl oz stock and reduce to 50 ml/2 fl oz. Stir in the cream and simmer briefly. Pass through a sieve, return to the rinsed pan and reheat gently, then over a very low heat gradually swirl in the remaining butter, making sure each piece is fully incorporated before adding the next. Season and keep warm.

Place the reserved beans in a steamer over a pan of simmering water to warm.

Spread about 1 tbsp broad bean purée over each of 4 slices of lamb. Cover with slices of lamb. Spread with another 1 tbsp broad bean purée and top with the remaining lamb slices, cover and keep warm.

Gently heat the remaining broad bean purée with the remaining wine and cream until bubbling gently.

Spoon the purée onto 4 warmed plates, place the lamb on top, spoon the other sauce around the purée and garnish with the broad beans and sprigs of savory.

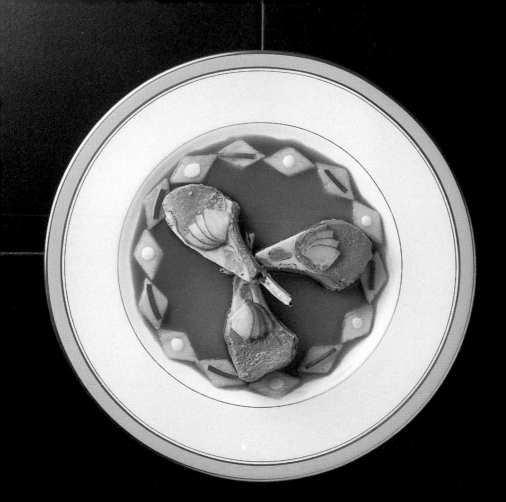

STRIPS OF LAMB WITH

ROSEMARY SAUCE

INGREDIENTS *(serves 4)*
350 g/12 oz green noodles (see p.78)
1 tbsp oil
salt and freshly ground black pepper
200 ml/7 fl oz full-bodied dry white
  wine
75 ml/3 fl oz dry vermouth
1 tbsp finely chopped shallot
375 ml/13 fl oz chicken stock
450 g/1lb loin of lamb, cut into strips
3 tsp finely chopped rosemary
2 small spinach leaves
150 ml/5 fl oz double cream

FOR THE GARNISH
small sprigs of rosemary, with flowers
  if possible
coriander leaves

Picture: page 215

The spinach leaves do not flavour the sauce, just tint it a delicate shade of green. If you are feeling adventurous, tie the noodles into knots.

Cook the noodles in boiling salted water with the oil until just tender.

Pour the wine, vermouth, shallot and 75 ml/3 fl oz stock into the bottom of a steamer and bring to the boil.

Season the lamb and put into the top half of the steamer. Put this in place on the bottom part of the steamer and cook for about 5 minutes. The lamb will still be pink in the centre.

Meanwhile, simmer the rosemary and spinach leaves in the remaining stock for 4 minutes, then reduce to 100 ml/4 fl oz.

Remove the lamb from the steamer, cover and keep warm. Add the rosemary, spinach and liquid to the bottom part of the steamer and reduce to 75 ml/3 fl oz. Stir in the cream.

Process briefly in a blender, then pass through a sieve. Season and heat gently.

Drain the noodles and arrange them on 4 warmed plates. Put the lamb in the centre and pour the sauce over the lamb. Arrange the sprigs of rosemary in the noodles and garnish with coriander leaves.

NOISETTES OF LAMB WITH

ROSEMARY AND WALNUTS

INGREDIENTS *(serves 4)*
2 tbsp walnut oil
150 g/5 oz butter, diced
salt and freshly ground black pepper
8 noisettes of lamb
1 tsp finely chopped shallots
150 ml/¼ pt red wine
600 ml/1 pt brown lamb stock
1 tsp finely chopped rosemary
12 walnuts, shelled or 50 g/2 oz
  chopped walnuts
100 g/4 oz tomato flesh, diced

FOR THE GARNISH
12 small courgettes, 'turned' (see p.65)
8 small carrots, 'turned' (see p.65)
small sprigs of rosemary
walnut halves

Picture: page 214

Heat half the oil and 15 g/½ oz butter in a sauteuse or large frying pan. Season the noisettes, add to the pan and cook for 3-4 minutes on each side so they are still pink in the centre. Remove with a slotted spoon, cover and keep warm.

Tip the excess fat from the pan, stir in the shallots, wine and stock and boil until reduced to a quarter. Add the rosemary. Reduce the heat to very low and gradually whisk in 50 g/2 oz butter. Season and keep warm but do not allow to boil.

Heat the remaining butter and oil, add the walnuts and tomatoes and cook for 2-3 minutes. Season.

Blanch, refresh and drain the courgettes and carrots.

Cut the noisettes in half and arrange on 4 warmed plates. Spoon the sauce around and divide the walnuts between the plates. Garnish with courgettes, carrots and rosemary.

CASSOLETTE OF SWEETBREADS AND KIDNEYS

INGREDIENTS (serves 4)
450 g/1 lb calves sweetbreads, soaked
    in several changes of cold water
    until the water is clear
1 tbsp lemon juice
120 g/4½ oz butter, diced
salt and freshly ground black pepper
2 crisp dessert apples, peeled, cored
    and chopped
2 shallots, finely chopped
450 g/1 lb veal kidneys, cut into
    2.5 cm/1 inch cubes
5 tbsp calvados
50 ml/2 fl oz dry vermouth
350 ml/12 fl oz veal stock
1 tbsp tarragon mustard

FOR THE GARNISH
julienne of lemon peel and red apple
    skin tossed in lemon juice
tarragon leaves

This is another Cuisine Vivante adaptation of a traditional French dish.

Simmer the sweetbreads with the lemon juice and covered by 5 cm/2 inches of salted water for 15 minutes. Refresh and drain well. Remove the membrane and any gristle, place in a cloth between 2 weighted boards and leave to cool.

Cut the sweetbreads into 2.5 cm/1 inch cubes. Heat 25 g/1 oz butter in a sauteuse or large frying pan. Add the sweetbreads, apples, shallots and seasoning. Cover and cook over a low heat for 15 minutes.

Heat 25 g/1 oz butter in another sauteuse or large frying pan. Season the kidneys, add to the pan and cook for 2 minutes, stirring. Transfer to a warmed dish, cover and keep warm.

With a slotted spoon, transfer the sweetbreads, apples, shallots and kidneys to a warmed dish, cover and keep warm.

Pour the excess fat from the pan in which the sweetbreads were cooked, stir in the calvados and ignite with a taper. When the flames have died down, stir in the vermouth and reduce by half. Stir in the stock and reduce by half. Reduce the heat to very low, then gradually whisk in the mustard, then the remaining butter, making sure that each piece is completely incorporated before adding the next. Season.

Meanwhile, blanch, refresh and drain the julienne of lemon and apple.

Divide the sauce between 4 warmed plates. Arrange the sweetbreads and kidneys on the sauce and garnish with lemon and apple julienne and tarragon leaves.

Noisettes of lamb with rosemary and
walnuts
Recipe: page 212

Strips of lamb with rosemary sauce
Recipe: page 212

LAMBS LIVER IN RED WINE

INGREDIENTS (serves 4)
450 g/1 lb piece of lambs liver
1 tbsp chopped thyme
1 tbsp chopped basil
salt and freshly ground black pepper
250 ml/9 fl oz chicken stock
225 ml/8 fl oz red wine
1 stick of celery, chopped
1 carrot, chopped
2 tbsp single cream
2 tbsp cognac
40 g/1½ oz butter, diced

FOR THE GARNISH
'turned' mushrooms
sprigs of parsley
red pepper petals

Picture: page 218

Lambs liver is not as delicate as calves but it is quite suitable for this recipe where the liver is gently steamed and the accompanying sauce has quite a full flavour.

———————————

Remove any membrane from the liver and coat with the herbs and seasoning. Put into a steaming basket.

Pour the stock and the wine into the base of the steamer, add the celery and carrot and bring to the boil. Put the steamer over the base, cover tightly and steam for 15 minutes.

Transfer the liver to a warmed serving plate, cover and keep warm.

Boil the steaming liquor until reduced to 225 ml/8 fl oz. Pass through a sieve and return to the pan. Reheat, then stir in the cream and cognac. Reduce the heat to very low and gradually stir in the butter, making sure that each piece is completely incorporated before adding the next. Season and keep warm, but do not allow to boil.

Slice the liver thinly and arrange on 4 warmed plates. Spoon the sauce around and garnish with 'turned' mushrooms, sprigs of parsley and red pepper petals.

LAMBS TONGUES AND MORELS

FEUILLETES

INGREDIENTS (serves 4)

8 lambs tongues, soaked for 3-4 hours
    in several changes of cold water
1 carrot, chopped
½ stick of celery, chopped
bouquet garni of 1 bay leaf, 4 parsley
    stalks, sprig of thyme and 4 basil
    leaves
salt
175 g/6 oz puff pastry (see p.79)
beaten egg yolk
100 g/4 oz butter, diced
2 shallots, finely chopped
100 g/4 oz morels or other wild
    mushrooms
225 ml/8 fl oz red wine
300 ml/½pt lamb stock
50 g/2 oz skinned red pepper,
    blanched and cut into diamond
    shapes.
1 tsp chopped sage
freshly ground black pepper

FOR THE GARNISH
diamond shapes of blanched red
    pepper
mint leaves

Picture: page 219

It may be necessary to order fresh lambs tongues from the butcher in advance — do not use frozen ones. Pickled, smoked or canned tongues are also unsuitable.

———————————

Cover the lambs tongues with water, add the carrot, celery, bouquet garni and salt and simmer very gently, removing any scum as necessary, for $1\frac{1}{4}$-$1\frac{1}{2}$ hours.

Allow the tongues to cool slightly, remove the skins, then cut the tongues into strips.

Roll the pastry out to a rectangle 5 mm/¼ inch thick. Trim the edges with a large sharp knife, then cut into 4 rectangles. Transfer to a baking tray, cover and leave in a cool place for at least 30 minutes.

Heat the oven to 220°C/425°F/Gas 7.

Brush the pastry with beaten egg yolk and bake for about 8 minutes until it is crisp, golden and well risen.

Meanwhile, heat half the butter, add the shallots and cook over a moderate heat, shaking the pan occasionally, until they are soft. Add the mushrooms and cook for 2-3 minutes. Stir in the wine and reduce by half, then stir in the stock and reduce until slightly thickened. Add the tongue and red pepper and heat gently for a few minutes. Add the sage, reduce the heat to very low and gradually stir in the remaining butter, making sure that each piece is completely incorporated before adding the next. Season and keep warm, but do not allow to boil.

Leave the pastries to cool very slightly on a wire rack, then carefully slit them in half horizontally. Carefully remove any very soft pastry. Return to the oven briefly.

Place the bottom halves of the feuilletés on 4 warmed plates. Spoon the filling over and cover with the tops. Garnish with diamonds of red pepper and mint leaves.

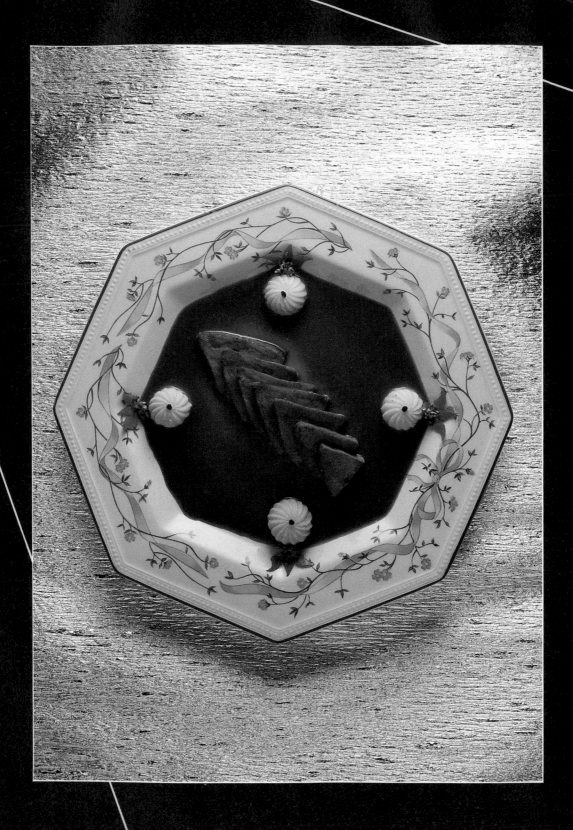

S L I C E S   O F   L A M B   W I T H   A S P A R A G U S

INGREDIENTS (serves 4)
50 g/2 oz butter, diced
2 shallots, chopped
½ carrot, chopped
600 ml/1 pt brown veal stock
bouquet garni of 5 parsley stalks,
   1 bay leaf, a sprig of thyme and a
   sprig of chervil
4 lamb steaks (1.25 mm/½ thick),
   weighing 150-175 g/5-6 oz, cut
   from the top of the leg and cut in
   half if large
salt and freshly ground black pepper
175 ml/6 fl oz red wine
2 tsp finely chopped chives
2 tsp finely chopped parsley
16—20 asparagus tips

FOR THE GARNISH
sprigs of parsley

If each slice of lamb is cut in half, making a total of 8, cook them in 4 batches, as they must be cooked in a single layer and not crowded in the pan. If fat white Argenteuil asparagus is used, halve the number of spears and slice each one in half lengthways just before it is served.

Heat 15 g/½ oz butter, add the shallots and carrot, cover and cook over a moderate heat, shaking the pan occasionally, until the shallots are soft. Stir in the stock and bouquet garni, then simmer until reduced to 225 ml/8 fl oz. Pass through a sieve.

Place each piece of lamb between 2 sheets of clingfilm and beat to a thickness of 6mm/¼ inch, retaining the oval shape. Season.

Heat 15 g/½ oz butter in a sauteuse or large frying pan. Add half the lamb and cook for 1 minute each side. Transfer to a warmed plate with a slotted spoon. Cover and keep warm. Cook the remaining lamb for 1 minute each side. Cover and keep warm. Lay the slices in a single layer — do not stack them.

Pour the excess fat from the pan, stir in the wine and reduce to 50 ml/2 fl oz. Stir in the reduced stock and reduce to 175 ml/6 fl oz. Pass through a sieve into a clean pan, add the chives and parsley and reheat gently over a very low heat. Gradually swirl in the remaining butter, making sure each piece is fully incorporated before adding the next. Season.

Meanwhile, blanch, refresh and drain the asparagus tips.

Spoon the sauce over the plates. Lay the slices of lamb on the sauce. Arrange the asparagus tips on the lamb and garnish with sprigs of parsley around the edge of the lamb.

RACK OF LAMB WITH LEEK PUREE

INGREDIENTS (serves 4)
2 racks of lamb, with 6 bones,
    trimmed
4 cloves of garlic, crushed
450 g/1 lb untrimmed leeks
100 g/4 oz butter, diced
2 tbsp chicken stock
2 tsp finely chopped parsley
salt and freshly ground black pepper
75 g/3 oz shallots, chopped
175 ml/6 fl oz dry vermouth
425 ml/15 fl oz veal stock
1 tsp chopped rosemary

FOR THE GARNISH
mint leaves
tomato 'flowers'

Picture: page 222

If this dish is prepared towards the end of the year or before the lambing season, when lambs are larger and more fatty, 2 cutlets per person will be sufficient. In the spring and early summer the cutlets will only have a fine layer of fat, and more will be needed.

———————

Heat the oven to 220°C/425°F/Gas 7.

Rub the lamb with 2 of the garlic cloves, protect the ends of the bones with foil and roast for 30 minutes until pink and still moist.

Transfer the lamb to a warmed plate, cover and keep warm.

Trim the leeks, leaving on 5 cm/2 inches of the green part. Slice thinly.

Heat the butter, stir in the leeks, stock and parsley, season lightly, cover and cook gently until the liquid has almost completely evaporated and the leeks are tender, but do not allow them to colour. Purée the leeks and keep warm.

Boil the shallots and remaining garlic in the vermouth until reduced by three quarters. Stir in the stock and reduce by one third. Add the rosemary and simmer gently for 5 minutes. Check the seasoning, keep warm.

Divide the lamb into cutlets.

Place the leek purée in the centre of 4 warmed plates, arrange the cutlets on top and spoon the sauce around. Garnish with mint leaves and tomato 'flowers'.

NOISETTES OF LAMB WITH RED, GREEN AND YELLOW PEPPER SAUCE

INGREDIENTS (serves 4)
50 g/2 oz red peppers, skinned and
    diced
50 g/2 oz green peppers, skinned and
    diced
50 g/2 oz yellow peppers, skinned and
    diced
600 ml/ 1 pt vegetable stock (see p.74)
425 ml/15 fl oz dry white wine
75 ml/3 fl oz double cream
40 g/1½ oz butter
12 noisettes of lamb
salt and freshly ground black pepper

FOR THE GARNISH
strips of red, green and yellow
    peppers, skinned and blanched

Picture: page 223

Simmer each of the peppers separately in a third of the stock for 2-3 minutes, then boil each until the liquid is reduced to 25 ml/1 fl oz. Stir a third of the wine into each and reduce to 50 ml/2 fl oz. Stir a third of the cream into each, then simmer for 1-2 minutes. Pureé, then pass through a sieve.

Heat the butter, add the noisettes and cook for about 2 minutes. Turn them over and cook for a further 2 minutes.

Meanwhile, gently reheat the sauces separately. Season each one. Place a spoonful of each sauce on 4 warmed plates and place a noisette on each bed of sauce. Garnish with contrasting colours of peppers.

MEDALLIONS OF LAMB WITH LIGHT

MUSTARD SAUCE

INGREDIENTS (serves 4)
50 g/2 oz butter, diced
450 g/1 lb wild mushrooms
225 ml/8 fl oz veal stock
1 tsp mustard seeds
2 tsp wholegrain mustard
175 ml/6 fl oz double cream
salt and freshly ground black pepper
a squeeze of lemon juice
16 medallions of lamb, about 40 g/1½
   oz each

FOR THE GARNISH
5-6 long carrots, cut into julienne of
   even lengths
20 chives
16 sprigs of chervil

Heat 15 g/½ oz butter, add the mushrooms and cook over a moderate heat, stirring occasionally, until all the moisture has evaporated. Transfer to a warmed plate with a slotted spoon, cover and keep warm.

Stir the stock and mustard seeds into the pan and reduce to about 50 ml/2 fl oz.

Stir in the mustard and cream and simmer until slightly thickened. Reduce the heat to very low and gradually whisk in 15 g/½ oz butter, making sure each piece is fully incorporated before adding the next. Season and add a squeeze of lemon juice to taste. Keep warm over a very low heat but do not allow to boil.

Meanwhile, blanch the carrot julienne for the garnish, refresh and drain well.

Season the medallions, heat the remaining butter in a sauteuse or large frying pan, add the medallions and cook for 2 minutes each side. They should still be pink and moist in the centre. Transfer to a warmed plate, cover and keep warm.

Whilst the lamb is cooking, group the carrot julienne into 20 bundles and tie a chive around the centre of each bundle.

Spoon the sauce over 4 warmed plates. Place the mushrooms in the centre of the plates. Arrange the medallions around. Place a bundle of carrots in between the medallions and place a sprig of chervil on each medallion.

LAMB WITH ARTICHOKE SAUCE

INGREDIENTS (serves 4)
1 large or 2 small globe artichokes,
   trimmed
lime juice
1 tbsp crème fraîche
550 g/1¼ lb fillet of young lamb,
   sliced
a few sprigs of lemon balm
225 ml/8 fl oz double cream
salt and freshly ground white pepper

FOR THE GARNISH
1-2 small courgettes
concassé tomatoes
leaves of flat-leaved parsley
slices of lime

Picture: page 226

This is really a dish for late spring or early summer, when the flavour of lamb is still delicate enough not to dominate the artichokes and lemon balm is just beginning to grow.

Place the artichoke in a pan of water, add a squeeze of lime juice and bring to the boil. Cover and cook for 35-45 minutes until tender.

Remove the artichoke from the pan and leave to drain upside down. When cool enough to handle, remove the leaves, scraping the edible flesh into a bowl. Discard the hairy choke. Purée the artichoke bottom, and the scrapings in a food processor or blender with the crème fraîche and 1 tsp lime juice.

Steam the lamb over a pan of water scented with lemon balm for 3-4 minutes or until the inside is pale pink. Remove from the heat and keep warm.

Boil the double cream until reduced by a quarter, then

whisk in the artichoke purée and season.

Blanch the courgettes for the garnish. Refresh and drain well and cut into fine slices.

Spoon the sauce over 4 warmed plates, add the lamb and garnish with the slices of courgette, concassé tomatoes and parsley and slices of lime.

◆ L O I N   O F   L A M B   W I T H   S W E E T B R E A D S

A N D   B A S I L

INGREDIENTS (serves 4)
1 bunch of basil
2 loin of lamb
2 cloves of garlic, crushed
bones from loin
2 shallots, chopped
1 carrot, chopped
1 stick of celery, chopped
2 pigs cauls
225g/8oz lambs sweetbreads, soaked
   for 3-4 hours in frequent changes of
   cold water
salt and freshly ground black pepper
100 g/4 oz butter, diced
16 button mushroom caps, turned (see
   p.65)
a squeeze of lemon juice
225 ml/8 fl oz light red wine
flesh of 2 firm ripe tomatoes, cut into
   concassé

FOR THE GARNISH
thin strips of cucumber

Picture: page 230

Chop the stalks of the basil and scatter over and around the lamb with the garlic. Cover and leave for 3-4 hours.

Place the bones in a roasting tin and brown under a hot grill, then tip into a saucepan, add the vegetables and garlic and basil stalks from the lamb. Place the roasting tin over the heat and stir in about 300 ml/$\frac{1}{2}$ pt water, dislodging the sediment. Pour the water into the saucepan — add more if necessary to cover the bones. Bring to the boil, remove the scum from the surface, then simmer for about an hour.

Pass through a conical strainer, pressing down well on the vegetables to extract as much liquid as possible.

Heat the oven to 220°C/425°F/Gas 7.

Lay the pigs cauls out on a warm surface and place a piece of lamb at one end of each.

Drain, dry and slice the sweetbreads and place over the remaining area of caul. Finely chop the basil leaves (3-4 tbsp)and sprinkle over the sweetbreads with salt and pepper. Starting with the end on which the lamb is placed, roll up the cauls like a Swiss roll. Tie the ends with string and loosely tie around the body in two places along its length.

Heat 15 g/$\frac{1}{2}$oz butter in a roasting tin, add the lamb roll and sear evenly. Place in the oven for about 8 minutes, turning occasionally, to cook evenly.

Transfer to a warmed plate, cover and keep warm.

Heat 25 g/1 oz butter, add the mushrooms and a squeeze of lemon juice and cook until slightly softened but not coloured.

Boil the stock and wine until reduced to 175 ml/6 fl oz, reduce the heat to very low and gradually stir in the remaining butter, making sure that each piece is completely incorporated before adding the next. Add the tomato, check the seasoning and add more finely chopped basil, if necessary. Keep warm but do not allow to boil.

Cut off the end pieces from the rolls of lamb, then cut the rolls into 12 slices.

Spoon the sauce over 4 warmed plates and arrange the slices of lamb and the mushrooms. Place thin strips of cucumber around the rims of the plates.

ABOVE *Lamb with artichoke sauce*
Recipe: page 224
OPPOSITE *Sweetbreads with leek and*
spinach sauce
Recipe: page 228

SWEETBREADS WITH LEEK AND SPINACH SAUCE

INGREDIENTS (serves 4)
4 veal sweetbreads, approximately
    225 g/8 oz each, soaked in several
    changes of cold water, until the
    water is clear
salt and freshly ground black pepper
15 g/½ oz butter, diced
1 tbsp olive oil

FOR THE SAUCE
90 g/3½ oz butter, diced
4 leeks, white part only, chopped
300 ml/½ pt chicken stock
50 g/2 oz spinach
150 ml/¼ pt double cream
salt and freshly ground black pepper

FOR THE GARNISH
mangetouts, trimmed down
spinach leaves
slices of truffle

Picture: page 227

Bring the sweetbreads slowly to the boil in a large saucepan of salted, acidulated water, then simmer for 5-6 minutes. Refresh and drain them carefully, remove the membrane and any gristle and fat. Place between two cloths, then press under a lightly weighted board until cold.

For the sauce, heat 15 g/½ oz butter, add the leeks, cover and cook over a moderate heat, shaking the pan occasionally, for about 3 minutes. Stir in the stock and simmer until almost tender. Stir in the spinach and simmer for 2-3 minutes, then reduce the liquid by just over a half. Stir in the cream and simmer until slightly thickened. Purée, then reheat gently and gradually whisk in the remaining butter, making sure that each piece is completely incorporated before adding the next. Season and keep warm but do not allow to boil.

Slice and season the sweetbreads.

Heat the butter and oil, add the sweetbreads and cook lightly for 2-3 minutes each side. Remove with a slotted spoon.

Meanwhile, separately blanch, refresh and drain the mangetouts and spinach — this should be blanched very briefly and drained very well. Cut the spinach into julienne.

Place the sweetbreads on 4 warmed plates and spoon the sauce around. Arrange the mangetouts and truffles in the centre of the sweetbreads and scatter the spinach julienne on the sauce.

NOISETTES OF LAMB WITH MINT

INGREDIENTS (serves 4)
16 noisettes of lamb (from the best
    ends), about 2.5 cm/1 inch thick
salt and freshly ground black pepper
50 g/2 oz butter, diced
225 ml/8 fl oz full-bodied dry white
    wine
450 ml/¾ pt lamb stock
2 tbsp finely chopped mint

FOR THE GARNISH
2 tbsp butter, diced
1 tbsp sugar
salt and freshly ground black pepper
1 cucumber, 2-3 carrots and 2-3
    turnips, peeled and cut into 5cm/2
    inch batons of uniform thickness
4 small courgettes, cut into slices
mint leaves

Picture: page 231

An old favourite that has been given an entirely new look. For the best effect, serve on really large plates. When preparing the garnish measure the batons against the plates you are to use to make sure they fit.

———————

Season the noisettes.

Heat half the butter in a sauteuse, add the noisettes and cook for about 3 minutes each side. They will be pink in the centres. Transfer to a warmed plate with a slotted spoon. Cover and keep warm.

Tip the excess fat from the sauteuse. Stir in the wine and reduce to about 3 tbsp. Stir in the stock and reduce to about 175 ml/6 fl oz.

Melt the butter and sugar for the garnish with the seasoning in 200 ml/7 fl oz water, then bring to the boil and cook the vegetables separately in it until they are just tender but still crisp. Remove with a slotted spoon, refresh, drain and keep warm.

Pass the sauce through a sieve, reheat, then, over a very low heat, swirl in the remaining butter. Add the mint. Season.

Spoon the sauce over 4 warmed plates. Place the batons in the shape of a cross. Place the noisettes in the 4 corners and garnish with mint and courgette slices.

STRIPS OF PORK WITH ORANGE AND
GREEN PEPPERCORNS

INGREDIENTS (serves 4)
finely grated rind and juice of 2
    oranges
1 tsp ground ginger
salt and freshly ground black pepper
550 g/1¼ lb pork fillet, cut into strips
50 g/2 oz butter, diced
2 tbsp cognac
150 ml/5 fl oz veal stock
150 ml/5 fl oz Gewürztraminer wine
1 tbsp finely chopped peeled fresh root
    ginger
1½ tbsp green peppercorns

FOR THE GARNISH
spring onion tassels (see p.71)
small segments of tangerine or orange
julienne of orange rind, blanched
julienne of cucumber, blanched

An Oriental influence can be detected in the flavourings used in this dish.

———————

Mix the orange rind, ground ginger and seasoning together.

Coat the pork in the orange mixture.

Heat half the butter, add the pork and cook for 2-3 minutes, stirring frequently. Remove with a slotted spoon, cover and keep warm.

Stir the cognac into the pan and ignite with a taper. When the flames die down, stir in the stock, wine, orange juice and root ginger. Reheat gently. Stir in the peppercorns, then gradually swirl in the remaining butter, making sure each piece is fully incorporated before adding the next. Season. Spoon the sauce over 4 warmed plates. Arrange the strips of pork on the sauce, then arrange the garnish.

Noisettes of lamb with mint
Recipe: page 229

BEEF WITH SHALLOTS

INGREDIENTS (serves 4)
2 tbsp oil
salt and freshly ground black pepper
550 g/1¼ lb fillet of beef, trimmed
25 g/1 oz butter, diced
2 shallots, finely chopped

FOR THE SAUCE
50 g/2 oz butter, diced
2 shallots, chopped
½ stick of celery, chopped
1 sprig of thyme
1 small bay leaf
1 tomato, chopped
1 tsp tomato purée
7 g/¼ oz black peppercorns, crushed
300 ml/½ pt full-bodied red wine
25 ml/1 fl oz red wine vinegar
300 ml/½ pt brown veal stock
salt

FOR THE GARNISH
slices of carrot
small sprigs of parsley

Picture: page 234

Heat the oven to 220°C/420°F/Gas 7.

Heat half the butter for the sauce, add the shallots and celery, cover and cook over a moderate heat, shaking the pan occasionally, until softened. Stir in the herbs, tomato, tomato purée, peppercorns and wine and simmer until reduced to about 3—4 tbsp. Stir in the vinegar and stock and reduce by half.

Meanwhile, heat the oil, season the beef, add to the oil and sear evenly, then place in the oven for 15 minutes, so that it remains rare. Transfer to a warmed plate, cover and keep warm.

Pass the sauce through a fine sieve, reheat gently and gradually stir in the remaining butter, making sure each piece is completely incorporated before adding the next. Add salt and keep warm, but do not allow to boil.

Cook the slices of carrot for the garnish, refresh and drain.

Heat the butter, add the shallots and cook over a moderate heat, stirring occasionally until just beginning to soften. Remove with a slotted spoon and drain on absorbent paper.

Cut the beef into 24 slices. Spoon the sauce over 4 warmed plates. Arrange the beef on top and scatter the shallots over the sauce. Garnish with the slices of carrot and the sprigs of parsley.

BEEF WITH SAGE

INGREDIENTS (serves 4)
25 g/1 oz butter, diced
salt and freshly ground black pepper
4 fillet steaks

FOR THE SAUCE
50 g/2 oz butter, diced
1 tbsp finely chopped shallot
16 sage leaves
100 ml/4 fl oz sercial madeira
425 ml/¾ pt brown veal stock
salt and freshly ground black pepper

FOR THE GARNISH
Brussels sprout leaves
½ quantity cauliflower purée (see
   p.301)
sage leaves

Picture: page 235

The sage leaves are simmered with the sauce ingredients so they give out their delicate flavour, but they are then sieved out, as they can taste bitter when bitten into.

For the sauce, heat 15 g/½ oz butter, add the shallot, cover and cook over a moderate heat, shaking the pan occasionally, until just soft. Stir in the sage leaves and madeira, simmer for 10 minutes, then reduce to about 1 tbsp. Stir in the stock and reduce by half. Pass through a sieve, reheat, then, over a very low heat, stir in the remaining butter. Season and keep warm, but do not allow to boil.

Heat the butter, season the steaks, add to the pan and cook for 2—3 minutes on each side so that they are rare. Remove with a slotted spoon.

Meanwhile, for the garnish, blanch the Brussels sprout leaves, refresh and drain well. Warm the cauliflower mousseline in a bowl over a pan of hot water, stirring occasionally.

Spoon the sauce over 4 warmed plates. Place the steaks on top. Add the sage leaves and cauliflower purée wrapped in Brussels sprout leaves.

BEEF WITH HORSERADISH AND SHALLOTS

INGREDIENTS (serves 4)
approximately 600 g/1 lb 6 oz fillet
   of beef
salt and pepper
100 g/4 oz butter, diced
12 firm, even sized shallots, unpeeled
   but roots and tops trimmed
1 carrot, chopped
½ onion, chopped
½ stick of celery, chopped
25 g/1 oz fresh horseradish root,
   peeled and shredded
2 tbsp cognac
600 ml/1 pt brown veal stock
half quantity turnip purée (see p.300)

FOR THE GARNISH
4 potato baskets (see p.302)

A very traditional combination of ingredients given a new look in the way it is cooked and presented. Fresh horseradish is not always easy to buy, but it *is* easy to grow — even a small piece of root will take shoot. But, be warned whilst preparing it — it produces strong fumes that can make the eyes and nose run.

———————————

Heat the oven to 220°C/425°F/Gas 7.

Season the beef. Heat 25 g/1 oz butter in a roasting tin, add the beef and sear evenly. Place in the oven and cook for about 15 minutes until rare, then transfer to a warmed plate, cover and keep warm.

Meanwhile, wrap the shallots in a parcel of foil, sealing the seam well. Spread 1.25 cm/½ inch salt in a heavy ovenproof dish and place the parcel of shallots on it. Place in the oven for 20-30 minutes until tender.

Heat 25 g/1 oz butter in a flameproof dish, add the vegetables and horseradish and cook in the oven until browned, turning frequently.

Drain off the surplus fat, stir in the cognac and ignite with a taper. Stir in the stock and reduce by two thirds. Pass through a sieve and measure the liquid — there should be about 100 ml/4 fl oz.

Pour into a clean saucepan, reheat, reducing further if necessary then, over a very low heat, gradually swirl in the remaining butter, making sure each piece is fully incorporated before adding the next. Season and keep warm but do not boil.

Warm the turnip purée and cook the potato baskets.

Cut the beef into 24 slices. Re-form and keep warm. Cut the shallots into halves.

Spoon the sauce over 4 warmed plates. Lay the slices of beef on it, arrange the shallots and add the turnip purée and potato baskets.

◆

Beef with shallots
Recipe: page 232

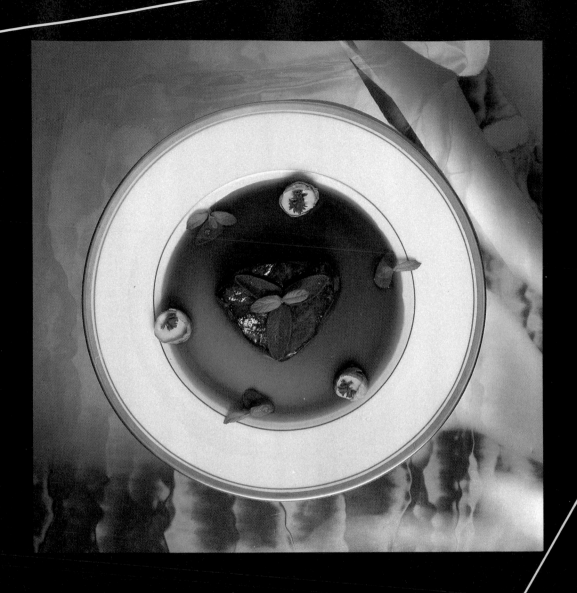

◆

Beef with sage
Recipe: page 232

BEEF WITH GLAZED VEGETABLES

INGREDIENTS (serves 4)
100 g/4 oz butter, diced
2 shallots, chopped
2 small carrots, chopped
2 sticks of celery, chopped
50 g/2 oz wild mushrooms
salt and freshly ground black pepper
4 fillet steaks, approximately
    150 g/5 oz
150 ml/¼pt ruby port
425 ml/¾pt brown veal stock
4 tsp chopped tarragon

FOR THE GARNISH
potato galettes (see p.303)
glazed 'turned' baby carrots (see
    p.63)
glazed 'turned' baby turnips (see
    p.63)
glazed chestnuts (see p.63)
sprigs of parsley

Picture: page 238

No extra vegetables are necessary with this dish as it is a complete meal in itself.

Heat 2 tbsp butter in a sauteuse or a large frying pan, add the shallots, carrots, celery and mushrooms, cover and cook over a moderate heat, shaking the pan occasionally, until just soft. Remove the lid and cook the vegetables more rapidly to evaporate the moisture.

Push the vegetables to one side. Season the beef, add to the pan and cook for about 3 minutes each side. Stir the vegetables occasionally to prevent them from burning. Transfer the beef to a warmed dish, season, cover and keep warm.

Carefully remove the excess fat from the surface of the pan, then stir in the port and boil until reduced to a syrupy glaze. Stir in the stock and tarragon and reduce by three quarters. Pass through a sieve, pressing down well on the vegetables to extract as much liquid as possible. Return to the rinsed pan and reheat gently.

Meanwhile, prepare the potato galettes and glaze the vegetables for the garnish.

Gradually swirl the remaining butter into the sauce, making sure that each piece is completely incorporated before adding the next. Season and keep warm but do not allow to boil.

Slice the beef. Spoon the sauce over 4 warmed plates, arrange the beef on top and add the vegetables. Garnish with sprigs of parsley.

BEEF WITH BASIL AND TOMATOES

INGREDIENTS (serves 4)
4 fillets of beef, approximately
    150-175 g/5-6 oz
salt and freshly ground black pepper
25 g/1 oz butter
100 ml/4 fl oz full-bodied dry white
    wine
225 ml/8 fl oz veal stock, boiled down
    to 100 ml/4 fl oz
100 ml/4 fl oz crème fraîche
1½ tbsp finely chopped fresh basil
flesh from approximately 100 g/4 oz
    tomatoes, chopped

FOR THE GARNISH
small basil leaves

A simple dish that has the unmistakable flavour of the South of France.

Season the beef, heat the butter, add the beef and cook for about 3 minutes each side until rare. Transfer to a warmed plate, cover and keep warm.

Pour the excess fat from the pan, stir in the wine and stock and reduce by half. Stir in the crème fraîche and simmer until slightly thickened.

Reduce the heat to very low and stir in the basil and tomatoes. Season.

Cut the beef diagonally into slices, re-form and keep warm.

Divide the sauce between 4 warmed plates. Place the beef on top and garnish with small basil leaves.

STEAK WITH OYSTER AND MUSHROOM FILLING

INGREDIENTS (serves 4)
75 g/3 oz butter, diced
2 shallots, finely chopped
175 g/6 oz button mushrooms,
    chopped
8 oysters
90 ml/6 tbsp dry white wine
1½ tbsp lemon juice
1 tsp chopped thyme
salt and freshly ground black pepper
4 fillet steaks, approximately
    175 g/6 oz
150 ml/¼pt dry oloroso sherry
600 ml/¼pt brown veal stock
celeriac purée (see p.301)

FOR THE GARNISH
4 oysters

Picture: page 239

The Australian carpet-bag steak provided the inspiration for this dish.

Heat 25g/1 oz butter, add the shallots, cover and cook over a moderate heat, shaking the pan occasionally, until softened. Stir in the mushrooms and cook, stirring occasionally, until softened.

Meanwhile, open and drain the oysters (see p.61). Heat the wine, add the oysters and poach for 30 seconds. Remove with a slotted spoon, cut each oyster into 4 and, off the heat, add to the mushrooms with the lemon juice, thyme and seasoning.

With a small, sharp knife, cut a pocket in each steak and fill with the mushroom mixture. Cover and chill.

Heat 25 g/1 oz butter, season the steaks, add to the pan and cook for about 3 minutes each side. Transfer to a warmed plate, cover and keep warm.

Tip the surplus fat from the pan, stir in the sherry and stock and reduce by three quarters. Reduce the heat to very low and gradually whisk in the remaining butter, making sure that each piece is completely incorporated before adding the next. Season. Keep warm, but do not allow to boil.

Meanwhile, gently warm the celeriac purée. Open the oysters for the garnish and put them on the side of the stove so they warm gently.

Place the celeriac purée on 4 warmed plates, spreading it out to make circles that are larger than the steak and thicker around the edge than in the centre. Add the steaks and spoon the sauce around. Place an oyster on each steak.

ABOVE *Beef with glazed vegetables*
Recipe: page 236
OPPOSITE *Steak with oyster and*
mushroom filling
Recipe: page 237

FILLETS OF BEEF WITH SOFT GARLIC SAUCE

INGREDIENTS (serves 4)
8 cloves of garlic
225 ml/8 fl oz dry white wine
100 ml/4 fl oz white wine vinegar
600 ml/1pt double cream
225 g/8 oz butter, diced
salt and freshly ground white pepper
4 fillets of beef, approximately
   175 g/6 oz, trimmed

FOR THE GARNISH
sprigs of broccoli
meat glaze (see p.74)

Picture: page 242

Cooking garlic in this way produces a very delicate flavoured sauce without any trace of harshness or bitterness. A simpler, yet still most effective way to garnish the dish with meat glaze is to trickle a thin stream around the edge of the sauce and plate or around the beef.

———————————

Boil the garlic cloves for 2 minutes, then refresh and drain. Repeat 4 times.

Reduce the wine and wine vinegar to about 1 tbsp, then stir in the cream and simmer for 3—4 minutes. Mix 25 g/1 oz butter with 6 of the garlic cloves in a food processor or blender for 30 seconds. Pass through a fine sieve. Season. Keep warm, but do not allow to boil.

Heat the remaining butter in a large sauteuse or frying pan, season the beef and cook for about 3 minutes each side to keep it rare.

Remove with a slotted spoon, cover and keep warm.

Cook the broccoli for the garnish until just tender, refresh and drain well. Gently warm the glaze in a small saucepan or bowl placed over a pan of hot water.

Spoon some of the sauce over 4 plates. Arrange the beef on top and garnish with the sprigs of broccoli and the glaze.

BEEF WITH COURGETTE AND TOMATO PLATTERS

INGREDIENTS (serves 4)
600 g/1lb 6 oz piece of fillet of beef
salt and freshly ground black pepper
100 g/4 oz butter, diced
2 courgettes, quite thinly sliced
3 small firm tomatoes, peeled, seeded
   and sliced
3 tsp finely chopped thyme
75 ml/3 fl oz dry vermouth
400 ml/14 fl oz veal stock

FOR THE GARNISH
50 g/2 oz small broad beans
sprigs of chervil

Heat the oven to 220°C/425°F/Gas 7.

Season the beef. Heat 40 g/1$\frac{1}{2}$ oz butter, add the beef and sear evenly. Place in the oven for 15 minutes. The beef will be rare. Transfer to a warmed plate, cover and keep warm.

Meanwhile, blanch, refresh and drain the courgettes.

Arrange overlapping slices of courgette and tomatoes in a single layer over the bases of 4 small buttered ovenproof dishes, sprinkle with thyme and seasoning, cover, then place on the bottom shelf of the oven for 10 minutes.

Pour the excess fat from the pan then stir in the vermouth, bring to the boil and reduce by half. Stir in the stock and reduce to about 150 ml/$\frac{1}{4}$ pt. Pass through a sieve, then reheat in a clean saucepan over a very low heat and gradually whisk in the remaining butter, making sure each piece is fully incorporated before adding the next. Season and keep warm but do not allow to boil.

Meanwhile, cook the beans for the garnish in simmering salted water until just tender. Refresh and drain well then pop the tender centres from the outer skin by pressing between thumb and forefinger.

Cut the beef into 20 slices, re-form and keep warm.

Carefully turn the courgette and tomato platters onto 4 warmed plates, keeping them in shape. Spoon the sauce over the plates, add the slices of beef and garnish with the broad beans and chervil.

FILLET OF BEEF WITH PARSLEY

INGREDIENTS (serves 4)
4 fillets of beef, approximately
    175 g/6 oz
salt and freshly ground black pepper
70 g/2¾ oz butter, diced
175 ml/6 fl oz red wine
425 ml/¾ pt brown veal stock
50 ml/2 fl oz sercial madeira
1 bay leaf
a sprig of thyme
65 g/2½ oz parsley leaves
7 g/¼ oz butter

FOR THE GARNISH
tiny sprigs of cauliflower

Picture: page 243

Season the fillets on both sides. Heat three quarters of the butter and cook the fillets for 3 minutes each side so that they remain pink inside. Transfer to a warmed plate, cover and keep warm.

Tip the butter from the pan. Stir the wine into the pan and reduce to 2 tbsp. Stir in the stock, madeira, bay leaf and thyme and simmer until reduced by a quarter. Pass through a sieve, then reheat gently and gradually whisk in the remaining butter, making sure each piece is completely incorporated before adding the next. Season and keep warm.

Gently cook the parsley in a very little water until tender, boiling rapidly at the end of the cooking to evaporate off excess moisture if necessary. Purée, then blend in the butter. Season.

Blanch the cauliflower sprigs for the garnish, then refresh and drain well.

Cut the fillets into 6 slices. Spoon the sauce over 4 warmed plates, place a spoonful of the parsley purée in the centre and arrange the cauliflower around. Arrange the slices of beef on the sauce.

Fillets of beef with soft garlic sauce
Recipe: page 240

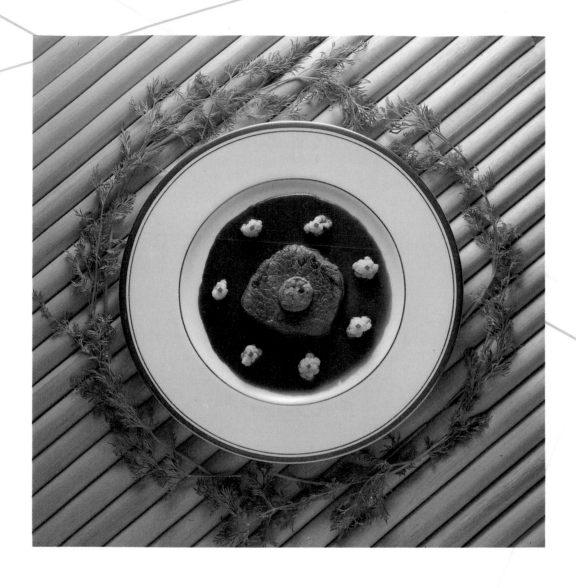

Fillet of beef with parsley
Recipe: page 241

BEEF WITH SPRING VEGETABLES

INGREDIENTS (serves 4)
175 ml/6 fl oz full-bodied dry white
  wine
4 shallots, freshly chopped
750 ml/26 fl oz veal stock
6 fl oz veal stock
2½ tbsp Dijon mustard
150 ml/5 fl oz double cream
1½ tbsp coarse grain mustard
1½ tsp freshly chopped chervil
1½ tsp finely chopped chives
1 tsp finely chopped tarragon
salt and freshly ground white pepper
550 g/1¼ lb fillet of beef
8 small carrots, turned
8 small turnips, turned
1 small courgette, turned
100 g/4 oz French beans

A dish that shows off the first of the new season's vegetables to their best advantage. Choose whichever vegetables are the best and freshest to make a colourful display.

Reduce the wine with the shallots by half. Add 175 ml/6 fl oz stock and the Dijon mustard and reduce by half again. Stir in the cream and simmer for 3 minutes. Pass through a sieve into a clean pan. Add the coarse grain mustard, herbs and seasoning.

Bring the remaining stock to the boil. Cut the beef into 4, season, add to the stock, reduce the heat and poach the beef for 3—4 minutes until rare. Drain well, cover and keep warm. Meanwhile blanch, refresh and drain all the vegetables separately.

Reheat the sauce gently but do not boil.

Cut each piece of beef in half, re-form and keep warm.

Spoon the sauce over 4 warmed plates. Arrange the beef and the vegetables in the sauce.

FILLET OF BEEF WITH REDCURRANTS

INGREDIENTS (serves 4)
225 ml/8 fl oz redcurrant vinegar
1 onion, chopped
1 carrot, chopped
2 tbsp oil
2 bay leaves
2 sprigs of marjoram
8 black peppercorns, crushed
600 g/1 lb 6 oz fillet of beef
25 g/1 oz butter
salt and freshly ground black pepper
175 g/6 oz redcurrants

FOR THE SAUCE
25 g/1 oz butter
2 tbsp finely chopped shallot
1 tbsp finely chopped carrot
2 tbsp finely chopped leek
425 ml/¾ pt veal stock
2 tbsp redcurrant jelly

Bring the vinegar, onion, carrot, oil, bay leaves, marjoram and peppercorns to the boil, then leave to cool. Pour over the beef, cover and leave in a cool place to marinate for 24 hours, turning occasionally.

For the sauce, heat the butter, add the shallot, carrot and leek, cover and cook over a moderate heat until soft and very lightly coloured, shaking the pan occasionally. Stir in the stock, bring to the boil then reduce to 300 ml/½pt. Stir in the redcurrant jelly and 175 ml/6 fl oz strained marinade. Simmer until reduced to about 300 ml/½ pt.

Meanwhile, heat the oven to 230°C/450°F/Gas 8.

Dry the beef very well. Heat half the butter, add the beef and sear evenly all over. Season the beef, then place in the oven for 7—8 minutes until rare.

Remove the beef, cover and keep warm.

Stir the sauce into the pan in which the beef was cooked, dislodging the sediment, then reduce until slightly thickened. Pass through a sieve then return to a very low heat and swirl in the remaining butter and the redcurrants. Season and keep warm, but do not boil.

Cut the beef into 12 slices, re-form, cover and keep warm. Spoon the sauce over 4 warmed plates. Arrange the beef on the sauce.

FILLET OF BEEF WITH TURNIPS AND MORELS

INGREDIENTS (serves 4)
550 g/1¼ lb fillet of beef
2 tbsp olive oil
2 sprigs of thyme
salt and freshly ground black pepper
75 g/3 oz butter, diced
300 ml/½ pt sercial madeira
300 ml/½ pt brown veal stock
3 shallots, finely chopped
200 g/7 oz morels
12 baby turnips with green tops,
    turned (see p.65)
25 g/1 oz demerara sugar

FOR THE GARNISH
parsley leaves

The simple olive oil and thyme marinade ensures the beef is succulent and imparts an additional depth to the flavour.

————————————

Marinate the beef with the olive oil, thyme and seasoning, covered, in a cool place overnight.

Heat the oven to 230°C/450°F/Gas 7.

Remove the beef from the marinade and dry well.

Heat 25 g/1 oz butter in a roasting tin, add the beef and sear evenly, then place in the oven for about 7 minutes. It will be rare.

Transfer the beef to a warmed plate, cover and keep warm.

Stir the madeira into the roasting tin and reduce by just over two thirds. Stir in the stock and reduce by half. Keep warm.

Heat 25 g/1 oz butter, add the shallots, cover and cook over a moderate heat, shaking the pan occasionally, until soft. Add the morels and cook for 3 minutes. Strain in the reduced stock. Season and keep warm.

Meanwhile, cook the turnips in gently boiling salted water until just tender. Refresh and drain.

Dissolve the sugar in the remaining butter over a low heat, add the turnips and carefully turn in the butter/sugar until evenly glazed.

Cut the beef into 24 slices. Re-form, cover and keep warm. Remove the morels from the sauce with a slotted spoon. Spoon the sauce over 4 warmed plates. Place the morels in circles around the centre, then arrange the slices of beef around the outside. Add the turnips and finish with the parsley.

POULTRY

AND GAME

◆ The term 'poultry' encompasses two quite different but equally delicious types of bird - chicken and duck - that require a different method of preparation and cooking in order to make full use of their unique characteristics. Light, lean chicken benefits from gentle cooking and responds well to steaming and poaching, while duck, with its richer flesh, responds better to short, fiercer cooking. Likewise, chicken is enhanced by light flavoured and textured accompaniments, while duck benefits from ingredients that have a sharp note to them, such as spinach and sorrel. All game is lean but there are quite marked differences between the flavours and textures of animals and birds. No game should be hung for so long that it becomes 'high'. Not only will this mask the flavour but it may also deter people from eating it.

CHICKEN WITH FENNEL SAUCE

INGREDIENTS (serves 4)
4 chicken breasts
salt and freshly ground black pepper
25 g/1 oz butter

FOR THE SAUCE
1 small bulb of fennel with some
    feathery leaves
25 g/1 oz parsley leaves
50 g/2 oz butter, diced
1 shallot, finely chopped
75 ml/3 fl oz dry white wine
100 ml/4 fl oz chicken stock
250 ml/9 fl oz double cream
salt and freshly ground white pepper
a squeeze of lemon juice

FOR THE GARNISH
broccoli purée (see p.62)
sprigs of fennel

Picture: page 250

Parsley not only adds colour to the sauce, and therefore the dish, but also gives a new dimension and 'roundness' to the flavour of fennel.

For the sauce, chop 100 g/4 oz of the centre of the fennel bulb. Chop the fennel leaves with the parsley very finely and mix with a very little water to give a soft purée.

Heat half the butter in a heavy pan, add the shallot, cover and cook over a moderate heat until soft. Add the chopped fennel, cover and cook over a low heat for 6-7 minutes until the fennel is soft.

Stir in the wine and stock and reduce to 3 tbsp, then stir in the cream and simmer for 2-3 minutes. Purée and simmer again if necessary, to give a smooth sauce.

Wrap the parsley/fennel purée in a cloth and squeeze the juice into the sauce to give a delicate green colour. Over a very low heat, gradually swirl in the remaining butter. Season, adding a little lemon juice if necessary. Keep warm, but do not allow to boil.

Beat the chicken breasts to flatten them slightly. Season.

Heat the butter, add the chicken and cook for about 3 minutes each side.

Remove with a slotted spoon and drain on absorbent paper. Cut into slices. Heat the broccoli purée.

Spoon the sauce over 4 warmed plates and arrange the slices of chicken on top. Garnish with sprigs of fennel and add the broccoli purée, formed into mounds.

STUFFED POUSSINS

INGREDIENTS (serves 6)
75 g/3 oz chicken breast meat
salt and lemon juice
½ tbsp dry vermouth
¼ egg white
175 ml/6 fl oz double cream, chilled
freshly ground white pepper
6 poussins, approximately 400 g/14
    oz each
freshly ground black pepper
35 g/1¼ oz red pepper, skinned,
    blanched and diced
4 tbsp finely chopped
    basil
1 L/1¾ pt chicken stock

FOR THE SAUCE
lettuce sauce (see p.261) or
light mustard sauce (see p.224)

Purée the chicken breast meat in a food processor or liquidiser until smooth. Add salt and lemon juice and vermouth, then mix in the egg white. Pass through a sieve into a bowl placed over a bowl of ice, then gradually beat in the cream and season. Cover and chill for at least 30 minutes.

Cut through the poussins' legs at the first joint - use the ends for stock. Place the poussins breast downwards and cut along the backbone with a small sharp knife. Then cut the flesh away from the carcass with short clean movements, taking care not to pierce the skin. Cut out the thigh bones but leave the lower leg and wing-bones in place.

Mix the red pepper into the chicken mixture, then divide between the poussins, spreading it out evenly. Sprinkle the basil along the length of the mixture, adding just enough to give a green centre to the slices when the poussins are sliced. Tuck the skin over the filling, reshape the birds and tie them up securely with string, but do not pull the string too tightly,

FOR THE GARNISH
basil leaves
double cream

Picture: page 251

so that the filling can expand during cooking.

Bring the stock to the boil in a saucepan that is large enough to hold all 6 birds, or use 2 smaller ones. Reduce the heat to simmering, lower in the poussins, cover with greaseproof paper and poach for 10 minutes.

Prepare the sauce.

Remove the poussins from the poaching liquor. Drain them in a cloth, then trim the legs. Place them on a large warmed plate, cover and leave in a warm place for 3-4 minutes. Then remove the string and cut into neat slices.

Spoon the sauce over 6 large, warmed plates, carefully arrange the slices, overlapping, on the plates and garnish with basil leaves. Swirl thin lines of cream in the sauce.

CHICKEN BREASTS WITH PINK LEEK SAUCE

INGREDIENTS *(serves 6)*
15 g/½ oz butter
white part of 1 leek, sliced
1 tsp finely chopped shallot
2 tbsp dry vermouth
250 ml/9 fl oz chicken stock
120 ml/4½ fl oz double cream
salt and freshly ground black pepper
6 chicken breasts, skinned
15 g/½ oz skinned red
   pepper, chopped
2 egg yolks

FOR THE GARNISH
diced red pepper
small sprigs of thyme

A small amount of red pepper is used to lift the colour of the light sauce without spoiling the delicacy of the flavour.

———————————

Heat the butter in a heavy flameproof casserole, add the leek and shallot, cover and cook over a low heat, shaking the pan occasionally, until softened. Stir in the vermouth, stock and cream and simmer for 10 minutes.

Season the chicken breasts. Place in the casserole, cover and poach for 8-10 minutes.

Transfer the chicken breasts to a warmed plate, cover and keep warm.

Purée the contents of the casserole with sufficient red pepper to give a light pink colour. Pour into a saucepan and reduce to 300 ml/½pt. Reduce the heat and keep warm.

Whisk the egg yolks with 3 tbsp cold water until foamy. Pour into the hot, but not boiling pink leek liquor, whisking constantly. Season.

Cut the chicken breasts into slices, re-form and keep warm.

Divide the sauce between 6 warmed plates. Arrange slices of chicken breasts on the sauce. Garnish with diced red pepper and sprigs of thyme.

Chicken with fennel sauce
Recipe: page 248

Stuffed poussins
Recipe: page 248

CHICKEN WITH CARROT SAUCE

INGREDIENTS (serves 4)
2 large chicken breasts, cut in half
salt and freshly ground black pepper
3 tbsp butter
2 tbsp Pernod

FOR THE SAUCE
2 tbsp butter
225 g/8 oz baby carrots, finely
    chopped
50 g/2 oz finely chopped tart apple
2 shallots, finely chopped
½ stick of celery, finely chopped
bouquet garni of 6 parsley stalks,
    sprig of fresh thyme, ½ bay leaf and
    3 tsp fennel seeds, crushed
salt and freshly ground black pepper
225 ml/8 fl oz chicken stock
50 ml/2 fl oz crème fraîche

FOR THE GARNISH
slim corkscrews of apple peel
feathery leaves from the carrots
'turned' carrots

Picture: page 254

For the sauce, heat the butter, add the carrot, apple, shallots, celery, bouquet garni and salt and pepper, cover and cook over a moderate heat, shaking the pan occasionally, for 5 minutes.

Stir in the stock and simmer for 10 minutes, stirring occasionally, until the vegetables are tender. Remove the bouquet garni and purée the carrot mixture in a food processor or blender, then pass through a fine sieve. Return to the rinsed food processor or blender and, with the motor running, slowly pour in the crème fraîche.

Season the chicken breasts. Heat 2 tbsp butter, add the chicken breasts and cook for 3 minutes each side.

Transfer the chicken breasts to a warmed plate, cover and keep warm.

Stir half the Pernod into the cooking juices, dislodging the sediment, then stir in the carrot sauce and simmer gently for 5 minutes.

Reduce the heat and stir in the remaining butter. Season. Add the remaining Pernod, if necessary, then spoon over 4 warmed plates. Arrange the chicken breasts on top and garnish with the apple peel corkscrews, carrot leaves and 'turned' carrots.

CHICKEN BREASTS WITH

ARTICHOKES AND MANGETOUTS

INGREDIENTS (serves 4)
50 g/2 oz butter, diced
4 chicken breasts, skinned
salt and freshly ground black pepper
2 tbsp chopped shallots
225 ml/8 fl oz chicken stock, boiled
    down to 100 ml/4 fl oz
100 ml/4 fl oz dry vermouth
4 tsp chopped basil
2 cooked artichoke bottoms (see
    p.64) sliced
100 g/4 oz mangetouts
40 g/1½ oz pistachio nuts

Heat half the butter. Beat the chicken breasts to flatten them slightly. Season the chicken and the butter, cook for about 3 minutes each side until just cooked through. Transfer to a warmed plate with a slotted spoon, cover and keep warm.

Stir the shallots into the pan and cook over a moderate heat, stirring frequently. Stir in the stock, vermouth and basil and reduce to 175 ml/6 fl oz. Pass through a sieve into a clean pan and reheat gently. Over a very low heat gradually swirl in the remaining butter.

Lay the slices of artichoke in the top of a steamer and place over a pan of simmering water to warm.

Blanch the mangetouts, refresh and drain well.

Slice the chicken breasts and arrange on 4 warmed plates. Spoon the sauce around and arrange the mangetouts, slices of artichoke and pistachio nuts.

BREASTS OF CHICKEN WITH

PERNOD

INGREDIENTS (serves 4)
150 ml/5 fl oz full-bodied white wine
150 ml/5 fl oz fino sherry
bouquet garni of 2 sprigs of fennel, 4
  basil leaves, 4 mint leaves, sprig
  of lemon thyme, small strip of
  lemon peel and 2 sprigs of tarragon
4 chicken breasts, skinned
salt and freshly ground black pepper
1 tbsp Pernod
2 bay leaves
300 ml/½ pt double cream

FOR THE GARNISH
cucumber balls
puff pastry fleurons (see p.79)
leaf shapes of cucumber skin
sprigs of fennel

Picture: page 255

Only a little Pernod is used so that its fairly pervasive flavour enhances the other flavours without dominating them.

———————

Gently heat the wine, sherry and bouquet garni to just below simmering point in a covered pan. Remove from the heat and leave to infuse for about an hour. Remove and reserve the bouquet garni.

Beat the chicken breasts to flatten slightly, then season. Lay in a single layer in a heavy flame-proof casserole and pour the wine/sherry and Pernod over. Add the bay leaves, cover with foil and poach gently for 7-10 minutes until tender.

Transfer the chicken breasts to a warmed plate, cover and keep warm.

Return the bouquet garni to the poaching liquor and reduce by three quarters. Stir in the cream and simmer until slightly thickened. Remove the bay leaves and bouquet garni. Season and keep warm.

Meanwhile, steam the cucumber balls for 2 minutes and warm the puff pastry fleurons.

Cut the chicken breasts into slices. Spoon the sauce over 4 warmed plates, arrange the chicken breasts on top and garnish with the cucumber balls, cucumber 'leaves', sprigs of fennel and fleurons.

ABOVE *Chicken with carrot sauce*
Recipe: page 252
OPPOSITE *Breasts of chicken with Pernod*
Recipe: page 253

SMALL CHARTREUSE OF PIGEON AND CHICKEN

INGREDIENTS (serves 4)
100 g/4 oz chicken breast meat,
*   chopped and chilled*
salt and freshly ground black pepper
50 g/2 oz butter, diced
50 ml/2 fl oz double cream
1 egg yolk
pinch of freshly grated nutmeg
2 pigeons
2 sprigs of thyme
2 tbsp oil
50 g/2 oz carrots, cut into julienne
50 g/2 oz French beans, cut into
*   julienne*
50 g/2 oz celery, cut into julienne
50 ml/2 fl oz ruby port
500 ml/18 fl oz chicken stock
100 g/4 oz chicken liver parfait

FOR THE GARNISH
julienne strips of carrot, celery and
*   French beans*
individual leaves of herbs

Picture: page 258

This is a good illustration of how Cuisine Vivante has adapted a traditional dish to fall into line with modern trends of eating. If serving this dish for a dinner party, choose recipes that do not require too much last-minute attention for the other courses.

Heat the oven to 220°C/425°F/Gas 7.

Mix the chicken, seasoning, 35 g/1¼ oz butter, the cream, egg and nutmeg together in a food processor until smooth. Cover and chill.

Season the pigeons, place a sprig of thyme inside each one, spoon the oil over and roast for 15 minutes until they are pink inside and still moist.

Remove the pigeons and drain the excess oil from the roasting tin.

Blanch, refresh and drain the vegetables.

Cut the breasts and legs from the pigeons and chop up the carcasses. Stir the port into the roasting tin, add the carcasses and simmer until reduced by half. Stir in the chicken stock and reduce again to one third. Strain, then stir in half the chicken liver parfait and season.

Arrange the vegetables alternately in the bottom and sides of 4 buttered ramekin dishes and chill for 10 minutes.

Carefully spoon a layer of the chicken mixture into the bottom of the dishes.

Cut the pigeon breast and leg meat into neat rounds, to fit the dishes, and place on top of the chicken with the remaining parfait. Moisten with a little of the sauce, then cover with the remaining chicken mixture.

Place the dishes in a baking or roasting tin, pour boiling water around them, then place in the oven for 20 minutes.

Gently reheat the remaining sauce over a very low heat. Gradually swirl in the remaining butter, keep the sauce warm, but do not allow it to boil.

Blanch, refresh and drain the vegetables for the garnish.

Leave the chartreuse to stand for a few minutes before unmoulding onto 4 warmed plates. Spoon the sauce around, arrange the vegetables neatly in stacks and garnish with herb leaves.

CHICKEN BREASTS WITH VEGETABLE

FILLING AND VEGETABLE SAUCE

INGREDIENTS (serves 4)
2 chickens, approximately 1.5 kg/3½
  lb each
1 carrot, chopped
1 onion, quartered
1 stick of celery, chopped
1 leek, chopped
1 tomato, peeled, seeded and chopped
1 sprig of tarragon
1 sprig of thyme

FOR THE SAUCE
475 ml/17 fl oz crème fraîche
1 carrot, cut into fine julienne
½ small fennel bulb, cut into fine
  julienne, with a little green left on
3 mangetouts, cut into fine julienne
salt and 1 tsp green peppercorns,
  crushed
8 morels, chopped

FOR THE FILLING
salt and freshly ground black pepper
1 small carrot, cut into fine julienne
½ small leek, cut into fine julienne
½ stick of celery, cut into fine julienne
1 tsp finely chopped parsley
1 tsp finely chopped chives
8 morels
25 g/1 oz butter, diced

Picture: page 259

Slit the chickens along the breast bone, remove the skin and wishbones. Cut off the fillet from the breasts and reserve. Cut off the legs and use in another dish. Remove and chop the wings and chop the carcass. Remove all visible fat.

Place the carcasses and the remaining ingredients in a large saucepan, cover with water, cover the pan and bring to the boil. Simmer for 1 hour.

For the sauce, strain off 750 ml/1¼ pt of stock (reserve the remainder) and boil until reduced by half. Stir in the crème fraîche and reduce again to 350 ml/12 fl oz.

Blanch the vegetable julienne, refresh, drain and dry very well, then add to the reduced stock with salt, green peppercorns and morels. Remove from the heat but keep warm.

With the point of a sharp knife, cut a horizontal pocket in each chicken breast, leaving 1.25 cm/½ inch at each end. Sprinkle salt and pepper inside the pocket.

Blanch the carrot, leek and celery for the filling. Refresh and drain well. Mix with the parsley and chives.

Divide the vegetables between the pockets in the chicken and top each with 2 morels. Close carefully and secure with a cocktail stick. Place a small knob of butter on each breast, then wrap securely in foil, but do not pull the foil too tightly across the breasts. Poach for 8-10 minutes, turning carefully twice.

Remove the breasts from the heat and leave for a few minutes before cutting each breast into 4 slices.

Spoon some of the sauce onto 4 warmed plates, then arrange the pieces of chicken on top.

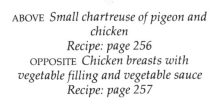

ABOVE *Small chartreuse of pigeon and chicken*
Recipe: page 256
OPPOSITE *Chicken breasts with vegetable filling and vegetable sauce*
Recipe: page 257

CHICKEN BREASTS WITH SHERRY VINEGAR SAUCE, WHITE WINE SAUCE AND WILD MUSHROOMS

INGREDIENTS *(serves 4)*
4 chicken breasts, skinned
salt and freshly ground black pepper
65 g/2½ oz butter, diced
1 small shallot, finely chopped
100 ml/4 fl oz dry white wine
300 ml/1½pt chicken stock
150 ml/¼pt double cream
1 tbsp oil
150 g/5 oz chanterelles or other wild
  mushrooms
1 tbsp chopped parsley

FOR THE SHERRY VINEGAR SAUCE
50 ml/2 fl oz sherry vinegar
175 ml/6 fl oz dry white wine
300 ml/½pt chicken stock
50 g/2 oz butter, diced
salt and freshly ground black pepper

FOR THE GARNISH
leaves of flat parsley

Picture: page 262

A wetted meat cleaver will do just as well as a meat bat for beating the chicken breasts. Beat them firmly but take care not to break the flesh fibres.

Beat the chicken breasts to flatten them slightly. Season.

Heat the butter in a sauteuse or a large frying pan, add the shallot in a single layer, cover and cook over a moderate heat, shaking the pan occasionally until they are soft. Place the chicken breasts on top and cook until they have just stiffened. Remove.

Tip off excess fat, stir in the wine and reduce to 2 tbsp. Stir in the stock. Bring to the boil, lower the heat, add the chicken and poach until tender. Remove the chicken, cover and keep warm.

Pour the liquor from the pan and reserve.

For the sauce, stir the vinegar and wine into the pan and reduce to 2 tbsp. Stir in the stock and boil until it coats the back of a spoon. Pass through a sieve, then reheat gently and gradually whisk in the butter, making sure each piece is completely incorporated before adding the next. Season and keep warm but do not allow to boil.

Reduce the cooking liquor by half. Stir in the cream and simmer for 2-3 minutes. Pass through a fine sieve, then reheat gently and gradually whisk in the remaining butter. Season and keep warm.

Heat the oil, add the chanterelles and parsley and cook, shaking the pan occasionally for 3-4 minutes. Remove with a slotted spoon and drain on absorbent paper.

Spoon the vinegar sauce over one half of 4 warmed plates and spoon the white wine sauce over the other. Slice the chicken breasts. Arrange the chicken breasts on top.

Add the mushrooms and garnish with flat-leaved parsley.

CHICKEN BREASTS WITH LIGHT TOMATO SAUCE

INGREDIENTS *(serves 4)*
75 g/3 oz butter, diced
1 shallot, very finely chopped
flesh of 2 tomatoes, chopped

Heat 15 g/½ oz butter in a small saucepan and add the shallot. Cover and cook over a moderate heat, shaking the pan occasionally, until the shallot is soft. Stir in the tomatoes and simmer gently until reduced to about 50 ml/2 fl oz. Pass

salt and freshly ground black pepper
4 chicken breasts, skinned
2 tbsp cognac
150 ml/5 fl oz medium-bodied dry
   white wine
50 ml/2 fl oz dry vermouth
175 ml/6 fl oz chicken stock

FOR THE GARNISH
celery leaves
julienne of celery

through a sieve. Season.

Season the chicken breasts. Heat 25 g/1 oz butter in a sauteuse or large frying pan, add the chicken and cook for 3 minutes each side. Transfer to a warmed plate with a slotted spoon, cover and keep warm.

Pour the excess fat from the pan, stir in the cognac and ignite with a taper. When the flames have died down, stir in the wine, vermouth, stock and tomato and reduce 120 ml/4½fl oz. Reduce the heat to very low and gradually swirl in the remaining butter, making sure each piece is fully incorporated before adding the next. Season.

Meanwhile, blanch and refresh the celery julienne and drain well.

Cut the chicken breasts into slices, re-form and keep warm.

Divide the sauce between 4 plates. Arrange the slices of chicken overlapping down the centre of the plates. Garnish with celery leaves and the celery julienne randomly in piles.

BREAST OF CHICKEN WITH LETTUCE SAUCE AND THYME

INGREDIENTS (serves 4)
75 g/3 oz wild rice
15 sprigs of thyme
salt and freshly ground pepper
4 chicken breasts, skinned

FOR THE SAUCE
35 g/1¼ oz butter, diced
1 shallot, finely chopped
100 g/4 oz Iceberg lettuce, shredded
25 g/1 oz spinach, shredded
225 ml/8 fl oz chicken stock
100 ml/4 fl oz dry white wine
100 ml/4 fl oz double cream
salt and freshly ground pepper

FOR THE GARNISH
sprigs of thyme
tomato 'diamonds'

Picture: page 263

Bring a pan of salted water to the boil, add the wild rice, stir once, cover and boil for 40-45 minutes until just tender.

Lay half of the sprigs of thyme in the bottom of a steamer or colander. Season the chicken breasts and place them on top of the thyme, place the remaining thyme on top then cover with greaseproof paper.

Place the steamer or colander over a pan of simmering water and steam the chicken for 15-20 minutes until tender.

Meanwhile, for the sauce, heat 7 g/¼ oz butter, add the shallot, cover and cook over a moderate heat, shaking the pan occasionally, until soft. Stir in the lettuce, spinach, stock and wine and cook until tender then boil to evaporate off the excess moisture. Stir in the cream and simmer for 2-3 minutes. Purée then pass through a sieve. Return to the rinsed pan and reduce further if too thin. Reduce the heat to very low and gradually stir in the remaining butter, making sure each piece is fully incorporated before adding the next. Season and keep warm but do not boil.

Strain the wild rice. When the chicken is cooked, remove it from the heat, keep covered and warm for a few minutes before cutting into slices.

Spoon the sauce over 4 warmed plates. Arrange the chicken on top of the wild rice and garnish with the sprigs of thyme and tomato 'diamonds'.

ABOVE *Chicken breasts with sherry
vinegar sauce, white wine sauce and
wild mushrooms
Recipe: page 260*
OPPOSITE *Breast of chicken with lettuce
sauce and thyme
Recipe: page 261*

STEAMED POUSSINS WITH SHERRY

SAUCE

INGREDIENTS (serves 4)
2 leeks, sliced lengthways
2 carrots, chopped
2 shallots, chopped
500 ml/18 fl oz chicken stock
200 ml/7 fl oz fino sherry
6 sprigs of chervil
2 cloves
salt and freshly ground white pepper
4 poussins
4 strips of lemon peel
50 g/2 oz butter, diced

FOR THE GARNISH
concassé tomatoes
fresh chervil

Put the leeks, carrots, shallots, stock, sherry, chervil, cloves and seasoning into the base of a steamer and bring to the boil.

Season the poussins inside and out and put a strip of lemon peel in each cavity. Place in the top of the steamer.

Put the top of the steamer in place on the base, cover and steam the poussins for 20-25 minutes. Transfer the poussins to a warmed plate, cover and keep warm.

Simmer the liquid for about 5 minutes, pass through a conical sieve, then reduce to 150 ml/5 fl oz. Reduce the heat to very low then gradually swirl in the butter, making sure that each piece is fully incorporated before adding the next. Season and keep warm but do not boil.

Remove the strips of lemon peel from the poussins. Spoon the sauce over 4 warmed plates. Place a poussin in the centre of each and garnish the birds and the sauce with concassé tomatoes and chervil.

DUCK BREASTS WITH CALVADOS

SAUCE AND NUTMEG SAUCE

INGREDIENTS (serves 4)
2 ducks
1 carrot, chopped
1 onion, chopped
2 sticks of celery, chopped
bouquet garni of a sprig of thyme,
   3 sprigs of chervil, 3 parsley stalks
   and a bayleaf
40 g/1½ oz butter, diced
2 tbsp finely chopped shallots
100 ml/4 fl oz dry cider
50 ml/2 fl oz calvados

FOR THE NUTMEG SAUCE
225 ml/8 fl oz dry white wine
225 ml/8 fl oz veal stock
175 ml/6 fl oz double cream
a pinch of grated nutmeg
25 g/1 oz butter, diced
salt and freshly ground black pepper

FOR THE GARNISH
1 crisp apple
2 tbsp sugar

Picture: page 266

This recipe is a development of the traditional theme of apples, cream and nutmeg, the characteristic flavours of Normandy. The base for the calvados sauce can be prepared in advance.

Remove the breasts and legs from the ducks (keep the legs for another dish). Chop the carcasses, put them in a roasting tin and brown under a hot grill. Transfer the carcasses to a large pan and pour off the excess fat from the roasting tin. Put the vegetables into the roasting tin, brown under a hot grill, then add them to the carcasses with the bouquet garni and about 900 ml/1½ pt water. Bring to the boil slowly, skim the fat from the surface and simmer for 2-3 hours, skimming the surface occasionally.

Strain the stock and reduce by three quarters.

Heat 15 g/½ oz butter, add the shallot, cover and cook over a moderate heat, shaking the pan occasionally, until soft. Stir in the cider and reduce by half. Add the calvados and reduce to 50 ml/2 fl oz. Stir in the stock and simmer until syrupy. Remove from the heat.

Heat the grill.

Season the duck breasts and cook under the grill, skin-side

up, for 3-4 minutes. Turn over and cook the other side for 3-4 minutes.

Meanwhile, reduce the wine to 2 tbsp. Stir in the stock and reduce by three quarters. Stir in the cream and nutmeg and simmer for 2-3 minutes. Reduce the heat and gradually swirl in the butter, making sure that each piece is completely incorporated before adding the next. Season and keep warm, but do not allow to come to the boil.

When the duck is cooked, transfer to a warmed plate. Cover and keep warm.

'Turn' the apple for the garnish (see p.65). Heat the sugar, add the apple and cook for about 2 minutes, shaking the pan frequently so that the apple cooks evenly. Remove with a slotted spoon and drain on absorbent paper.

Pass the calvados sauce through a sieve and reheat gently. Reduce the heat to very low and swirl in the remaining butter. Season.

Remove the skin from the duck and cut the breasts into slices. Arrange them on 4 warmed plates. Spoon the calvados sauce over one half of each plate, the nutmeg sauce over the other. Garnish with apple shapes.

BREAST OF DUCK WITH COGNAC
AND PINK PEPPERCORN SAUCE
AND CRISPY DUCK SALAD

INGREDIENTS (serves 4)
4 large duck breasts
salt and freshly ground pepper
½ tbsp oil
20 g/¾ oz pink peppercorns
200 ml/7 fl oz cognac
300 ml/½ pt double cream
50 g/2 oz butter, diced
1 tsp soy sauce

FOR THE SALAD
lamb's lettuce
julienne of red pepper
julienne of courgette
julienne of fennel
small sprigs of chervil
vinaigrette dressing (see p.76)

Heat the oven to 230°C/450°F/Gas 8. Remove the excess fat from the duck breasts and reserve. Season the breasts.

Heat the oil, add the breasts skin side up, and cook over a high heat until just browned. Transfer to a rack placed in a roasting tin and place in the oven for about 4 minutes.

Transfer the breasts to a warmed plate and keep warm. Pour the excess fat from the roasting tin. Add the peppercorns and stir in the cognac. Stir in the cream and reduce until the sauce coats the back of a spoon. Gradually whisk the butter into the boiling sauce, making sure each piece is fully incorporated before adding the next. Season and keep warm but do not allow to boil.

Arrange small portions of salad on 4 side plates.

Remove the skin from the breasts. Shred it, then cook in a small pan over a high heat until golden brown. Pour off the excess fat. Add the soy sauce and toss over the heat. Divide between the salads.

Slice the duck breasts thinly. Re-form and keep warm.

Spoon the sauce over 4 warmed plates. Arrange the duck breasts in a fan shape on the sauce. Spoon some of the dressing over the salads and serve with the duck.

ABOVE *Duck*
breasts with Calvados
sauce and nutmeg sauce
Recipe: page 264
OPPOSITE *Breast of duck with spinach*
filling and tarragon sauce
Recipe: page 268

BREAST OF DUCK WITH SPINACH FILLING AND TARRAGON SAUCE

INGREDIENTS *(serves 4)*
2 ducks
1 duck liver
1 tbsp cognac
salt and freshly ground black pepper
35 g/1¼ oz butter, diced
50 g/2 oz celery, finely chopped
50 g/2 oz shallot, finely chopped
100 g/4 oz spinach, shredded
50 g/2 oz Iceberg lettuce, shredded

FOR THE SAUCE
1 shallot, finely chopped
1 tbsp lemon juice
4 tbsp finely chopped tarragon leaves
75 ml/3 fl oz double cream
75 g/3 oz butter, diced
salt and freshly ground black pepper

FOR THE GARNISH
tarragon leaves

Picture: page 267

A little Iceberg lettuce added to the spinach mellows and softens its flavour without destroying that characteristic sharp note that blends so well with duck.

Heat the oven to 220°C/425°F/Gas 7.

Remove the breasts, whole, from the ducks.

Mash the duck liver with the cognac and season. Spread in the natural cavities formed by the two halves of the breasts.

Heat the butter, add the celery and shallot, cover and cook over a moderate heat, shaking the pan occasionally until the shallot is just soft. Stir in the spinach and lettuce, cover and cook, shaking the pan frequently until the spinach has 'fallen'. Remove from the heat, season and leave to cool.

Divide the spinach mixture between the breasts and secure the two halves of each breast together with trussing string.

Score the skin with the point of a sharp knife. Heat the remaining butter, add the duck breasts and sear evenly all over, then place in the oven for about 15 minutes.

Transfer the breasts to a warmed plate, cover and keep warm.

For the sauce, cook the shallot in the lemon juice over a moderate heat for 3 minutes, then boil to evaporate the liquid. Stir in the tarragon and cream and simmer for 1 minute. Reduce the heat to very low and gradually swirl in the butter, making sure that each piece is completely incorporated before adding the next. Season and keep warm but do not allow to boil.

Remove the trussing string from the breasts and cut them into slices. Arrange on 4 warmed plates, add the sauce and garnish with tarragon leaves.

DUCK WITH FLEURIE

INGREDIENTS (serves 4)
4 duck breasts
salt and freshly ground black pepper
small pinch of grated nutmeg
20 g/¾ oz butter

FOR THE SAUCE
40 g/1½ oz butter, diced
2 tbsp shallot, finely chopped
450 ml/¾ pt Fleurie
100 ml/4 fl oz sauternes
2 sage leaves
2 sprigs of thyme
175 ml/6 fl oz duck stock
salt and freshly ground black pepper

FOR THE GARNISH
25 g/1 oz butter, diced
75 g/3 oz chanterelles
green grapes, peeled, pips removed,
    quartered

Picture: page 270

Fleurie is the most charming and feminine of the single villages Beaujolais and is well worth looking for for this recipe. However, if your searches should prove unsuccessful, Chiroubles or Juliennas could be used instead.

For the sauce, heat 15 g/½ oz butter, add the shallot, cover and cook over a moderate heat, shaking occasionally until soft. Stir in the Fleurie, sauternes and herbs and reduce by half. Stir in the stock and reduce to 350 ml/12 fl oz. Remove from the heat.

With the point of a sharp knife, slash the skin of the duck breasts in a lattice pattern. Season and sprinkle with a little nutmeg. Heat the butter, add the duck breasts and sear the skin side for 30 seconds. Remove and tip the fat from the pan. Return the breasts to the pan and cook for 3-4 minutes each side until still pink in the centre. Transfer to a warmed plate with a slotted spoon. Cover and keep warm.

Meanwhile, remove the herbs from the sauce, then purée the sauce and pass it through a sieve. Reheat gently. Then, over a very low heat, gradually stir in the remaining butter, making sure that each piece is completely incorporated before adding the next. Season and keep warm but do not allow to boil.

For the garnish, heat the butter, add the chanterelles and cook for about 3 minutes, shaking the pan occasionally. Remove with a slotted spoon,

Remove the skin from the duck breasts. Slice the breasts, re-form and keep warm. Spoon the sauce over 4 warmed plates. Arrange the slices of duck on top and place the chanterelles and grapes around the edge of the plate.

Breast of duck with figs
Recipe: page 272

ROAST DUCK WITH ESSENCE OF MUSHROOMS

INGREDIENTS (serves 4)
2 ducks, legs, wings and backbones
    removed
90 g/3½ oz butter, diced
2½ tbsp cognac
4 shallots, chopped
flesh of 2 tomatoes
450 ml/¾ pt red wine
500 ml/18 fl oz brown veal stock,
    reduced by a half
bouquet garni of a bay leaf, sprig of
    thyme, sprig of rosemary, 4 parsley
    stalks
salt and freshly ground black pepper
150 ml/¼ pt double cream
500 g/1 lb 2 oz wild mushrooms
50 ml/2 fl oz ruby port
2 tbsp finely chopped parsley

FOR THE GARNISH
short, slim batons of carrot
leaves of flat-leaved parsley

Chop the duck legs, wings and backbones. Heat 20 g/¾ oz butter, add the bones and brown them. Drain off the excess fat. Ignite the cognac and pour over the bones. Stir in 3 of the shallots, the tomatoes, wine, reduced stock and bouquet garni. Bring to the boil and simmer for 1 hour, skimming the surface, if necessary.

Heat the oven to 220°C/425°F/Gas 7. Pass the stock through a conical sieve, pressing down well on the bones to extract as much liquid as possible.

Heat 15 g/½ oz butter. Season the duck and cook with breasts downwards, for 1-2 minutes until they are slightly golden and crisp. Place in the oven for 5 minutes until the breasts are pink. Transfer to a warmed dish, cover and keep warm.

Pour the stock into a clean pan and reduce to 150 ml/¼ pt. Stir in the cream and simmer until slightly thickened. Season and keep warm, but do not allow to boil.

Cook the mushrooms in their own juices in a covered pan for 2 minutes. Drain well. Heat the remaining butter, add the remaining shallot and the mushrooms and cook for 2-3 minutes. Stir in the port and cook rapidly until the moisture has evaporated. Stir in the parsley and season.

Blanch, refresh and drain the carrot batons.

Slice the duck breasts, re-form and keep warm.

Spoon the sauce over 4 warmed plates. Place the mushrooms in the centres and arrange the duck breasts on top. Garnish with the carrot batons and parsley.

BREAST OF DUCK WITH FIGS

INGREDIENTS (serves 4)
4 duck breasts, skinned
salt and freshly ground black pepper
8 medium sized figs, sliced
2 tbsp eau-de-vie de framboise
1 tsp icing sugar
100 ml/4 fl oz good quality dessert
    wine
250 ml/9 fl oz duck stock
50 g/2 oz butter, diced

FOR THE GARNISH
kumquats, cut into wedges

Picture: page 271

When kumquats are not available, small segments of orange, with every last trace of pith and peel removed, can be used instead.

Heat the grill.

Season the duck breasts and cook, skinned-side uppermost, under the hot grill for 1 minute. Turn over and cook for a further minute, then turn over and cook for 1 minute more. Remove from the heat, cover and keep warm.

Poach the slices of fig in the framboises, sugar and dessert wine for about 2 minutes, then carefully remove with a slotted spoon, cover and keep warm.

Boil the poaching liquor to reduce it slightly, then stir in the stock and reduce by one third. Reduce the heat to very low, then gradually whisk in the butter, making sure that each piece is completely incorporated before adding the next. Season.

Cut the duck breasts into thin slices. Arrange them on 4 warmed plates. Spoon on the sauce, arrange the figs and garnish with the kumquats.

DUCK WITH TURNIPS

INGREDIENTS (serves 4)
2 ducks
salt and freshly ground black pepper
50 g/2 oz butter, diced
2 shallots, finely chopped
150 ml/¼ pt sherry vinegar
600 ml/1 pt duck stock
4 small even sized turnips, peeled
75 g/3 oz spinach, trimmed
1 tbsp double cream

FOR THE GARNISH
½ quantity of white butter sauce (see p.66)

Heat the oven to 220°C/425°F/Gas 7.

Season the duck, then place in the oven for 25 minutes until very pink and moist inside.

Cut the legs and the breasts in one piece from the carcasses. Cover and keep warm.

Heat 25 g/1 oz butter, add the shallots and carcasses, then cook over a moderately high heat. Stir in the vinegar, then the stock and reduce to 150 ml/¼ pt.

Meanwhile, cut the tops off the turnips and hollow out the turnips slightly. Decorate the outside with a cannelle knife or ordinary knife. Place in the top half of a steamer or colander.

Bring some water to the boil in the bottom half of the steamer; put the top half of the colander in place, cover and cook for about 10 minutes until tender.

Wash the spinach, shake off the water, then cook in a small, covered saucepan over a low heat until soft. Purée with the cream. Season and return to the rinsed pan and keep warm.

Pass the sauce through a conical sieve, pressing down well on the carcasses to extract as much flavour as possible. Reheat over a very low heat and stir in the remaining butter, making sure that each piece is completely incorporated before adding the next. Season and keep warm, but do not allow to boil.

Prepare the white butter sauce for the garnish.

Place the duck legs and breast, skin-side uppermost, under a hot grill for a minute or two. Cut the breasts into slices. Re-form and keep warm. Divide the spinach between the hollows in the turnips. Keep warm.

Spoon the sauce over 4 warmed plates. Add the duck breasts and legs. Place a circle of white butter sauce that is larger than the turnips on each plate and place a turnip in each circle so that there is a halo of sauce around it.

DUCK QUENELLES WITH DUCK

BREASTS

INGREDIENTS (serves 4)
225 g/8 oz duck leg meat, chopped
salt and lemon juice
1 egg white
225 g/8 fl oz double cream
1 tbsp ruby port
1 tsp finely chopped thyme
freshly ground black pepper
2 duck breasts
½ tbsp redcurrant jelly, melted
900 ml/1½ pt chicken stock

FOR THE SAUCE
600 ml/1 pt duck stock
100 ml/4 fl oz raspberry vinegar
a strip of lemon peel
175 g/6 oz butter, diced
salt and freshly ground black pepper
1-2 tbsp eau-de-vie de framboise

FOR THE GARNISH
4 filo tartlet cases (see p.81)
flageolet purée (see p.62)
petits pois
mint leaves

Picture: page 274

The quenelle part of this dish is an especially useful addition to the cook's repertoire as it calls for the use of duck leg meat, and many Cuisine Vivante recipes only use the breast.

Purée the duck leg meat in a food processor or blender. Mix in the salt and lemon juice followed by the egg white. Pass through a sieve into a bowl over a bowl of ice and gradually work in the cream. Lastly, add the port, thyme and pepper. Cover and chill.

Heat the grill.

Season the duck breasts and brush the skin with melted redcurrant jelly. Grill, skin-side up, for 4—5 minutes. Turn over and grill for a further 4—5 minutes. Transfer to a warmed plate. Cover and keep warm.

Meanwhile, heat the chicken stock in a shallow pan until just simmering. Use 2 tablespoons to shape the duck leg mixture into 8 ovals and carefully lower them into the stock. Poach gently for about 3—4 minutes. Turn over and poach for another 3—4 minutes. Lift out with a slotted spoon and drain on a cloth.

For the sauce, boil the stock, raspberry vinegar and strip of lemon peel until reduced by three quarters. Remove the lemon peel and reduce the heat to very low. Gradually stir in the butter, making sure that each piece is completely incorporated before adding the next. Season and keep warm but do not allow to boil.

Meanwhile, warm the tartlet cases and flageolet purée separately and blanch, refresh and drain the petits pois. Fill the tartlets with the flageolet purée.

Ignite the framboise and spoon over the duck breasts. Cut into slices and arrange on warmed plates. Spoon on some of the sauce. Add the quenelles and tartlets, then the petits pois. Finish with the mint leaves.

WILD DUCK WITH SUMMER FRUITS

INGREDIENTS (serves 4)
2 wild ducks, hung for 3 days
40 g/1½ oz butter
1 carrot, chopped
1 onion, chopped
1 stick of celery, chopped
3 juniper berries, crushed
bouquet garni of a sprig of thyme,
    sprig of rosemary and 1 bay leaf
1 tbsp sugar
1 tbsp red wine vinegar
200 ml/7 fl oz cognac
100 ml/4 fl oz ruby port
300 ml/½ pt full-bodied dry white
    wine
juice of 4 oranges
100 ml/4 fl oz meat glaze (see p.74)
400 ml/14 fl oz duck stock
1 tbsp lemon juice
½ oz redcurrant jelly
salt and pepper

FOR THE GARNISH
apricots, halved and stoned
sweet white wine
redcurrants
sliced figs
orange rind julienne

Picture: page 275

The fruits can be varied according to what is available; the dish illustrated on p.275 shows kiwi fruits, plums and strawberries.

Remove the legs, backbones and wishbones from the ducks.

Melt 25 g/1 oz butter, add the duck legs, backbones and wishbones and cook until well browned. Add the vegetables and cook until lightly browned, stirring occasionally. Add the juniper berries, bouquet garni, sugar and vinegar and boil rapidly until the liquid has evaporated. Stir in 100 ml/4 fl oz cognac, the port and the wine. Reduce by half.

Boil the orange juice until reduced by half. Strain onto the bones. Add the meat glaze and stock and simmer for 2 hours, skimming the surface occasionally.

Heat the oven to 230°C/450°F/Gas 6. Pass the stock through a conical sieve, pressing down well on the bones to extract as much liquid as possible. Remove the fat from the surface then reduce to 350 ml/12 fl oz. Add lemon juice, redcurrant jelly and seasoning to taste.

Heat the remaining butter. Season the duck and cook, breast downwards for 1-2 minutes until lightly golden and crisp. Place in the oven for 5 minutes until pink and moist.

Lightly poach the apricots in the wine then add the redcurrants and sliced figs to cook very slightly.

Drain off the surplus fat from the roasting tin, ignite the remaining cognac and pour over the duck. Remove the breasts in one piece then carve into thin slices. Re-form, cover and keep warm.

Remove the fruits from the wine with a slotted spoon and arrange on four warmed plates with the orange julienne. Spoon the sauce over the plates and arrange the slices of duck breast on the sauce.

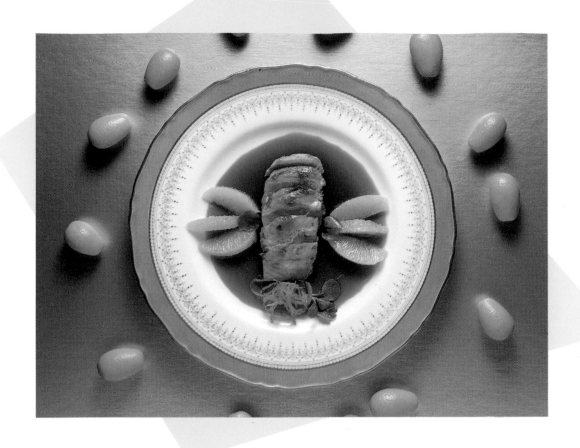

OPPOSITE *Breast of guinea fowl in an*
apple jacket
Recipe: page 281
ABOVE *Breast of pheasant with white*
wine and orange
Recipe: page 289

PIGEON BREASTS WITH PORT SAUCE AND CHESTNUTS

INGREDIENTS *(serves 4)*
4 pigeons
salt and freshly ground black pepper
65 g/2½ oz butter
2 carrots, finely chopped
2 leeks, finely chopped
2 shallots, chopped
600 ml/1 pt chicken stock
1 bay leaf
4 sage leaves
6 black peppercorns
1 tbsp very finely chopped shallot
5 black peppercorns, crushed
4 tbsp red wine vinegar
50 ml/2 fl oz ruby port
50 ml/2 fl oz crème de cassis
1 tbsp redcurrant jelly
3 tbsp orange juice
chestnut purée (see p.300)
40 g/1½ oz sugar
6 cooked chestnuts

FOR THE GARNISH
50 g/2 oz cranberries

Young wild wood pigeon are ideal in this full-flavoured dish. The sauce can be prepared in advance up to the addition of the butter, and the purée up to the addition of the cream and butter.

Carefully remove the breasts from the pigeons, skin the breasts and beat lightly to flatten them. Season.

Heat 25 g/1 oz butter, add the carrots, leeks and shallots and cook over a moderate heat, stirring occasionally, for 4-5 minutes. Add the pigeon carcasses, stock, bay leaf, sage leaves and peppercorns. Bring to the boil, remove the scum from the surface, then simmer gently for about 45 minutes. Reduce to 100 ml/4 fl oz. Pass through a conical sieve, pressing down well on the bones to extract as much liquid as possible.

Gently simmer the chopped shallots with the crushed peppercorns in the vinegar, port, crème de cassis and stock until the shallots are softened, then reduce the liquid by half, stir in the redcurrant jelly and the orange juice. Simmer briefly then reduce the heat to very low and gradually swirl in 25 g/1 oz butter, making sure each piece is incorporated before adding the next.

Heat the remaining butter, add the pigeon breasts and cook for 30 seconds on each side. Transfer to a warmed plate, cover and keep warm.

Prepare the cranberries and warm the chestnut purée.

Dissolve the sugar in a little water in a small saucepan, then stir in the chestnuts to coat them in syrup and heat through.

Slice the pigeon breasts, re-form and keep warm.

Spoon the sauce over 4 warmed plates. Arrange the breasts on the sauce and place the purée in neat mounds around the breasts.

Chop the chestnuts and place on the mounds. Remove the cranberries from the liquid with a slotted spoon, drain well and scatter over the sauce.

BREAST OF GUINEA FOWL IN AN APPLE JACKET

INGREDIENTS (serves 4)
4 breasts, from guinea fowl,
    approximately 900 g/2 lb each
guinea fowl carcasses and trimmings,
    coarsely chopped
100 g/4 oz butter, diced
2 shallots, chopped
1 carrot, chopped
1 tbsp tomato purée
225 ml/8 fl oz dry white wine
50 ml/2 fl oz ruby port
salt and freshly ground black pepper
2 tbsp sirop de framboise
2 crisp dessert apples
2 tbsp caster sugar
75 ml/3 fl oz calvados
4 pâté brisée tartlet cases (see p.80),
    cooked
100 g/4 oz raspberries
1 tsp icing sugar
75 ml/3 fl oz full-bodied dry white
    wine

FOR THE GARNISH
mint leaves

Picture: page 278

The jacket of apple slices keeps the breasts of guinea fowl beautifully moist and gives them an additional succulence. The sauce can be prepared in advance but the apples must be left whole until they are required.

———————————

Heat 75 g/3 oz butter, add the carcasses and trimmings, shallots and carrot and cook, stirring occasionally, until well browned. Stir in the tomato purée, wine and port and sufficient water to cover the bones. Simmer for about one hour until the liquid is reduced by half, skimming the surface occasionally.

Pass through a conical sieve, pressing down well on the bones and vegetables to extract as much liquid as possible. Reduce the liquid to about 150 ml/$\frac{1}{4}$ pint. Season and add the sirop. Keep warm.

Heat the oven to 200°C/400°F/Gas 6.

Heat the remaining butter, add the guinea fowl breasts and cook, skinned side down, for 30 seconds, turn over and cook for one minute. Turn over again, cover and place in the oven for about 6 minutes until pink and moist. Transfer to a warmed plate, cover and keep warm.

Peel, core and slice the apples. Gently dissolve the sugar in the calvados, add the apple slices and poach until just becoming tender.

Put the tartlet cases into the oven to warm through but do not allow to burn.

Carefully lift the apple slices from the liquid with a slotted spoon and arrange neatly over the guinea fowl breasts to cover them like a jacket. Brush the apples lightly with the calvados syrup and place the breasts in a hot oven for a few minutes.

Gently warm the raspberries, lightly sweetened with icing sugar, in the wine in a covered pan, then remove with a slotted spoon, allowing the excess juice to drain off. Place in the tartlet cases and garnish with the mint leaves.

Transfer the guinea fowl breasts to 4 warmed plates. Add the raspberry tartlets. Spoon the sauce around.

OPPOSITE
*Medallions of hare
with blackberry
sauce
Recipe: page 292*
ABOVE *Medallions
of rabbit with basil
Recipe: page 290*

LEFT *Medallions of
hare with beetroot
Recipe: page 293*

283

GROUSE WITH CHICORY

INGREDIENTS (serves 4)
3 shallots, chopped
1 stick of celery, chopped
1 carrot, chopped
3 juniper berries, crushed
4 coriander seeds, lightly toasted and
   crushed
425 ml/$\frac{3}{4}$ pt brown veal stock
4 young grouse, trussed
salt and freshly ground black pepper
4 rashers of bacon
25 g/1oz butter, diced
250 ml/9 fl oz full-bodied red wine

FOR THE CHICORY
40 g/1$\frac{1}{2}$ oz butter, diced
4 heads of chicory, thickly sliced
1 tsp sugar
salt and freshly ground black pepper
75 ml/3 fl oz whipping cream

FOR THE GARNISH
16 chicory leaf tips
4 tsp tomato concassé

For how to choose chicory see p.31. This recipe mellows the natural bitterness of chicory.

———————

Simmer the shallots, celery, carrot, juniper berries and coriander seeds in the stock for an hour until the stock is reduced to 225 ml/8 fl oz.

Heat the oven to 220°C/425°F/Gas 7.

Meanwhile, heat half the butter for the chicory, add the chicory and sugar and cook, stirring frequently until very soft and lightly coloured. Turn into a cast iron flameproof casserole, cover with water, add the remaining butter and cook over a moderate heat for 15—20 minutes until tender.

Season the grouse inside and out and tie a rasher of bacon over the breasts.

Heat the butter in a roasting tin, add the grouse and sear evenly. Cover closely with buttered greaseproof paper and place in the oven for 10 minutes. Remove the bacon and return to the oven for 10 minutes. Remove the grouse from the tin with a slotted spoon, cover and keep warm.

Pour most of the fat from the tin, then stir in the wine and reduce by half. Stir in the stock and reduce to 200 ml/7 fl oz. Season.

Meanwhile, drain the chicory well, then turn into an ovenproof dish that it just fits, season and pour over the cream. Put into the oven for about 10—15 minutes until the cream has almost evaporated.

Blanch, refresh and drain the chicory leaf tips for the garnish.

Cut the legs from the grouse and cut off the lower part of the leg at the joint. Remove the breasts in one piece, then carve into slices. Re-form and keep warm with the thighs.

Divide the sauce between 4 warmed plates. Arrange the grouse, chicory and chicory tips, placing the concassé tomatoes on the stems of the tips.

PARTRIDGE WITH JUNIPER SAUCE
AND CABBAGE

INGREDIENTS (serves 4)
4 partridges, trussed
salt and freshly ground black pepper
4 sprigs of thyme
4 rashers of bacon
1 tbsp olive oil

FOR THE SAUCE
100 ml/4 fl oz sercial madeira
300 ml/½pt full-bodied red wine
5 juniper berries, crushed
a sprig of thyme
1 bayleaf
225 ml/8 fl oz chicken stock
50 ml/2 fl oz double cream
25 g/1 oz butter, diced
salt and freshly ground black pepper

FOR THE CABBAGE
15 g/½ oz butter, diced
350 g/12 oz hard white cabbage,
*   finely shredded*
100 ml/4 fl oz bual madeira
salt and freshly ground black pepper

Heat the oven to 220°C/425°F/Gas 7.

Season the partridges inside and out. Place a sprig of thyme in the cavity of each and tie a rasher of bacon over the breasts.

Heat the oil, add the partridges and sear evenly. Place in the oven and cook for 10 minutes. Remove the bacon and cook for a further 5 minutes.

Meanwhile, heat the butter for the cabbage, add two thirds of the cabbage and the madeira, cover tightly and cook over a very low heat until softened, shaking the pan occasionally. Season.

Transfer the partridges to a warmed plate, cover and keep warm.

For the sauce, stir the madeira into the partridge cooking juices and reduce by half. Stir in the wine, add the juniper berries, thyme and bayleaf and reduce the liquid to about 3 tbsp. Stir in the stock and reduce by half. Stir in the cream and simmer briefly. Pass through a sieve into a clean pan. Reheat gently, over a very low heat, and gradually stir in the butter. Season, and keep warm, but do not allow to boil.

Blanch and refresh the remaining cabbage and drain well.

Divide the sauce between 4 warmed plates. Place the cooked cabbage in the centres to form a bed and place the partridges on the beds. Scatter the remaining cabbage on the sauce.

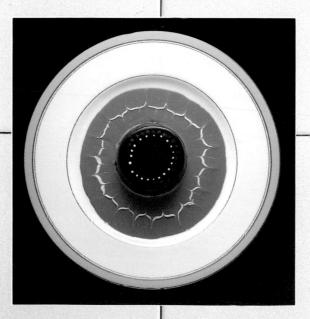

OPPOSITE
Medallions of venison with apples and celeriac
Recipe: page 294

ABOVE *Loin of venison with pears and cranberries*
Recipe: page 295

LEFT *Venison medallions in port jelly and beetroot purée*
Recipe: page 296

RABBIT WITH CELERIAC AND APRICOTS

INGREDIENTS (serves 4)
12 dried apricots soaked in 225 ml/8
    fl oz medium-bodied dry white
    wine for at least 4 hours
1 large head of celeriac
50 g/2 oz butter, diced
1½ tbsp lemon juice
salt and freshly ground black pepper
2 large saddles of rabbit
75 ml/3 fl oz white wine vinegar
1½ tbsp finely chopped shallot
600 ml/1 pt brown veal stock

FOR THE GARNISH
sprigs of chervil

Simmer the apricots in the wine until tender.

Heat the oven to 220°C/425°F/Gas 7.

Peel the celeriac and scoop into balls with a melon baller, or cut into cubes. Place immediately in a saucepan with 15 g/½ oz butter, the lemon juice, salt and sufficient water to cover. Bring to the boil, cover then simmer until tender.

Meanwhile, heat half the remaining butter in a roasting tin. Season the rabbit, add to the pan and sear evenly. Place in the oven for about 15 minutes until pink and moist in the centre. Transfer to a warmed dish with a slotted spoon, cover and keep warm.

Pour the excess fat from the tin, stir in the wine vinegar and shallot and reduce by two thirds. Stir in the stock and reduce to 175 ml/6 fl oz. Remove from the heat and gradually swirl in the remaining butter. Pass through a sieve, season and reheat gently, but do not allow to boil.

Remove the fillets from the saddles and cut each one diagonally into slices. Re-form and keep warm. Remove the apricots from the wine with a slotted spoon and cut into quarters.

Spoon the sauce over four warmed plates. Place the slices of rabbit down the centre of each one. Arrange the apricot quarters and balls of celeriac in groups around the slices. Garnish the rabbit with sprigs of chervil.

SALMIS OF PHEASANT

INGREDIENTS (serves 4)
425 ml/¾ pt Beaujolais
3 shallots, chopped
1 leek, sliced
1 carrot, sliced
12 juniper berries, crushed
bouquet garni of 4 parsley stalks,
    1 sprig of marjoram, 1 bayleaf
2 basil leaves
4 tbsp good quality Marc de
    Bourgogne
2 hen pheasants
75 g/3 oz seedless muscat or other
    white grapes, peeled, halved and
    seeded, if necessary
75 g/3 oz black grapes, peeled, halved
    and seeded
100 g/4 oz butter, diced
425 ml/¾ pt game stock
25 ml/1 fl oz double cream
salt and freshly ground black pepper

Bring the wine, shallots, leek, carrot, juniper berries and bouquet garni to the boil then simmer until reduced by a quarter. Leave to cool then stir in 2 tbsp Marc. Pour over the pheasants, cover and leave in a cool place for 12-18 hours turning the pheasants over occasionally.

Marinate the grapes separately in the remaining Marc for 2 hours at room temperature.

Remove the pheasants and the vegetables separately from the marinade. Drain and dry well.

Heat the oven to 220°C/425°F/Gas 7. Heat 50 g/2 oz butter in a roasting tin, add the pheasants and sear evenly. Place in the oven for 20 minutes, basting occasionally. Remove with a slotted spoon and pour most of the fat from the tin.

Add the vegetables to the tin and cook over a moderate heat, stirring frequently until lightly browned. Stir in the marinade, bring to the boil and reduce to 175 ml/6 fl oz. Stir in the stock and reduce to 200 ml/7 fl oz. Stir in the cream then pass through a conical sieve. Reheat gently and then, over a

FOR THE GARNISH
4 small spring green leaves or larger
ones, neatly trimmed

very low heat gradually stir in the remaining butter. Season and keep warm but do not allow to boil.

Meanwhile remove the grapes from the Marc with a slotted spoon, place in a single layer on a warmed plate, cover and put in the oven to warm. Remove the trussing strings from the pheasant. Cut each bird into quarters. Remove all the bones except the main ones in the legs and wings. Pack the pieces of pheasant, skin side up, in a large, heavy, buttered casserole. Cover and keep warm.

Heat a deep fat frying pan of oil to about 200°C/400°F, spread two of the spring green leaves out in the basket, lower them into the oil and fry briefly until crisp. Remove and drain on absorbent paper. Cook the remaining leaves in the same way.

Arrange the pheasant on 4 warmed plates. Spoon some of the sauce over half of the pheasant and spoon the remainder over most of the plates. Place the spring green leaves on the parts of the plates without sauce.

Garnish the plates with black and green grapes.

BREAST OF PHEASANT WITH WHITE WINE AND ORANGE

INGREDIENTS (serves 4)
75 g/3 oz butter
2 shallots, finely chopped
4 oranges, rind cut into julienne, juice squeezed
250 ml/9 fl oz full-bodied dry white wine
breasts of 3 young pheasants
8 tbsp cognac
5 tbsp good quality bitter orange marmalade
salt and pepper

FOR THE GARNISH
orange segments, skin and pith removed
strips of blanched orange rind
individual watercress leaves

Picture: page 279

Heat the oven to 220°C/425°F/Gas 7.

Heat the butter in a heavy flameproof casserole, add the shallots and cook over a low heat, stirring frequently, until soft but not coloured. Remove with a slotted spoon.

Increase the heat to moderate, then stir in half the orange juice. Season the pheasant breasts and place, skin-side down, in the orange butter for 1 minute. Turn them over to coat them and remove with a slotted spoon.

Stir half the wine into the casserole and boil it until almost evaporated. Place the pheasant breasts, skin side up, in the casserole, cover closely with buttered greaseproof paper, cover the casserole and cook in the oven for 4—5 minutes. They should be still pink and moist.

Transfer the pheasant breasts to a warmed plate, cover and keep warm.

Place the casserole on a high heat, pour in the cognac and remaining wine and boil rapidly. Scrape down the sides and add the remaining orange juice and the orange julienne. Boil until the sauce is dark, then whisk in the marmalade.

Pass the sauce through a sieve, pressing down well on the orange julienne to extract as much flavour as possible. Season.

Cut the breasts into slices and arrange them on 4 warmed plates. Pour the sauce around and garnish with orange segments, orange rind and watercress leaves.

RABBIT MILLE FEUILLES

INGREDIENTS *(serves 4)*
300 g/10 oz puff pastry (see p.79)
salt and freshly ground black pepper
2 small saddles of rabbit
50 g/2 oz butter, diced
75 ml/3 fl oz cider vinegar
100 ml/4 fl oz full-bodied dry white
* wine*
500 ml/18 fl oz rabbit stock
½ cinnamon stick
100 ml/4 fl oz double cream
1 tbsp clear honey
2 crisp juicy apples
lemon juice

FOR THE GARNISH
sage leaves
corkskrews of caramelized orange peel

Divide the pastry in half, roll each half out very thinly to a rectangle about 32.5 × 12.5 cm/13 × 5 inches. Trim the edges with a sharp knife, then carefully transfer each piece to a wetted baking tray. Prick the top well with a fork to minimize the amount of rising. Cover and leave in a cool place for at least 30 minutes.

Heat the oven to 220°C/425°F/Gas 7.

Uncover the pastry and bake for 12—15 minutes until crisp and golden.

Season the rabbit. Heat half the butter in the roasting tin, add the saddles and sear evenly. Place in the oven for about 20 minutes. They should be still pink and moist. Transfer to a warmed plate, cover and keep warm.

Stir the vinegar and wine into a roasting tin then reduce to about 1 tbsp. Stir in the stock and cinnamon stick and reduce to 75 ml/3 fl oz. Stir in the cream and honey then pass through a sieve into a clean saucepan. Reheat gently, then over a very low heat gradually swirl in the remaining butter. Season and keep warm but do not boil.

Meanwhile, core and slice the apples and brush with lemon juice. Lay in a single layer in the top half of a steamer or a colander. Cover and place over a pan of simmering water for about 2 minutes — they should remain crisp. Then remove from the heat.

With a large, sharp knife cut each piece of pastry into 6 rectangles approximately 10 × 5 cm/4 × 2 inches. Then remove the fillets from the saddles and carve into slices along their length. Trim the slices to fit the pastry.

Place a rectangle of pastry on each of 4 warmed plates, cover with rabbit slices and spoon a little sauce over the rabbit. Then repeat the layering ending with a rectangle of pastry. Spoon the remaining sauce around the pastries. Arrange some of the apple slices on the pastry and arrange the remaining slices in the sauce. Garnish with sage leaves and corkscrews of caramelized orange peel.

MEDALLIONS OF RABBIT

WITH BASIL

INGREDIENTS *(serves 4)*
2 saddles of rabbit, filleted
salt and freshly ground black pepper
25 g/1 oz butter, diced

FOR THE SAUCE
150 ml/¼ pt sercial madeira
12 basil leaves

Blackcurrants and cranberries can be added to the garnish for extra colour and richness.

———————

Cut each piece of rabbit into 12 medallions. Season.

Heat the butter, add the rabbit and cook for about 2—3 minutes each side so the medallions remain pink inside.

150 ml/¼ pt dry white wine
300 ml/½ pt veal stock
300 ml/½ pt double cream
75 g/3 oz butter, diced
salt and freshly ground black pepper

FOR THE GARNISH
basil leaves

Picture: page 283

Transfer to a warmed plate with a slotted spoon, cover and keep warm.

Tip the excess fat from the pan. Stir in the madeira, basil and wine and reduce to about 3 tbsp. Stir in the stock and reduce by three quarters. Stir in the cream and simmer until slightly thickened. Reduce the heat to very low, then gradually whisk in the butter, making sure each piece is fully incorporated before adding the next. Season.

Spoon the sauce onto 4 warmed plates, arrange the rabbit on top and garnish with the basil leaves.

SADDLE OF HARE WITH CELERIAC MOUSSES AND ORANGE

INGREDIENTS (serves 4)
celeriac mousse (see p.309)
2 tbsp oil
2 saddles of hare
225 ml/8 fl oz ruby port
50 ml/2 fl oz brandy
75 ml/3 fl oz sercial madeira
2 sprigs of thyme
40 ml/1½ fl oz orange juice
8 juniper berries, crushed
3 black peppercorns, crushed
200 ml/7 fl oz game stock
julienne of orange rind cut into short
    strips
25 g/1 oz butter, diced
salt and freshly ground black pepper

Only a very simple vegetable accompaniment is necessary to complete this main course. To minimize last-minute preparation, prepare the orange rind in advance and have the dishes for the mousses set ready in the baking tin.

─────────

Prepare the celeriac mousse, cover and keep cool.

Heat the oven to 230°C/450°F/Gas 8.

Heat 1½ tbsp oil, add the saddles, sear evenly, then cook in the oven for 9—10 minutes until pink and still moist in the centre. Reduce the heat to 180°C/350°F/Gas 4.

Transfer the saddles to a warmed plate, cover and keep warm.

Pour the excess fat from the roasting tin, stir in the port, brandy and madeira and heat to simmering point. Stir in the thyme, orange juice, juniper berries, peppercorns and stock and reduce to 200-225 ml/7-8 fl oz.

Divide the celeriac mousse mixture between 4 small buttered dishes, and place the dishes in a roasting or baking tin. Surround with boiling water, cover with buttered greaseproof paper and place in the oven for 15—20 minutes until just set.

Heat the remaining oil, add the orange rind and cook until beginning to curl. Remove with a slotted spoon and drain on absorbent paper.

Pass the sauce through a sieve, then reheat gently. Gradually swirl in the butter over a low heat. Season and keep warm but do not boil.

When the mousses are set, remove them from the heat and leave to stand for a few minutes. Cut the saddles lengthways into slices. Re-form and keep warm.

Unmould the mousses onto 4 warmed plates, spoon the sauce around. Arrange the slices of hare on the sauce. Place some of the orange julienne on the mousses and scatter the remainder over the sauce.

MEDALLIONS OF HARE WITH

BLACKBERRY SAUCE

INGREDIENTS (serves 6)
4 rashers of streaky bacon
4 saddles of hare, trimmed and
    seasoned
2 tbsp oil

FOR THE SAUCE
350 g/12 oz blackberries
100 g/4 oz granulated sugar
12 sugar lumps
2 tbsp red wine vinegar
200 ml/7 fl oz game stock
15 g/½ oz butter, diced

FOR THE GARNISH
blackberries
mint leaves

Picture: page 282

If the saddles of hare are large, 3 will be sufficient — unless appetites are very hearty. It is important to keep on tasting the sauce when the stock is being added to get the right balance of flavours.

Heat the oven to 220°C/420°F/Gas 7.

Tie a rasher of bacon over each saddle. Heat the oil in a roasting tin, add the saddles and seal quickly all over. Place in the oven for 15—20 minutes — the meat should remain pink inside. Transfer the saddles to a warmed plate, cover and keep warm.

Barely cover the blackberries with water, add the sugar and poach for 8—10 minutes, then pass through a fine sieve.

Heat the sugar lumps in a small, heavy-based pan, then stir in the vinegar and simmer for 2—3 minutes. Stir in the blackberry purée and reduce until fairly syrupy.

Stir a spoonful of stock at a time into the blackberry sauce, checking constantly to avoid adding too much, as the flavour should be rich yet still with a tang to it. When the right amount has been added, simmer for 3—4 minutes. Remove from the heat and swirl in the butter.

Cut each saddle into 5—6 slices and arrange on 6 warmed plates. Spoon the sauce around and garnish with blackberries and mint leaves.

MEDALLIONS OF VENISON WITH

HARLEQUIN PEPPERCORN SAUCE

INGREDIENTS (serves 4)
1.2 L/2 pt game stock
bouquet garni of 4 parsley stalks,
    1 bayleaf, a sprig of thyme, 2 sprigs
    of chervil, a sprig of tarragon
1 small leek, sliced
2 shallots, chopped
1 small carrot, chopped
3 tomatoes, chopped
¼ tsp black peppercorns, finely crushed
¼ tsp white peppercorns, finely
    crushed
4 venison steaks, approximately
    150g/5 oz and 2.5 cm/1 inch thick
salt
75 g/3 oz butter, diced

Simmer the stock with the next 5 ingredients for 2 hours, then reduce to about 225 ml/8 fl oz. Pass through a conical strainer, pressing down well on the vegetables to extract as much liquid as possible. Measure out 175 ml/6 fl oz.

Mix the black and white peppercorns together. Season the venison with salt and the mixed peppercorns.

Heat 40 g/1½ oz butter in a sauteuse or large frying pan. Add the venison and cook for about 3—4 minutes each side until pink and moist inside. Transfer to a warmed plate with a slotted spoon, cover and keep warm.

Pour the excess fat from the pan. Pour the cognac into the pan and ignite with a taper. When the flames have died down, stir in the reduced stock and reduce again by half. Stir in the cream and boil again until slightly thickened. Reduce the heat

3 tbsp cognac
75 ml/3 fl oz double cream
1 tsp green peppercorns
1 tsp pink peppercorns

FOR THE GARNISH
cooked flageolet beans (see p.305)
½ quantity of white butter sauce (see
p.66)

to very low and gradually stir in the remaining butter, making sure that each piece is completely incorporated before adding the next. Stir in the green and pink peppercorns and add salt to taste.

Meanwhile, warm the beans in a steamer. Prepare the white butter sauce.

Cut each piece of venison into 6 slices. Re-form and keep warm. Spoon the sauce over 4 warmed plates. Arrange the slices of venison, overlapping, so that they form three quarters of a circle. Place the flageolet beans in a single layer in the semi-circular space formed in front of the venison. Carefully spoon the sauce around the circumference of the venison.

MEDALLIONS OF HARE WITH

BEETROOT

INGREDIENTS (serves 4)
2 saddles of hare, trimmed
salt and freshly ground black pepper
2 tbsp oil

FOR THE MARINADE
500 ml/18 fl oz red wine
1 large carrot, diced
1 onion, chopped
bouquet garni of a sprig of thyme,
*   a sprig of rosemary, a bayleaf and*
*   4 parsley stalks*
8 black peppercorns, crushed
8 juniper berries, crushed
2 cloves

FOR THE SAUCE
1 tbsp chopped shallot
1 tbsp red wine vinegar
175 g/6 oz freshly cooked beetroot,
*   chopped*
75 ml/3 fl oz double cream
1 tsp creamed horseradish

FOR THE BEETROOT
100 g/4 oz freshly cooked small
*   beetroot, thinly sliced*
2 tsp red wine vinegar

FOR THE GARNISH
75 g/3 oz plain noodles
1 tbsp oil
sprigs of chervil

Picture: page 283

A dish that succeeds even when hare is not quite at its best. Start the preparation the day before it is to be served and do be sure to dry the hare well after removing it from the marinade.

Mix the ingredients for the marinade together. Pour over the saddles, cover and leave in a cool place for 24 hours, turning occasionally.

Heat the oven to 230°C/450°F/Gas 8.

Remove the saddles from the marinade with a slotted spoon, drain and dry well. Strain the marinade.

Season the saddles. Heat the oil, add the saddles and sear all over, then cook in the oven for 9—10 minutes, so they are pink inside and moist. Transfer to a warmed plate, cover and keep warm.

Tip most of the oil from the pan in which the saddles were cooked.

Stir the shallots and vinegar into the pan, cover and cook over a moderate heat, shaking the pan occasionally until the shallots have softened. Add the beetroot and 3 tbsp of the marinade and reduce by three quarters. Stir in the cream and reduce by half. Stir in the horseradish and seasoning. Keep warm.

Meanwhile, cook the noodles in boiling salted water with the oil until just tender. Drain well.

Gently warm the beetroot slices in the vinegar in a covered pan.

Cut the saddles into slices and arrange on 4 plates. Divide the sauce between the plates and arrange the slices on the sauce, then finish with a small mound of noodles on each plate and garnish with sprigs of chervil.

MEDALLIONS OF VENISON

WITH APPLES AND CELERIAC

INGREDIENTS (serves 6)
1.25 kg/2½ lb saddle of venison, boned
bones and trimmings from the saddle
4 carrots, chopped
4 small leeks, chopped
2 sticks of celery, chopped
10 juniper berries, crushed
rind of 1 orange
bouquet garni of 3 sprigs of thyme,
 1 bay leaf and 6 parsley stalks
salt and freshly ground black pepper
75 cl/26 fl oz bottle of fruity dry
 white wine
50 g/2 oz butter, diced
50 ml/2 fl oz calvados
300 ml/½ pt crème fraîche
100 g/4 oz redcurrant jelly
2 crisp green dessert apples
50 ml/2 fl oz Scotch apple liqueur, or
 fruity dry white wine
2.5 cm/1 inch cinnamon stick

FOR THE GARNISH
julienne of celeriac

Picture: page 286

The tang of crème fraîche is essential for this dish, so if you are unable to buy it, make your own according to the method on p.51.

Cut the venison into 6 lean medallions, place in a shallow dish, add 2 carrots, 2 leeks, 1 stick of celery, the juniper berries, orange rind, bouquet garni and seasoning and pour half the wine over it. Cover and leave in a cool place for 8 hours, turning occasionally.

Place the bones, remaining carrots, leeks and celery in a roasting tin and brown under a hot grill, turning occasionally. Tip the bones and vegetables into a large saucepan. Stir the remaining wine into the roasting tin and bring to simmering point, stirring. Pour into the saucepan with about 1 L/1¾ pt water and season. Bring to the boil, skim the scum from the surface and simmer for about 2 hours, skimming off the scum occasionally and at the end of the 2 hours. Leave to cool and remove the fat from the surface.

Pass through a conical sieve, pressing down well to extract as much flavour as possible. Reduce to 300 ml/½ pt.

Remove the venison from the marinade with a slotted spoon and dry well.

Heat the butter in a large sauteuse or frying pan and cook the medallions for about 3 minutes each side so that they remain pink and moist. Remove with a slotted spoon, place on a warmed plate, cover and keep warm.

Tip the surface fat from the pan. Stir in the calvados and ignite with a taper. Stir in the sauce and reduce by half. Stir in the crème fraîche and redcurrant jelly. Season. Keep warm but do not boil.

Meanwhile, peel, core and slice the apples and poach for about 5 minutes in the Scotch apple liqueur, or wine, with the cinnamon stick. Remove the apple slices with the slotted spoon and drain.

Blanch, refresh and drain the celeriac.

Spoon the sauce over 6 warmed plates. Arrange the venison on top and add the apple slices and celeriac julienne.

LOIN OF VENISON WITH

PEARS AND CRANBERRIES

INGREDIENTS (serves 4)
700 g/1½ lb loin of venison
bones from the loin
1 carrot, chopped
1 onion, chopped
2.25 L/4 pt veal stock
10 juniper berries, crushed
3 sprigs of thyme and 3 sprigs of
   chervil, tied together
2 tbsp tomato purée
50 g/2 oz butter, diced
salt and freshly ground black pepper
50 g/2 oz cranberries
15 g/½ oz sugar
2 tbsp brown sugar
75 ml/3 fl oz Gewürztraminer wine
25 ml/1 fl oz poires William
2 pears

Picture: page 287

The stock can be prepared in advance. If a Gewürztraminer wine is not available, another full-bodied, fruity dry white wine could be used instead; in place of poires William you could use cognac.

———————————

Brown the venison bones under a high grill, then stir in the vegetables and brown these. Tip into a large saucepan, stir in the stock, juniper berries, herbs and tomato purée and bring to the boil, skimming off the scum as it rises. Simmer for 2½ hours, removing the scum occasionally.

Strain the stock and reduce to one third. Leave to cool and remove the excess fat from the surface.

Heat the oven to 220°C/425°F/Gas 7.

Heat half the butter, add the venison and sear all over, then place in the oven for 15—20 minutes until pink and moist inside.

Meanwhile, put the cranberries into a saucepan and pour 40 ml/1¼ fl oz boiling water over. Cover and leave for 5 minutes. Bring to simmering point and simmer for 3 minutes. Turn off the heat and leave for 5 minutes. Stir in the white sugar.

Remove the venison from the roasting tin, cover and keep warm.

Bring the venison sauce to the boil, reduce if necessary, then reduce the heat to very low and gradually whisk in the remaining butter. Season and keep warm, but do not allow to boil.

Dissolve the brown sugar in the wine and poires William over a gentle heat. Peel, core and cut the pears into batons. Add to the wine and cook gently for 2 minutes. Remove with a slotted spoon and reduce the liquor until syrupy. Remove from the heat and return the pear batons to the pan.

Cut the venison into slices and arrange on 4 warmed plates. Spoon the sauce around. Remove the cranberries and pears from their liquors with a slotted spoon and arrange on the sauce.

VENISON MEDALLIONS IN PORT

JELLY WITH BEETROOT PUREE

INGREDIENTS (serves 6)
350 g/12 oz boned venison saddle,
* trimmed*
salt and freshly ground black pepper
25 g/1 oz butter
600 ml/1 pt game stock (see p.76)
200 ml/7 fl oz red wine
200 ml/7 fl oz ruby port
1½ tsp gelatine
25 g/1 oz caster sugar
2 tsp red wine vinegar
1½ tsp pink peppercorns

FOR THE PUREE
175 g/6 oz freshly cooked beetroot,
* chopped*
2 tsp red wine vinegar
75 ml/3 fl oz double cream
¾ tsp horseradish cream
salt and freshly ground black pepper

FOR THE GARNISH
crème fraîche

Picture: page 287

This is a very versatile recipe as it can be served as a fairly substantial first course, a main course, as part of a buffet or as part of a picnic. Pack the venison unmoulded and the purée in a sealed container. A cobweb design of cream can be piped into the sauce for colour contrast.

Heat the oven to 220°C/425°F/Gas 7.

Tie the venison into a neat cylindrical shape. Season. Heat the butter in a roasting tin, add the venison and sear evenly. Place in the oven and cook for 10—15 minutes, until pink and moist in the centre. Remove with a slotted spoon and leave to cool on a wire rack.

Reduce the stock, wine and port by half. Cool slightly, then stir a little into the gelatine. Stir until the gelatine has dissolved, then pour back into the reduced liquid.

Dissolve the sugar in the vinegar, then stir into the reduced stock. Leave to cool.

Spoon a layer of the cold reduced liquor into 6 cold ramekin dishes. Sprinkle the peppercorns around the circumferences of the dishes. Leave in the refrigerator for 1 hour.

Cut the venison into six 1.25—2 cm/½—¾ inch slices and place one in each ramekin. Spoon sufficient stock into the ramekins to just cover the venison and leave in the refrigerator for 2 hours.

For the purée, warm the beetroot in the vinegar, then purée with the cream. Add the horseradish cream and seasoning. Cover and chill lightly.

Unmould the venison onto 6 cold plates. Spoon the sauce around and swirl in the crème fraîche.

M E D A L L I O N S   O F   R O E - D E E R   W I T H

T U R N I P   M O U S S E S   A N D   P O R T   S A U C E

INGREDIENTS (serves 4)
12 medallions, approximately 40 g/1½
    oz each, from a saddle of roe deer
500 ml/18 fl oz full-bodied red wine
8 juniper berries, crushed
5 coriander seeds, toasted and
    crushed
a sprig of thyme
salt and freshly ground black pepper
120 g/4½ oz butter, diced
250 ml/9 fl oz ruby port
500 ml/18 fl oz game stock, boiled
    down to 250 ml/9 fl oz

FOR THE TURNIP MOUSSES
450 g/1 lb small turnips, halved
salt
2 egg whites
15 g/½ oz butter, diced and just melted
3 tbsp double cream
freshly ground white pepper
a small pinch of grated nutmeg

FOR THE GARNISH
3 tsp concassé tomato

As roe-deer produce the most delicately flavoured venison, keep the hanging time to the minimum and do not leave the medallions in the marinade for long. Be sure to dry them well before cooking.

———————————

Mix the wine, juniper berries, coriander, sprig of thyme and seasoning together. Pour over the venison and leave to marinate for 30 minutes.

Cook the turnips in simmering salted water until tender. Drain very well, pressing down well on the turnips to extract as much water as possible. Purée, then leave the purée to drain through a sieve.

Heat the oven to 180°C/350°F/Gas 4.

Remove the venison from the marinade and dry well.

Heat 50 g/2 oz butter in a sauteuse or large frying pan, add the venison and cook for about 2 minutes each side until they are pink and moist in the centre. Transfer to a warmed plate with a slotted spoon. Cover and keep warm.

Turn the turnip purée into a bowl in a bowl of ice. Gradually beat in the egg whites, then the butter, cream, pepper and nutmeg. Divide between 4 small buttered ramekin dishes. Place the dishes in a roasting or baking tin, surround with boiling water and place in the oven for 18—20 minutes.

Pour the excess fat from the sauteuse, stir in the port and reduce by half. Add the reduced stock and reduce by half again. Reduce the heat to very low and gradually stir in the remaining butter, making sure that each piece is completely incorporated before adding the next. Season and keep warm but do not allow to boil.

Leave the mousses to stand for a minute or two before unmoulding onto 4 warmed plates. Spoon the sauce around. Arrange the medallions and place a little concassé tomato on the top of each mousse.

VEGETABLE

DISHES

◆ It is a mistake to view vegetables as merely accompaniments to more important main courses. Cuisine Vivante vegetable dishes have a much more positive role to play in complementing the texture, colour, flavour and style of the main course. When combining a vegetable dish with a main course, whether it be fish, shellfish, meat, poultry or game, make sure that the method of preparation and cooking is one that will combine to bring out the best in both dishes. Vegetables should always be thoroughly drained and the plates and dishes warmed before serving. ◆

PEA PUREE

INGREDIENTS (serves 4)
25 g/1 oz butter
3 spring onions, finely sliced
200 g/7 oz petits pois
5 round lettuce leaves, finely shredded
2 tbsp double cream
salt and freshly ground pepper

Heat the butter, add the spring onions, cover and cook over a moderate heat, shaking the pan occasionally until they are softened. Stir in about 300 ml/½ pt water, bring to the boil, add the peas and lettuce and return to the boil for 1 minute.

Drain well then pass through a sieve into a clean saucepan. Reheat gently, beat in the cream and seasoning.

PEA AND MINT PUREE
Add 2 tbsp finely chopped mint with the lettuce.

CHESTNUT PUREE

INGREDIENTS (serves 4)
850 g/1¾ lb chestnuts
500 ml/18 fl oz milk
75 g/3 oz butter
a pinch of sugar
salt and freshly ground black pepper
1—2 tbsp cognac, optional

Split the chestnut skins with the point of a sharp knife.

Put the chestnuts into a heavy based saucepan or flameproof casserole and place over a moderate heat, turning them over constantly, until the skins dry and crack.

As soon as the chestnuts are cool enough to handle, peel off the skins.

Simmer the chestnuts in the milk for 20 minutes, then pass through a fine sieve.

Reheat the purée in a clean saucepan and beat in the butter. Add a pinch of sugar, seasoning and cognac to taste.

TURNIP PUREE

INGREDIENTS (serves 4)
450 g/1 lb small turnips, peeled and
  thinly sliced
salt and freshly ground white pepper
25 g/1 oz butter
50 ml/2 fl oz double cream, lightly
  whipped

Turnips can produce a surprising amount of water, even when small and young. So to make a good purée it really is important to dry it thoroughly before adding the butter and cream.

———————————

Cook the turnips in the minimum of simmering salted water until tender but not falling apart.

Drain very well, then purée. If the purée is too moist, turn it into a frying pan and boil rapidly, stirring, to evaporate the excess moisture.

Over a low heat, beat in the butter and pepper then fold in the cream.

CAULIFLOWER PUREE

INGREDIENTS *(serves 6)*
*1 medium sized cauliflower, trimmed
   and broken into florets*
salt
25 g/1 oz butter
50 ml/2 fl oz double cream
freshly ground black pepper
a pinch of grated nutmeg

Cook the cauliflower in simmering salted water until tender.
   Drain well and refresh under cold running water. Drain again and dry in a cloth or on absorbent paper.
   Pass through a mouli-légumes.
   Melt the butter in a non-stick pan. Stir in the cauliflower then beat in the cream and reheat gently. Season and add a pinch of nutmeg.

 # CELERIAC PUREE

INGREDIENTS *(serves 4)*
*700 g/1½ lb celeriac, peeled and
   chopped*
salt
300 ml/½ pt milk
25 g/1 oz butter
25 ml/1 fl oz double cream

Cook the celeriac in the salted simmering milk until tender.
   Drain well, reserving the milk.
   Pass the celeriac through a mouli-légumes or sieve.
   Heat the butter in a non-stick pan, add the celeriac purée, then beat in the cream and sufficient of the cooking milk to give a creamy consistency. Reheat gently. Season.

 # COURGETTE PUREE

INGREDIENTS *(serves 4)*
900 g/2 lb courgettes
salt
25 g/1 oz butter
40 g/1½ fl oz double cream
freshly ground white pepper
a squeeze of lemon juice, optional

Peel the courgettes and chop finely. Place in a colander, sprinkle with salt and leave to drain for 30 minutes.
   Rinse under cold running water. Drain well.
   Heat the butter, add the courgettes and cook over a moderately low heat for 3—4 minutes. Stir in sufficient water to just cover, cover the pan and simmer gently until tender.
   Drain well, then purée. Return to a non-stick pan and heat gently, to drive off excess moisture if necessary. Beat in the cream and season, adding a squeeze of lemon juice, if liked.

 # SAFFRON RICE TIMBALES

INGREDIENTS
a pinch of saffron threads
2 tbsp dry vermouth
25 g/1 oz long-grain rice per person
a pinch of salt

Adjust the amount of rice needed for each portion according to whether the timbales are to be used to garnish a dish or as a vegetable accompaniment.
   Soak the saffron threads in the vermouth.
   Measure water to three times the volume of the rice. Bring the water, with a pinch of salt, to the boil. Add the rice and saffron, with its liquid, return to the boil, stir once, cover, lower the heat and simmer for about 12-15 minutes until the rice is just tender and the liquid has been absorbed. Pack the rice into oiled dariole moulds. Leave to stand in a warm place for a minute or two then unmould onto warm plates.

CARROT PUREE

INGREDIENTS (serves 4)
450 g/1 lb carrots, peeled and sliced
salt
25 g/1 oz butter
40 ml/2½ fl oz double cream
freshly ground black pepper
a pinch of sugar

Cook the carrots in simmering salted water until tender.

Drain well and pass through a mouli-légumes into a bowl lined with a double thickness of muslin or cloth. Fold the muslin or cloth over the puréed carrots and squeeze out the excess moisture.

Heat the butter in a non-stick pan. Stir in the carrot purée, then beat in the cream and reheat gently, stirring. Season and add a pinch of sugar to taste.

BRUSSELS SPROUTS PUREE

INGREDIENTS (serves 4)
450 g/1 lb Brussels sprouts, trimmed
salt
25 g/1 oz butter
75 ml/3 fl oz double cream
freshly ground black pepper

Blanch the Brussels sprouts for 2 minutes. Refresh then cook in simmering salted water until tender.

Drain well, dry on absorbent paper then pass through a mouli-légumes.

Heat the butter in a non-stick pan, add the Brussels sprouts, then beat in the cream and reheat gently. Season.

FRESH TOMATO PUREE

INGREDIENTS (serves 4)
7 g/¼ oz butter
2 shallots, very finely chopped
flesh from 1.5 kg/3½ lb ripe tomatoes, chopped
bouquet garni of 3 parsley stalks, a sprig of chervil, a sprig of thyme and a bayleaf
salt and freshly ground black pepper
a pinch of caster sugar or squeeze of lemon juice to taste

The flavour of the tomatoes used for this recipe *must* really be good — see the notes on p.31.

Heat the butter in a heavy based saucepan, add the shallots, cover and cook over a moderate heat, shaking the pan occasionally, until the shallots are soft.

Stir in the tomatoes and bouquet garni and simmer gently until the moisture has evaporated. Remove the bouquet garni. Season and add sugar or lemon juice to taste. Leave to cool and store in a covered glass or earthenware container in a cool place.

POTATO BASKETS

INGREDIENTS (serves 4—6)
450 g/1 lb even sized floury potatoes
oil for deep frying
salt and freshly ground black pepper

The small baskets used here can be bought from good Chinese shops, hardware or kitchen shops or department stores.

Slice the potatoes very thinly in a food processor or with a mandolin cutter, then cut the slices into julienne.

Line a wire mesh ladle about 5-6.5 cm/2-2½ inches in diameter with a thin layer of potato julienne and hold them in place by placing another ladle on top.

Heat a deep fat frying pan to 200°C/400°F/, lower in the ladle and cook the potatoes for 1—2 minutes until crisp and golden. Carefully remove the potato basket from the ladle. Sprinkle with salt and pepper and keep warm whilst preparing the remaining baskets.

COURGETTE CUPS WITH PEAS

INGREDIENTS (serves 4)
4 fat courgettes, approximately 5-7
    cm/2-2½ inch diameter, about 9 cm/
    3½ inches long
7 g/¼ oz butter, diced
2 tsp finely chopped shallot
6 tbsp petits pois
1 tsp finely chopped mint
salt and finely ground white pepper
a squeeze of lemon juice

FOR THE GARNISH
small mint leaves

Peel lengthways strips from the courgettes to create a striped appearance with a cannelle knife or potato peeler.

Cut the ends from the courgettes and cut them into 6.5 cm/2½ inch lengths. Remove balls of the flesh with a small melon baller, leaving a narrow border.

Heat the butter, add the shallot and cook over a moderate heat, shaking the pan occasionally until soft. Add the balls of courgette and cook, stirring occasionally for 3 minutes until the flesh is just beginning to soften.

Add the peas, mint, seasoning and a squeeze of lemon juice and heat for about 1 minute, shaking the pan occasionally. Meanwhile, cook the courgette cups in simmering salted water for about 4 minutes until just tender. Refresh and drain well.

Spoon the courgette balls and peas into the courgette cups. Garnish with mint leaves.

POTATO GALETTES

INGREDIENTS (serves 4)
450 g/1 lb potatoes
olive oil
salt and freshly ground black pepper

Picture: page 306

Peel the potatoes, then slice thinly with a mandolin or in a food processor.

Heat some oil in a small frying pan over a high heat. Arrange a quarter of the potato slices in a single layer, overlapping, in a circle in the pan and fry on both sides until crisp and golden.

Quickly drain on absorbent paper. Cut into a neat circle with a plain 5 cm/2 inch pastry cutter.

Keep warm whilst preparing the remaining galettes. Sprinkle with salt and freshly ground black pepper just before serving.

POTATO FANS

INGREDIENTS *(serves 4)*
450 g/1 lb potatoes
1 tbsp oil
15 g/$\frac{1}{2}$ oz butter, diced
sea salt and freshly ground black
*   pepper*

Heat the oven to 200°C/400°F/Gas 6.

Peel the potatoes and cut into even shapes about 6.5 cm/ 2$\frac{1}{2}$ inches long. Slice the potatoes across their width at 5 mm/ $\frac{1}{4}$ inch intervals, cutting almost to the base, but leaving the sides joined. Rinse in cold water and drain well.

Heat the oil and butter in a roasting tin until very hot. Add the potatoes, turn them in the fat to coat them evenly, season well, then place in the oven for 50—60 minutes until crisp and golden and soft in the centre, turning them occasionally and basting.

POTATO CASTLES

INGREDIENTS *(serves 4)*
450 g/1 lb potatoes
oil
salt and freshly ground black pepper

Heat the oven to 190°C/375°F/Gas 5.

Peel the potatoes and trim to the width of a dariole mould. Cut into slices about 3 mm/$\frac{1}{8}$ inch thick.

Heat a thin layer of oil in a frying pan. Add a few potato slices at a time and cook for 1—2 minutes until soft but not coloured. Remove with a slotted spoon and drain on absorbent paper.

When all the slices have been fried, line the sides and base of 4 buttered dariole moulds with potato. Season well, then fill the centres with the remaining potato slices, packing them down well and doming the top slightly, as they will shrink when cooked.

Place the moulds in a baking or roasting tin of hot oil and place in the oven for about 20 minutes until the sides are golden and have shrunk away from sides of the moulds.

Run the point of a sharp knife around the edges of the moulds, then invert onto warmed plates.

ARTICHOKE AND POTATO GALETTE

INGREDIENTS *(serves 4)*
2 potatoes, about 175 g/6 oz each
6 tbsp clarified butter
2 tsp finely chopped thyme
salt and freshly ground black pepper
3 large or 5 small cooked artichoke
*   bottoms, thinly sliced*

FOR THE GARNISH:
short julienne of mangetouts

Heat the oven to 220°C/425°F/Gas 7.

Peel the potatoes and, using a mandolin or food processor, cut into very thin slices.

Over a moderate heat, heat a very thin layer of clarified butter in 4 small flameproof dishes or one large round dish. Arrange half the potato slices in concentric circles in the bottom of the dishes or dish, shaking occasionally to prevent the potato from sticking. Sprinkle half the thyme over. Season.

Cover the potato slices with slices of artichoke, sprinkle the remaining thyme over, season then cover with the remaining potato, continuing to shake occasionally. Season again and trickle 1—2 tsp clarified butter over the potatoes. Cover with foil and cook for 5 minutes to brown the bottom.

Place in the oven and cook for about 25 minutes for small dishes, or 20—25 minutes for a large one, until the potatoes are tender.

Blanch the mangetouts for the garnish, refresh and drain well.

Invert the galettes onto a warm plate and place a few julienne of mangetouts on the top of each one. If a large dish is used, cut the galette into slices to serve.

VEGETABLE SPIRALS

INGREDIENTS (serves 4)
2 carrots, approximately 200 g/7 oz
   each
2 turnips, approximately 200 g/7 oz
   each
1 cucumber, approximately 100 g/4 oz

Single-coloured spirals can be prepared in the same way using just one type of vegetable.

———————————

Blanch the carrots and turnips for 3 minutes. Refresh and drain well.

Cut each carrot into a 6 cm/2¼ inch long cylinder then, with a very sharp, thin bladed knife, peel off long strips around each cylinder. If the strips break, it does not matter as short pieces can still be used.

Repeat with the turnips and cucumber, but only cut down as far as the cucumber seeds.

Carefully blanch the strips in boiling water for 1 minute, then remove with a slotted spoon.

Lay the strips together to form long tri-coloured strips. Roll them together then fasten with thread or fine string.

Cook in boiling salted water for 5 minutes.

Lift the coils out from the water with a skimmer or slotted spoon and drain on absorbent paper.

Place on 4 warmed plates. Remove the threads or string. Unroll a short length of each coil and spread it out on the plate.

FLAGEOLET BEANS

INGREDIENTS (serves 4)
175 g/6 oz flageolet beans, soaked
   overnight in cold water
1 large shallot, quartered
a sprig of summer savory
25 g/1 oz butter
salt

Drain the beans well. Put into a saucepan with the shallot, summer savory and butter, add plenty of water and bring to the boil. Simmer for about an hour until tender but still retaining their shape.

Drain well, remove the pieces of shallot and sprinkle salt over the beans.

TOP LEFT *Flageolet beans in potato baskets*
Recipes: page 305 & 302
TOP RIGHT *Potato galettes*
Recipe: page 303
CENTRE *Spinach, cauliflower and carrot mousselines*
Recipe: page 308

DOME OF CAULIFLOWER AND BROCCOLI

INGREDIENTS (serves 6)
450 g/1 lb trimmed broccoli, broken
into florets
1 cauliflower, approximately 450 g/
1 lb, broken into florets
salt
25 g/1 oz butter, diced
1 shallot, finely chopped
freshly ground black pepper

A useful recipe to bear in mind for the occasions when serving a main course that requires a fair amount of last-minute attention to detail.

Cook the broccoli and cauliflower separately in simmering salted water until only just tender. Refresh and drain well.

Trim off the stems and cut them into 5 mm/¼ inch slices.

Heat the butter, add the shallot, broccoli and cauliflower stems and cook over a moderate heat, stirring occasionally until the shallot is soft. Season.

Place a large broccoli floret, stem-side up, in the bottom of a 1 L/2 pt pudding basin. Arrange a circle of small cauliflower florets around it, with the stems pointing towards the centre of the bowl. Continue arranging alternating rows of broccoli and cauliflower. Fill the centre with any remaining florets and the sliced stems.

Place a plate that is slightly smaller than the inside of the basin on top of the vegetables and place a 500 g/1 lb weight on top.

Thirty minutes before required, place the basin in a large saucepan and surround with boiling water. Cover the saucepan and place over a very low heat for 30 minutes.

Invert the bowl onto a warmed plate and carefully lift away from the dome of cauliflower and broccoli.

SPINACH MOUSSELINE

INGREDIENTS (serves 4)
700 g/1½ lb spinach
25 g/1 oz butter
1 shallot, finely chopped
salt and freshly ground black pepper
1 egg beaten with 1 egg yolk
50 ml/2 fl oz whipping cream, lightly
whipped

Picture: page 306

Heat the oven to 180°C/350°F/Gas 4.

Blanch and refresh the spinach. Drain well, pressing down firmly on the spinach with the back of a spoon to extract as much liquid as possible.

Heat the butter and add the shallot. Cover and cook over a moderate heat shaking the pan occasionally, until the shallot is soft. Stir in the spinach and heat through, stirring, to drive off the last of the moisture.

Purée, season, beat in the eggs, then fold in the cream.

Strain into 4 buttered ramekin dishes or dariole moulds. Place in a baking or roasting tin and surround with boiling water. Cover the top of the moulds with buttered greaseproof paper, place in the oven and cook for 15-20 minutes.

Remove the moulds from the heat and leave to stand for a minute or two before unmoulding onto warmed plates.

POTATO AND CELERIAC CAKES

WITH CHESTNUTS

INGREDIENTS (serves 4)
1 head of celeriac, approximately
450 g/1 lb
225 g/8 oz potatoes
50 g/2 oz butter
salt and freshly ground black pepper
4 cooked chestnuts, halved

Peel the celeriac, cut into dice, putting the dice into acidulated water as soon as they are prepared. Simmer for about 20 minutes until tender.

Peel and dice the potatoes and simmer in salted water for about 20 minutes until tender.

Drain the vegetables well, purée, then reheat together in a non-stick frying pan, stirring to drive off as much water as possible. Beat in half the butter and the seasoning.

Divide the mixture into 8. Form each piece into a flat cake enclosing a chestnut half in the centre. Mark the tops in a diamond pattern with the point of a sharp knife.

Heat the remaining butter in a frying pan, add the potato and celeriac cakes and cook until golden on each side.

CELERIAC MOUSSES

INGREDIENTS (serves 4)
1 head of celeriac, approximately
700 g/1½ lb
25 g/1 oz clarified butter
1 shallot, finely chopped
2 leaves of sage
350 ml/12 fl oz chicken stock
50 ml/2 fl oz medium-bodied dry
white wine
1 whole egg and 2 egg yolks, beaten
together
50 ml/2 fl oz double cream, lightly
whipped
salt and freshly ground white pepper

For a flavour variation the sage leaves can be omitted and a pinch of freshly grated nutmeg added instead.

Heat the oven to 180°C/350°F/Gas 4.

Peel the celeriac and cut into approximately 2.5cm/1 inch cubes. Put the cubes into acidulated water as soon as they are prepared.

Cook the celeriac in simmering acidulated water for 5 minutes. Drain.

Meanwhile, heat the butter, add the shallot, cover and cook until soft, shaking the pan occasionally. Stir in the celeriac, sage, stock and wine. Bring to the boil, then simmer for about 15 minutes until the celeriac is tender. Drain, reserving the liquid.

Boil the liquid until reduced to about 2 tbsp.

Remove the sage, then purée the celeriac with the reduced liquid. Beat in the eggs and fold in the cream. Season, then divide between 4 small buttered dishes.

Place the dishes in a roasting tin and surround with boiling water. Cover the tops of the moulds with buttered greaseproof paper and place in the oven for 15—20 minutes until just set.

Leave the mousses to stand for a minute or two before unmoulding.

DESSERTS

The dessert is as important as any other element in a Cuisine Vivante meal. If the rest of the meal has been well balanced the thought of a dessert will not be daunting. 'Dessert' is not a synonym for very rich, sweet cakes, pastries, creams and such-like creations but can, and should, be light, airy, refreshing and palate-cleansing. Desserts need present the cook with few problems since the majority can be largely prepared in advance. Any decorations that need to be added at the last minute can be completed in the pause that is usually welcome between the main or cheese course and the dessert.

APRICOTS AND ICE CREAM

INGREDIENTS (serves 4)
5-6 ripe apricots, depending on size
300 ml/½ pt dessert wine
350 g/12 oz raspberries
2 tbsp sifted icing sugar
1-2 tbsp kirsch
300 ml/½ pt vanilla ice cream (see
   p.336)

FOR THE GARNISH
orange segments
4 tiny sprigs of mint
175 g/6 oz small, firm strawberries,
   halved

Picture: page 314

A little cream can be piped into the sauce in a cobweb design for extra effect.

Cut the apricots into halves, remove the stones and poach in the wine for about 8 minutes until just becoming tender. Leave to cool in the wine, then remove with a slotted spoon. Drain well, peel and cut into quarters. Cover and chill.

Purée, then sieve the raspberries. Sweeten with icing sugar and add kirsch to taste. Chill.

About 30 minutes before serving, transfer the ice cream to the main part of the refrigerator. Chill 4 plates.

Place balls of ice cream in the centre of the plates. Arrange apricot slices on top of the ice cream. Spoon the raspberry purée around the ice cream and arrange the strawberries with the sprigs of mint around the edge of the plates.

WHITE WINE GRANITA WITH APRICOT ICE CREAM

INGREDIENTS (serves 4)
75 g/3 oz sugar
300 ml/½ pint good quality dessert
   wine
1 tbsp strained orange juice
½ quantity of apricot ice cream (see
   p.313)
2 oranges
2 pears
lemon juice

FOR THE SAUCE
2 egg yolks
100 ml/4 fl oz crème fraîche
50 ml/2 fl oz Grand Marnier
2 tbsp strained orange juice
1 tsp finely grated lemon rind

FOR THE GARNISH
mint leaves
chocolate shapes

Picture: page 315

Dissolve the sugar in 75 ml/3 fl oz water, bring to the boil and boil for one minute. Leave to cool, then stir in the wine and fruit juices.

Pour into a shallow metal container and freeze until just firm, forking through the mixture occasionally from the outside to the middle so that the mixture forms a mass of small crystals.

For the sauce stir all the ingredients together in a bowl over a pan of hot water and continue to stir until the mixture thickens. Remove from the heat and leave to cool, stirring frequently. Cover the surface with cling film and chill lightly.

When the granita is nearly ready, about 30 minutes before serving, transfer the apricot ice cream to the refrigerator.

Thinly pare the rind from one of the oranges, cut into julienne strips then blanch for 4 minutes. Refresh and drain.

Peel the oranges and divide into segments, removing all the pith and skin. Quarter and core the pears and cut each quarter into lengthways slices. Dip in lemon juice diluted with water to prevent discoloration.

Spoon a thin layer of the sauce over 4 cold plates. Place scoops of the apricot ice cream and white wine granita on the sauce. Dry the fruit well and arrange attractively. Garnish with mint leaves and chocolate shapes.

APRICOT ICE CREAM

INGREDIENTS (serves 4)
550 g/1¼ lb ripe apricots
a squeeze of lemon juice
75 g/3 oz icing sugar
300 ml/½ pt crème fraîche or
    double cream

Remove the stones from the apricots, purée and sieve the flesh.

Add lemon juice and sugar to the purée to give the right balance of sweetness and freshness, bearing in mind that freezing masks sweetness. Cover and chill for 1 hour.

Lightly whip the crème fraîche or cream, then carefully fold in the chilled purée until just evenly blended. Freeze in a sorbetière for 15—20 minutes, then spoon into a container, cover and place in the freezer. Or spoon the mixture into a shallow metal container, cover and freeze for 45 minutes. Tip the mixture into a cold bowl and beat well with a cold whisk. Return to the container, cover and chill for 45 minutes. Repeat the beating, return to the freezer, covered, and freeze until firm.

Transfer the ice cream to the refrigerator about 30 minutes before serving.

ORANGE CUSTARD WITH APRICOT

PUREE

INGREDIENTS (serves 6)
500 ml/18 fl oz single cream
zest of 6 clementines or satsumas
    (about 450 g/1 lb fruit)
1 vanilla pod
90 g/3½ oz caster sugar
2 eggs
2 egg yolks
450 g/1 lb fresh apricots, halved and
    stoned
sugar
a squeeze of lemon juice

Pour the cream into the top of a double boiler or a basin placed over a pan of hot water. Stir in the fruit zest and vanilla pod and heat gently to just below simmering point. Remove from the stove, cover and leave to infuse for 20 minutes. Remove the vanilla pod and leave for 40 minutes.

Heat the oven to 170°C/325°F/Gas 3.

Add the sugar to the cream and stir until dissolved.

Beat the eggs and egg yolks together then stir into the cream. Strain the liquid into a non-stick or lightly oiled 17.5 cm/7 inch sandwich tin. Place the tin on a pad of newspaper in a roasting or baking tin, surround with boiling water, cover and place in the oven for 40-50 minutes until just set.

Poach the apricots in the minimum of water until tender. Purée, then pass through a sieve. Add sugar and a squeeze of lemon juice to taste. The purée must be very thick — if necessary reheat it, stirring to drive off the excess moisture. Leave to cool then cover and chill.

Remove the custard from the roasting tin, carefully loosen around the edge and leave to cool, uncovered.

Carefully unmould the custard onto a cold serving plate just before serving. Gently spoon the purée over the surface. Cut into wedges to serve.

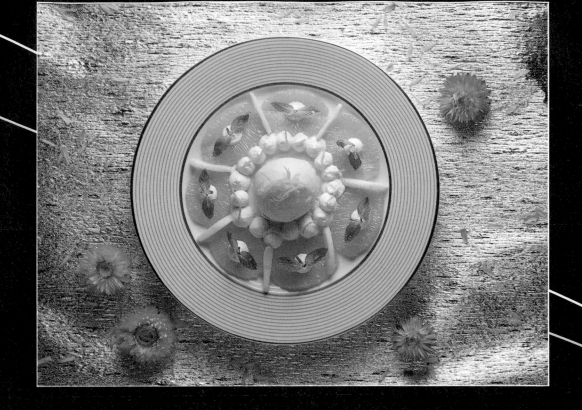

OPPOSITE *Apricots and ice cream·*
Recipe: page 312
ABOVE *White wine granita with apricot ice cream*
Recipe: page 312

LEFT *Gratin of fruits*
Recipe: page 317

S T R A W B E R R I E S   A N D   O R A N G E   C R E M E

INGREDIENTS *(serves 4)*
150 ml/¼ pt crème fraîche
1 egg white
2 tsp icing sugar, sifted
450 g/1 lb strawberries, hulled and
  halved

FOR THE DECORATION
small mint leaves

Picture: page 318

The whipped crème can just be spooned over the plates and the strawberries arranged on it for a very simple effect, or the crème can be piped over the plates, as in the photograph, for a more ornate appearance.

Very lightly whip the crème fraîche with the egg white and sugar, then fold in the orange juice.

Pipe the flavoured crème into the centre of 4-5 cold plates. Arrange layers of pink grapefruit and orange segments around the crème and decorate with strawberries and mint leaves.

S T R A W B E R R Y   M O U S S E S   W I T H

C O C O N U T   S A U C E

INGREDIENTS *(serves 4)*
450 g/1 lb strawberries
50 g/2 oz icing sugar
a squeeze of lemon juice
2½ tsp gelatine
2 egg whites
150 ml/¼ pt double cream, whipped

FOR THE SAUCE
1 coconut
50 g/2 oz caster sugar
150 ml/¼ pt milk
50 g/2 oz coconut cream
300 ml/½ pt double cream, whipped

FOR THE GARNISH
strawberries, sliced
mint leaves

Picture: page 319

Do not prepare the light, airy mousses more than a few hours in advance. Keep them covered with cling film until they are to be served.

Purée the strawberries then pass through a sieve. Add sugar and lemon juice to taste.

Dissolve the gelatine in 4 tbsp water in a small bowl placed over a pan of hot water. Leave to cool.

Whisk the egg whites until stiff but not dry.

Gradually whisk the gelatine into the strawberry purée, then fold in the cream, followed by the egg whites. Spoon into individual moulds and leave to set.

For the sauce, pierce 2 of the coconut eyes and drain out all the milk. Crack the coconut and scoop out the flesh. Cut the flesh into small pieces then cook over a low heat with the coconut milk, sugar, milk and coconut cream until soft. Pass through a fine sieve, then fold in the cream.

Unmould the mousses onto 4 cold plates, spoon the sauce over and decorate with sliced strawberries and mint leaves.

STRAWBERRY BISCUIT GATEAUX

INGREDIENTS (serves 4)
75 g/3 oz plain flour
2 egg whites, very lightly beaten
95 g/3¼ oz icing sugar, sifted
45 g/1½ oz butter, melted
125 g/6 oz strawberries
25-50 g/1-2 oz caster sugar
squeeze of lemon juice
75 ml/3 fl oz crème pâtissière (see
   p.81)
25 g/1 oz marzipan
1½ tbsp kirsch
150 ml/¼ pt double cream, whipped
350 g/12 oz wild strawberries, or
   small strawberries
icing sugar

Picture: page 318

To ensure the biscuits bake evenly it may be necessary to turn the baking sheets in the oven and swap shelves. Raspberries could replace all or some of the strawberries.

Heat the oven to 180°C/350°F/Gas 4.

Mix the flour, egg whites and icing sugar together, then stir in the melted butter. Spoon the mixture into 12 even circles on greased baking trays and bake for about 10 minutes until golden.

Remove the circles quickly from the baking trays and leave to cool.

Purée the strawberries, then pass through a sieve and add sugar and lemon juice to taste.

Mix the crème pâtissière, marzipan and kirsch together in a food processor or blender, then fold in the cream. Cover and chill.

Cut the wild strawberries into halves or slice the strawberries. Reserve some for the decoration.

Place 4 of the circles on individual plates. Spread with a layer of the marzipan mixture, then cover with wild strawberries.

Place another biscuit circle on these and repeat the layering, but, before putting on the final biscuit, sprinkle it liberally with icing sugar and mark a pattern with a very hot skewer. Spoon the sauce around and decorate with the reserved strawberries.

GRATIN OF FRUITS

INGREDIENTS (serves 4)
2-4 sweet, juicy grapefruit, preferably
   pink
2-4 sweet, juicy oranges
icing sugar
2 egg yolks
1 tbsp caster sugar
200 ml/7 fl oz champagne or good
   quality sparkling dry white wine

FOR THE DECORATION
fresh fruits, eg Cape gooseberries,
   strawberries
mint leaves

Picture: page 315

Adjust the number of oranges and grapefruit according to their size and the size of the portions you wish to serve.

Peel the grapefruit and oranges then divide into segments, making sure all the pith and membrane have been removed. Arrange on 4 plates.

Whisk the egg yolks and sugar together in a bowl placed over a pan of hot water. Whisk in the champagne or sparkling wine and continue to whisk until the mixture is light, fluffy and slightly thickened. Remove from the heat and whisk until cold.

Heat the grill to very high.

Spoon the sauce over the fruits. Sprinkle lightly with icing sugar and place briefly under the very hot grill until lightly coloured.

Decorate with the fruits and mint leaves.

ABOVE *Strawberries
and orange crème*
Recipe: page 316
RIGHT *Strawberry
biscuit gâteaux*
Recipe: page 317

OPPOSITE
*Strawberry mousses
with coconut sauce*
Recipe: page 316

NOUGAT GLACE WITH PASSIONFRUIT

INGREDIENTS (serves 6)
80 g/3¼ oz caster sugar
2 egg whites
850 ml/1½ pt crème fraîche
40 ml/1½ fl oz Cointreau
40 g/1½ oz crystallized orange peel,
    chopped
15 g/½ oz crystallized lemon peel,
    chopped
3 passionfruit
25 g/1 oz caster sugar
a squeeze of lemon juice

Picture: page 322

The light, fresh, citrus-orange flavour of the nougat glacé combines exceptionally well with the flavour of the passionfruit sauce. If preferred, it can be frozen in individual decorative moulds.

Dissolve 70 g/2¾ oz of the sugar in 25 ml/1 fl oz water, bringing it to the boil. Boil until the temperature reaches 120°C/250°F.

Meanwhile, whisk the egg whites with the remaining sugar until stiff but not dry, then slowly pour in the boiling syrup, whisking constantly. Continue whisking until the mixture is cold.

Whip the crème fraîche lightly with the Cointreau, then fold into the meringue with the crystallized peels.

Spoon into an oblong loaf tin, cover and freeze until firm.

Remove the pulp and seeds from the passionfruit. Dissolve the sugar in a little water, then simmer briefly to make a light syrup. Stir in the passionfruit pulp and seeds. Add a squeeze of lemon juice and adjust the sweetness. Leave to cool, then chill.

About 20 minutes before serving, unmould the ice cream and leave in the refrigerator.

Spoon the passionfruit over the mould and serve in slices.

ORANGE SORBET

INGREDIENTS (serves 4)
100 g/4 oz sugar
finely grated rind of 2 oranges
450 ml/¾ pt strained fresh
    orange juice
lemon juice

Picture: page 323

Dissolve the sugar in 100 ml/4 fl oz water and bring to the boil. Leave to cool, then stir in the orange rind, orange juice and lemon juice to taste.

Freeze in sorbetière for 10—12 minutes, then transfer to the freezer, covered. Or, alternatively, pour into a shallow metal container, cover and chill for 1 hour, then place in the freezer for 45 minutes. Tip the mixture into a cold bowl and beat well with a cold whisk. Return to the container, cover and freeze for 30 minutes. Repeat twice, then leave to freeze until firm.

Transfer the sorbet to the refrigerator about 40 minutes before serving.

APPLE AND BLACKCURRANT

TERRINE

INGREDIENTS (serves 6)
450 g/1 lb dessert apples, peeled, cored and sliced
2 slices of lemon
1 tbsp sugar
4 tbsp gelatine
3 tbsp calvados, optional
300 ml/½pt crème fraîche, lightly whipped
1 large egg, separated
450 g/1 lb blackcurrants
25-50 g/1—2 oz caster sugar

FOR THE SAUCE
225 g/8 oz blackcurrants
1-2 tbsp icing sugar
lemon juice

Blackberries or raspberries can be used in this terrine instead of blackcurrants. You could make it in a large decorative ring mould — simply form a deep channel in the apple mixture in the same way.

Cook the apples very gently with the slices of lemon, sugar and 1 tbsp water in a covered saucepan for 30 minutes. Remove the slices of lemon and purée the apples.

Dissolve 3 tbsp gelatine in the calvados, or water, in a small bowl over a pan of hot water. Remove from the heat, leave to cool, then beat into the apple purée.

Gently fold the crème fraîche into the apple mixture.

Whisk the egg white until stiff but not dry, then gently fold into the apple cream, cover and chill for one hour.

Cook the blackcurrants with 1-2 tbsp water in a covered pan over a very low heat for about 10 minutes until softened, purée, then pass through a sieve and add sugar to taste.

Bring the blackcurrant purée to the boil and simmer for 2-3 minutes to drive off excess moisture. Blend half of the hot purée with the egg yolk in a bowl. Place the bowl over a pan of hot water and cook, stirring until the mixture thickens slightly. Remove from the heat and beat in the remaining purée. Leave to cool slightly.

Dissolve the remaining gelatine in 2 tbsp of the purée in a small bowl over a pan of hot water. Remove from the heat and leave to cool.

Blend the blackcurrant gelatine into the blackcurrant purée, cover and chill.

Spoon the partially set apple mixture into a terrine rinsed out with cold water, pushing the mixture up the sides to coat them and leaving a deep channel down the centre. Spoon the blackcurrant mixture into the channel. Cover and refrigerate until set.

For the sauce, gently cook the blackcurrants with 1 tbsp water in a covered pan for about 10 minutes. Purée, pass through a sieve, then stir in icing sugar and lemon juice to taste, cool, cover and chill.

To serve, loosen around the edge of the apple mixture with the point of a sharp knife, then invert onto a cold plate. Spoon the sauce over 6 cold plates. Cut the terrine into slices and place one on each side.

OPPOSITE *Nougat glacé with passionfruit* Recipe: page 320
RIGHT *Orange sorbet* Recipe: page 320

BELOW *Blackcurrant rings* Recipe: page 324

BLACKCURRANT RINGS

INGREDIENTS (serves 4)
225 g/8 oz blackcurrants
50 g/2 oz caster sugar
2 egg yolks
100 ml/4 fl oz milk
1 tsp gelatine
25 ml/1 fl oz crème de cassis
lemon juice
150 ml/¼ pt double cream, whipped

FOR THE DECORATION
whipped cream
mint leaves

Picture: page 323

Cook the blackcurrants very gently in a covered saucepan with 1 tbsp water and 1 tbsp sugar for a few minutes until they are just softened but still whole.

Whisk the egg yolks with the remaining sugar until thick and light.

Bring the milk to the boil in a double boiler or a bowl placed over a pan of hot water, then pour onto the egg yolks in a slow stream, whisking continuously. Pour back into the double boiler or bowl and cook over hot water, stirring continuously until thickened. Strain into a bowl and leave to cool, stirring occasionally to prevent a skin forming.

Strain the blackcurrants. Reserve the juice. Purée half of the fruit, then pass through a sieve, pressing down well to extract as much juice as possible. Stir the purée and reserved juice into the cooled custard. Reserve the remaining blackcurrants.

Dissolve the gelatine in the crème de cassis in a bowl placed over a pan of hot water. Allow to cool slightly, then stir into the custard. Add lemon juice to taste. Place the custard over a bowl of ice and leave until it is just on the point of setting, stirring occasionally.

Fold in the cream.

Rinse 4 individual ring moulds in cold water, then fill them with the blackcurrant custard. Leave them to set.

Unmould the rings onto 4 cold plates and spoon some of the reserved blackcurrants into the centres. Arrange the remaining blackcurrants around the moulds and decorate with whipped cream and mint leaves.

GRAPES IN GINGERSNAP BASKETS

INGREDIENTS (serves 4)
grated rind of 1 lemon
grated rind of 1 lime
1½ tbsp lemon juice
1½ tbsp lime juice
1½ tbsp granulated sugar
150 ml/¼ pt medium white wine
1 egg, separated
1 tbsp caster sugar
225 g/8 oz green grapes, peeled and
    pips removed, if necessary
225 g/8 oz black grapes, peeled and
    pips removed, if necessary
4 gingersnap baskets (see p.332)

FOR THE DECORATION
long twisted strips of lime and lemon
    peel
small scoops of vanilla ice cream
    (see p.336)

The only last-minute preparation for this composite dessert is making the warm, frothy sauce. Vary the size of the baskets according to taste.

———————————

Stir the fruit rinds and juices, granulated sugar and wine together in a saucepan and heat gently until the sugar has dissolved. Bring to the boil and reduce by half. Cool slightly.

Put the grapes into a large shallow dish and pour the fruit syrup over. Cool completely then cover and chill for several hours.

Transfer the ice cream to the refrigerator 30 minutes before serving.

Just before serving strain the juices from the grapes and measure off 25 ml/1 fl oz.

Whisk the egg yolk with the caster sugar in a small bowl placed over a pan of hot water until thick and pale, then very gradually whisk in the 25 ml/1 fl oz of juice from the grapes.

Whisk the egg white until just beginning to hold shape, then fold into egg yolk mixture.

Place the gingersnap baskets onto 4 dessert plates. Place small scoops of vanilla ice cream in the bottom, add the grapes and spoon the sauce over.

I C E   C R E A M   W I T H   P E A C H E S

INGREDIENTS (serves 4)
6 egg yolks
100 g/4 oz icing sugar
50 ml/2 fl oz kirsch
vanilla flavouring
500 ml/18 fl oz whipping cream
5 peaches
2 slices of orange, pith and skin
*   removed*
500 ml/18 fl oz sauternes
200 g/7 oz caster sugar
¼ tsp peach brandy
juice of ½ orange

Picture: page 327

A recipe to choose for a special summertime occasion.

Whisk the egg yolks with the icing sugar and kirsch until light and fluffy, then whisk in 1 or 2 drops of vanilla flavouring. Gently fold in the cream and divide the mixture between 4 freezerproof dishes. Cover and freeze for 2 hours.

Poach 2 of the peaches and the orange slices in the wine with 100 g/4 oz of caster sugar and a few drops of vanilla flavouring for 10 minutes. Leave to cool in the syrup.

Peel and slice the remaining peaches.

Heat the remaining sugar in a small, heavy based saucepan until it begins to turn golden brown. Remove from the heat and stir in the peach poaching liquor. Heat gently, stirring to make sure all the caramel has dissolved. Add the sliced peaches and peach brandy and simmer for 10 minutes. Liquidize, then pass through a sieve and add sugar and orange juice to taste.

Peel the whole poached peaches, cut into halves and remove the stones.

Unmould the ice cream onto 4 cold plates. Cut almost across the centre and ease the 2 halves apart. Spoon the sauce around the ice cream. Lay a peach 'tail' on top of the ice cream and garnish the edge of the plate with whipped cream and dots of Grenadine.

Poached apples
Recipe: page 328

Ice cream with peaches
Recipe: page 325

POACHED APPLES

INGREDIENTS (*serves 4*)
4 dessert apples
100 g/4 oz sugar
150 ml/¼ pt dry cider
a strip of lemon peel
1 vanilla pod
100 ml/4 fl oz red Loire wine or
  Beaujolais Villages
4 egg yolks
100 g/4 oz caster sugar
1 tsp gelatine
1 tsp sirop de fraises
lemon juice

FOR THE DECORATION
mint leaves
blackcurrants

Picture: page 326

A soft red wine that is low in tannin must be used, otherwise the flavour of the dish will be spoilt.

Peel, halve and core the apples.

Dissolve the sugar in the cider and 425 ml/¾ pt water. Bring to the boil, add the apples, lemon peel and vanilla pod. Reduce the heat and poach the apples for about 8 minutes. Leave to cool in the liquid, then remove with a slotted spoon and drain well. Cover and chill.

Boil the wine until it is reduced by half.

Whisk the egg yolks, sugar and wine together in a bowl over a pan of hot water until light and thickened. Remove from the heat and whisk until cold.

Dissolve the gelatine in the sirop and 1 tbsp water in a bowl placed over a pan of hot water. Remove from the heat and leave to cool slightly, then lightly fold into the sauce. Taste and add a little lemon juice if necessary to 'lift' the flavour.

Spoon the sauce over 4 plates and leave to set — this will not take long.

Arrange the apple slices on the sauce and decorate with mint leaves and blackcurrants.

PILLOWS OF FRESH PEAR

INGREDIENTS (*serves 4*)
2 Comice pears
100 g/4 oz sugar
1½ tbsp lemon juice
50 ml/2 fl oz poires William
175 g/6 oz puff pastry (see p.79)
beaten egg
225 g/8 oz blackcurrants
225 g/8 oz caster sugar
pinch of ground cinnamon
crème pâtissière made from 300 ml/
  ½ pt milk and 2 egg yolks (see p.81)

FOR THE DECORATION
mint leaves
slices of peeled pear, dipped in lemon
  juice

Picture: page 330

The pastry can be cut into different shapes — round, diamond, square, scalloped, flower or heart.

Peel, core and halve the pears lengthways, then poach them in 425 ml/¾ pt water, with the sugar, lemon juice and poires William, for 5—10 minutes, until tender. Leave to cool in the liquor, then remove with a slotted spoon and drain well.

Meanwhile, roll out the pastry to 5 mm/¼ inch thick. Trim and straighten the edges, then cut into 4 rectangles, about 10 × 7.5 cm/4 × 3 inches. Transfer to a baking tray, cover and chill for at least 30 minutes.

Heat the oven to 220°C/425°F/Gas 7.

Brush the pastry with beaten egg, mark a pattern with the point of a sharp knife, and bake for about 7 minutes until crisp, golden and risen. Transfer to a wire rack to cool.

Purée the blackcurrants with 300 ml/½ pt of the poaching liquor, the caster sugar and cinnamon. Pass through a sieve, then chill.

Split the puff pastry rectangles in half lengthways. Carefully remove any pastry that is soft. Place the bottom halves on 4 cold plates. Reserve a little of the crème pâtissière for the decoration, then spread a layer onto each base.

Arrange the sliced pears on top, then drop the lids in place. Spoon the blackcurrant sauce around. Spoon the reserved crème pâtissière into a greaseproof paper piping bag, snip off the end and pipe a pattern on the sauce. Decorate with the mint leaves and slices of pear.

MANGO SORBET

INGREDIENTS (serves 4)
100 g/4 oz sugar
250 ml/9 fl oz ripe mango flesh, puréed and sieved
juice of 1 lemon, strained

Picture: page 331

Dissolve the sugar in 50 ml/2 fl oz water and bring to the boil. Leave to cool.

Blend the syrup with the mango purée and lemon juice. Freeze in a sorbetière for about 15 minutes, then transfer to the freezer. Alternatively, pour into a shallow metal container. Cover and chill for 1 hour, then place in the freezer for 45 minutes. Tip the mixture into a cold bowl, beat well with a cold whisk, then return to the container, cover and freeze for 30 minutes. Repeat the beating and freezing twice more. Leave the sorbet to freeze until firm.

Transfer the sorbet to the refrigerator about 30 minutes before serving.

MANGO ICE CREAM WITH

COCONUT SAUCE

INGREDIENTS (serves 4)
2 egg yolks
50 g/2 oz icing sugar
1 very large or 2 smaller ripe mangoes
lemon juice
150 ml/¼ pt double cream, whipped
coconut sauce (see p.316)

FOR THE DECORATION
grated coconut

Picture: page 330

Whisk the egg yolks and icing sugar together in a bowl over a pan of hot water until they are lukewarm. Remove from the heat and continue whisking until the mixture is cold and very thick and light.

Sieve the mango flesh and sharpen it with a little lemon juice.

Fold the mango flesh and cream together, then fold into the egg yolk mixture. Pour into a shallow metal container, cover and freeze until firm.

About 30 minutes before serving, transfer the ice cream to the main part of the refrigerator.

Spoon the sauce onto 4 cold plates. Scoop the ice cream into the centre and decorate with grated coconut.

ABOVE *Pillows of fresh pear*
Recipe: page 328
RIGHT *Mango ice cream with coconut sauce*
Recipe: page 329

OPPOSITE *Mango sorbet*
Recipe: page 329

G I N G E R S N A P   B A S K E T S

INGREDIENTS (makes 8—10)
50 g/2 oz golden syrup
50 g/2 oz butter
150 g/5 oz caster sugar
50 g/2 oz plain flour
1 tsp ground ginger
½ tsp finely grated lemon zest
½ tsp lemon juice

Heat the oven to 180°C/350°F/Gas 4.

Gently heat the syrup, butter and sugar until the sugar has dissolved. Remove from the heat and fold in the remaining ingredients.

Drop 3 spoonfuls of the mixture onto a lightly greased baking tray, leaving plenty of room for the mixture to spread.

Bake in the oven for 7—10 minutes until golden brown.

Quickly but carefully remove with a spatula or fish slice and mould around an orange or apple or small bowl.

When set, remove from the moulds and leave to cool on a wire cooling tray.

Bake the remaining mixture in the same way and shape as above.

W I N E   J E L L Y   W I T H   P E A C H E S

INGREDIENTS (serves 4)
3 tsp powdered gelatine
600 ml/1 pt fruity dry white wine
100 g/4 oz caster sugar
juice of 1 lemon
strips of lemon peel
small mint leaves
4 peaches
2 tbsp poires William

Picture: page 334

Dissolve the gelatine in a little of the wine in a small bowl over a pan of hot water. Remove from the heat and leave to cool slightly.

Gently heat half the remaining wine with the sugar and lemon juice, stirring constantly until the sugar has dissolved. Remove from the heat, stir into the gelatine. Reserve 50ml/2fl oz of the remaining wine and stir the gelatine mixture into the rest of the wine. Spoon a very thin layer over 4 cold plates. Leave until just beginning to set. Leave the remaining jelly in a cool place until just becoming syrupy.

Cut shapes out of the lemon peel with aspic cutters. Reserve some of the shapes and some of the mint leaves. Arrange the remainder on the plates. Leave to set in place, then cover with a thin layer of syrupy jelly, taking care not to dislodge the decoration. Leave to set.

Peel the peaches, remove the stones and cut the flesh into slices. Sprinkle with the reserved wine, cover and chill.

Just before serving, whisk the reserved jelly with the poires William until frothy.

Place the unwhipped jelly in the centre of the plates, then add the whipped jelly and arrange the slices of peach on top.

COUPELLES

INGREDIENTS (makes 8—10)
50 g/2 oz unsalted butter
2 egg whites
65 g/2½ oz caster sugar
50 g/2 oz plain flour

The baked biscuits set very quickly after they are removed from the oven, so it is advisable to cook only 3 at one time and to use 2 or 3 baking sheets in rotation. Handle with care after shaping, as they are brittle. Store in an airtight container and do not fill or place on a sauce until just before serving.

Heat the oven to 200°C/400°F/Gas 6.

Slowly melt the butter then allow to cool.

Whisk the egg whites until frothy, then whisk in the sugar and continue to whisk for 2—3 minutes until thick. Gently fold in the flour together with the melted butter.

Drop 3 spoonfuls of the mixture onto a lightly greased baking tray and spread each one out to a circle 10 cm/4 inches in diameter.

Bake in the oven for 5—7 minutes until the edges are light golden brown.

Carefully but quickly remove the biscuits with a spatula or fish slice and quickly shape around the bottom of an orange or apple or small dish such as a ramekin dish.

When set to shape, remove from the mould and leave to cool completely on a wire cooling rack.

Cook the remaining mixture in a similar way, using a cool baking sheet each time and shaping the biscuits as above.

Store carefully in tins or airtight containers.

KIRSCH ICE CREAM IN COUPELLES

INGREDIENTS (serves 4)
175 g/6 oz caster sugar
3 egg whites
40 ml/1½ fl oz good quality kirsch
200 ml/7 fl oz whipped crème fraîche
* or double cream*
4 coupelles

FOR THE DECORATION
whipped crème fraîche or double
* cream, optional*
pieces of fresh pineapple
strawberries
mint leaves

Picture: page 335

The ice cream goes equally well with raspberries — either whole, instead of the other fruits in the coupelles, or as a sauce with the ice cream served simply on top.

Dissolve the sugar in 150 ml/¼ pt water, then bring to the boil and boil for 3-5 minutes until the temperature reaches 110°C/230°F.

Whisk the egg whites until stiff but not dry, then gradually whisk in the syrup, whisking well after each addition. Continue whisking until cold.

Whisk in the kirsch, then carefully fold in the crème fraîche or double cream. Spoon into a shallow metal container, cover and chill for 30 minutes, then place in the freezer.

About 20 minutes before serving, transfer the ice cream to the main part of the refrigerator.

Place the coupelles on 4 cold plates and scoop ice cream into the centre. Garnish with the cream, if used, fruits and mint leaves.

Wine jelly with peaches
Recipe: page 332

Kirsch ice cream in coupelles
Recipe: page 333

FLOATING ISLANDS ON
BLACKCURRANT SAUCE

INGREDIENTS (serves 4)
2 tbsp sugar
225 g/8 oz blackcurrants
a squeeze of lemon juice
2 egg whites
50 g/2 oz caster sugar

FOR THE DECORATION
mint leaves

Dissolve the sugar in 2 tbsp water, add the blackcurrants and cook, covered, over a low heat for 2-3 minutes. Purée, then pass through a sieve and add lemon juice to taste.

Whisk the egg whites until stiff, then very gradually whisk in half the caster sugar, whisking well after each addition, and continue to whisk until the meringue is stiff. Whisk in the remaining caster sugar and whisk again until the meringue is very stiff.

Heat a wide pan of salted water until the water is just moving.

Form the meringue mixture into small mounds on a slotted spoon, then rest the spoon gently on the surface of the water. The mounds will gently float off the spoon onto the surface of the water. Cook for about 3-4 minutes, turning occasionally. Remove carefully with a slotted spoon and leave to drain on a cloth. Cook the remaining meringue in the same way.

Spoon the blackcurrant sauce over 4 plates and carefully transfer the meringue mounds to the surface of the sauce. Decorate with mint leaves.

VANILLA ICE CREAM

INGREDIENTS (serves 4)
½ vanilla pod, split
450 ml/¾ pt double cream
4 egg yolks
75 g/3 oz caster sugar

Heat the vanilla pod with the cream in a heavy based saucepan to just below boiling point. Remove from the heat, cover and leave for 30 minutes.

Lightly whisk the egg yolks with the sugar in a bowl. Strain in the cream, whisking constantly. Rinse the saucepan and pour in the cream/egg yolk mixture. Place over a low heat and cook gently, stirring constantly, until the mixture thickens. Do not allow it to boil.

Remove from the heat and leave to cool, stirring occasionally to prevent a skin forming, then pour into a shallow metal container. Cover and place in the freezer until a 2.5 cm/1 inch border of ice crystals have formed around the edge.

Tip the ice cream into a cold bowl and beat with a cold whisk to break up the ice crystals but do not allow the mixture to warm. Return the mixture to the container, cover and freeze until firm. Alternatively, freeze the ice cream in an ice cream maker.

About 35 minutes before serving transfer the ice cream to the main part of the refrigerator.

BAKED APPLES WITH BERRIES

INGREDIENTS (serves 4)
75 g/3 oz raspberries
75 g/3 oz strawberries
2½ tbsp eau-de-vie de Framboises
5 ml/1 tsp caster sugar
1 tbsp lemon juice
4 large, crisp, dessert apples
40 g/1½ oz butter, diced
65 g/2½ oz icing sugar
200 ml/7 fl oz crème fraîche

FOR THE DECORATION
slices of small strawberries
mint leaves

Put the raspberries and strawberries into a small bowl. Sprinkle 2 tbsp Framboises and the caster sugar over. Cover and leave for 1 hour, very gently folding the fruit over 2 or 3 times.

Acidulate a bowl of cold water with the lemon juice.

Peel the apples, leaving the stalks on. Cut a slice from the top of each apple and remove the cores. Put each one in the acidulated water as soon as it is finished.

Heat the oven to 200°C/400°F/Gas 6.

Remove the apples from the water and dry well. Place in an ovenproof dish and fill the cavities with some of the raspberries and strawberries. Pour the juices over the apples and reserve the fruit that remains.

Divide half of the butter between the apples and put the removed slices back in place. Sprinkle the apples with 20 g/¾ oz icing sugar. Scatter the remaining butter in the dish and surround the apples with about 175 ml/6 fl oz water.

Place in the oven and cook for 15-20 minutes.

Bake the apples with the cooking juices and sprinkle with a further 20 g/¾ oz icing sugar. Return to the oven for another 15 minutes until just cooked throughout. Leave to cool then chill for 1 hour.

Purée the remaining raspberries and strawberries then pass through a sieve. Whisk lightly with the crème fraîche, remaining Framboises and remaining icing sugar.

Remove the slices from the apples and spoon some of the berry sauce over the apples. Spoon the remaining sauce around the apples and decorate with strawberry slices and mint leaves.

CONVERSION CHARTS, GLOSSARY & INDEX

WEIGHTS AND MEASURES

SPOON MEASURES

In American recipes, when quantities are stated as spoons, 'level' spoons are meant. European recipes and those in this book usually call for rounded neither level, nor over-heaped) spoons, unless specifically stated otherwise. Also, American 'spoons' are standard cook's measuring spoons, whereas European 'spoons' tend to be any available kitchen or eating spoons. The best plan is to regard 2 American teaspoons or tablespoons as 1 English teaspoon or tablespoon. Dessertspoons are not often called for in recipes, but 1 dessertspoon is the equivalent of 2 teaspoons or half a tablespoon.

VOLUME			
Metric	Imperial		American
5 ml	—	1 tsp	1 tsp
10 ml	—	2 tsp	2 tsp
20 ml	—	1 tbsp	1½ tbsp
30 ml	1 fl oz	1½ tbsp	2 tbsp
50 ml	2 fl oz	3 tbsp	¼ cup
60 ml	2½ fl oz (½ gill)	3½ tbsp	¼C+2 tsp
75 ml	3 fl oz	4 tbsp	½C(6 tbsp)
100 ml	4 fl oz	¼ pint	½C(¼ pint)
150 ml	5 fl oz (1 gill)	¼ pint	¾C
175 ml	6 fl oz	—	¾C
200 ml	7 fl oz	—	—
250 ml	8 fl oz	⅓ pint	1C(½ pint)
300 ml	10 fl oz (2 gills)	½ pint	1¼C
350 ml	12 fl oz	—	1½C
400 ml	14 fl oz	⅔ pint	1¾C
450 ml	15 fl oz	¾ pint	—
500 ml	16 fl oz	—	2C (1 pint)
550 ml	18 fl oz	—	2¼C
575 ml	20 fl oz	1 pint	2½C
600 ml	21 fl oz	—	2¾C
700 ml	25 fl oz	1¼ pint	3C
750 ml	27 fl oz	—	3½C
800 ml	28 fl oz	—	3⅔C
850 ml	30 fl oz	1½ pints	3¾C
900 ml	32 fl oz	1⅔ pints	4C
1 litre	35 fl oz	1¾ pints	4½C
1.1 litre	40 fl oz	2 pints	5C
1.3 litre	48 fl oz	2⅔ pints	6C
1.5 litre	50 fl oz	2½ pints	6¼C
1.66 litre	56 fl oz	2¾ pints	7C
1.75 litre	60 fl oz	3 pints	7½C
1.8 litre	64 fl oz	3¼ pints	8C
2 litre	72 fl oz	3½ pints	9C
2.1 litre	76 fl oz	3⅔ pints	9½C
2.2 litre	80 fl oz	3¾ pints	10C
2.25 litre	84 fl oz	2 quarts	10½C

WEIGHTS			
Metric	**Imperial**	**Metric**	**Imperial**
8 g	¼ oz	325 g	11 oz
15 g	½ oz	350 g	12 oz
20 g	¾ oz	375 g	13 oz
25 g	1 oz	400 g	14 oz
30 g	1 oz	425 g	15 oz
45 g	1½ oz	450 g	16 oz (1lb)
50 g	1¾ oz	550 g	1¼ lb
55 g	2 oz	675 g	1½ lb
75 g	2½ oz	700 g	1⅔ lb
85 g	3 oz	800 g	1¾ lb
100 g	3½ oz	900 g	2 lb
115 g	4 oz	1 kg	2¼ lb
125 g	4½ oz	1.35 kg	3 lb
140 g	5 oz	1.5 kg	3½ lb
150 g	5½ oz	1.8 kg	4 lb
170 g	6 oz	2 kg	4½ lb
175 g	6½ oz	2.3 kg	5 lb
200 g	7 oz	2.5 kg	5½ lb
210 g	7½ oz	2.7 kg	6 lb
225 g	8 oz	3 kg	6½ lb
250 g	8½ oz	3.2 kg	7 lb
255 g	9 oz	3.5 kg	8 lb
275 g	9½ oz	4 kg	9 lb
285 g	10 oz	4.5 kg	10 lb
300 g	10½ oz	5 kg	11 lb

LENGTH	
Metric (cm)	**Imperial (in)**
0.3	⅛
0.6	¼
1	½
2	¾
2.5	1
5	2
15	6
30	12 (1 ft)
46	18
92	36 (1yd)
100 (1m)	39

TEMPERATURE								
°C	**°F**	**Gas mark**	**°C**	**°F**	**Gas mark**	**°C**	**°F**	**Gas mark**
27	80		71	160		130	275	1
29	85		77	170		140	285	
38	100		82	180		150	300	2(c)
41	105		88	190		160	325	3(w)
43	110		93	200		180	350	4
46	115		96	205		190	375	5(m)
49	120		100	212		200	400	6(lh)
54	130		107	225	¼(vc)	220	425	7
57	135		110	228		230	450	8(h)
60	140		115	238		250	475	9(vh)
66	150		120	250	½	260	500	

G L O S S A R Y

Acidify To add vinegar or lemon juice to a sauce or cooked dish.

Acidulated water Water to which lemon juice or vinegar has been added. Used for blanching sweetbreads etc. Also lemon juice and water mixed in equal quantities and added to apples, bananas, artichokes etc. to prevent them from going brown.

Aiguilette Thin strips of meat, most likely from the breast of poultry or game.

Aspic Jelly made from calfs foot or the bones of meat, fish or poultry. Vegetables, fish or meat can be served in aspic.

Bain marie A water bath in which delicate foods are stood in their dishes to cook away from direct heat in the oven. Can also be used to keep foods hot without spoiling.

Bake To cook in dry heat in the oven.

Bake blind To bake an empty pastry case. So that the case keeps its shape, it is filled with blind beans, *see* below.

Bard To cover meat, game or poultry in strips of pork or fatty bacon to prevent it drying out during roasting. Reduces the need for basting.

Baste To spoon the cooking liquid over the food as it cooks to add flavour and prevent it drying out.

Batter A beaten mixture used to make cakes, puddings or pancakes or to coat foods to be fried. Usually a liquid made from flour, eggs and milk.

Bavarois Dessert made with cream and eggs and set with gelatine.

Beat To mix energetically with a wooden spoon or in an electric mixer, incorporating air so that the mixture is light and smooth.

Beignets Fritters.

Beurre manié Flour and butter creamed together into a paste and used as a thickening for sauces etc.

Beurre noir Butter heated until it is dark brown — *not* black.

Beurre noisette Butter heated until it is light brown. Take care not to burn it.

Bind To thicken soups or sauces with eggs, cream etc.

Bisque A creamy soup made with puréed fish or shellfish.

Blanch To heat briefly in boiling water or steam. This can be done to whiten sweetbreads etc., to facilitate peeling vegetables or shelling nuts, to remove a strong or bitter flavour from certain meats and vegetables, or to prepare fruit and vegetables for preserving or freezing.

Blanquette A casserole made without prior frying of the meat to seal it. The meat is usually chicken, veal or lamb and the sauce thickened with cream or egg yolk.

Blend To mix together thoroughly.

Blind beans Dried beans (or can even be pebbles or marbles) used to fill a pastry

case for baking blind. Can be stored and reused.

Boil To cook in liquid brought to boiling point and kept there. Pasta is cooked at a full rolling boil in an open pan so that the water is agitated as much as possible to help stop the pasta sticking together. A tablespoon of oil added to the water helps too.

Bouquet garni Bunch of herbs used to flavour food during cooking and removed before serving.

Braise To cook slowly on a bed of vegetables in a covered pan.

Bread To coat in flour, egg, then breadcrumbs before frying.

Brochette (*see* Skewer).

Brunoise Finely diced root vegetables simmered in butter and stock until soft. Used to flavour soups and sauces and some fish dishes.

Caramelize To melt sugar into a syrup, either by boiling in a pan and stirring continuously, or by heating under the grill.

Chaudfroid A jellied white sauce made of butter and flour with egg yolks, stock, cream and gelatine. Used to give a white glaze to chicken etc. A brown chaudfroid is used on game and meat.

Chine To remove the backbone from a rack of ribs.

Chowder A fish stew or soup, often made with clams or oysters.

Clarified butter Butter that has been melted so that the clear oil can be separated from the milk particles and other impurities. It can then be heated to a higher temperature than unclarified butter without burning.

Clarify To clear a stock by adding lightly beaten egg whites and crushed egg shells. Bring the liquid to the boil, then cool and strain before using.

Cocotte A cast iron casserole with a lid, usually round or oval in shape. Also individual heatproof dishes for baking eggs.

Collops Small slices of meat.

Cool To allow to stand at room temperature. *Not* to put in the fridge.

Court bouillon Specially prepared cooking liquor for poaching fish and shellfish, and sometimes vegetables and meat. Water acidulated with a little vinegar and containing also herbs and seasoning, onion, garlic, carrot, celery, wine, stock, oil etc.

Cream To beat together certain foods until smooth and creamy. To cream butter and sugar, beat together in a bowl with a wooden spoon until soft and fluffy and light in colour, or use an electric mixer.

Croustade A bread case for hot savoury mixtures that is dipped in fat and baked or fried until crispy.

Croûte Crust or pastry case enclosing a filling. Usually made of rich brioche dough.

Croûton Trimmed bread cut into neat shapes and fried. Used as a garnish.

Dariole Small castle shaped mould used for both sweet and savoury mousses and sometimes for rice and cakes.

Deglaze To add boiling water, wine or stock to the meat sediment and cooking juices in the pan. Essential stage in making a sauce for fried meat.

Déglacer (*see* Deglaze).

Dégorger To remove strong or bitter tasting flavours from meat, fish or vegetables, usually by salting them, then soaking or washing. An alternative to blanching.

Dépouiller To add a little cold liquid to a pan of simmering stock, which will bring the fat and scum to the surface, making it easier to skim off.

Devil To grill food in a coating of butter and a hot sauce, such as Worcestershire.

Dice To cut into small cubes of even size.

Dredge To dust with flour, sugar etc.

Dropping consistency The consistency of a mixture that will fall reluctantly from a spoon when jerked — neither runny nor solid.

Duxelles A mixture of finely chopped mushroom and onion or shallot, sometimes mixed with ham. Used raw or cooked in butter until soft and dry to stuff or flavour poached fish, shellfish or meat, or to garnish a papilotte.

Emulsion A stable suspension of fat and another substance, eg mayonnaise.

Escalope A thin slice of meat, eg veal, often beaten flat to make it larger and thinner.

Farce Stuffing.

Fines herbes A combination of parsley, chives, tarragon and chervil.

Fillet A cut of prime meat or fish off the bone.

Flake To break down into small pieces with a fork.

Flamber To set light to alcohol poured over food. Adds flavour and drama to presentation.

Fold in To mix a heavy creamy mixture with a light and fluffy one, gently fold the first into the second with a large metal spoon in a three dimensional figure-of-eight motion. Do not beat or overwork, or you will lose all the air.

Fricassée Chicken or veal fried and then cooked in a sauce.

Fromage blanc Very soft low fat cheese.

Garniture Garnish or trimming. Neat shapes of vegetables, pasta, croûtons etc. used to enhance the flavour and appearance of a dish. An important part of presentation in Cuisine Vivante.

Giblets Gizzard, heart, neck and liver of poultry. The liver is very strong in flavour, but the others are often used in the making of stock.

343

Glacé de viande Concentrated meat glaze made by boiling brown stock to reduce. Used for colouring and flavouring sauces.

Glacé de poisson As above but of fish. (*See also* fish fumet.)

Glaze A thin coating of syrup or aspic that gives a shine to a finished dish (eg jellied meat juices on turkey, or melted jam on a fruit flan).

Gluten Proteins found in wheat important in the making of bread.

Gratin A gratin dish is oval and heatproof. Dishes cooked au gratin are dotted with butter, cheese and breadcrumbs and browned in the oven.

Grill To cook by direct heat.

Infuse To steep or heat through to extract a flavour, eg vanilla in milk.

Julienne Fine needleshreds or matchstick lengths of vegetable etc.

Knead To work dough, pressing it and stretching it until it reaches the right elasticity and consistency, and to distribute the yeast if there is any.

Knock back To knead dough for a second time and expel the air once it has risen.

Knock up To separate the edges of raw puff pastry so that it rises during cooking with as much air between the layers as possible.

Lard To thread strips of pork or anchovy through meat before roasting to make it juicy and flavoursome.

Lardons Strips of port fat used to line pâté tins or to thread through meat, *see* above.

Leavening Agent used to make mixtures rise in cooking — yeast, egg white, baking powder.

Liaison Thickening agent for sauces, either flour and butter or egg yolk, cream or blood.

Macédoine Diced mixed fruit for a fruit salad, or diced mixed vegetables for a garnish or hors d'oeuvre.

Macerate To soften or steep food in a liquid, especially of fruit, to let the flavours mingle.

Marinade The liquid in which food is marinated. *See* below.

Marinate To tenderize and flavour food, especially meat, by steeping in a liquid, usually red or white wine or a mixture of oil and lemon juice, flavoured with herbs and chopped vegetables.

Mask To cover food with a sauce.

Médallions Food trimmed into neat rounds, usually meat.

Mirepoix A bed of vegetables used for braising. Usually finely diced onion, carrot and celery, sometimes mixed with ham, which has been fried gently in butter until soft.

Mousseline A light, creamy, frothy mixture, a sauce with a mousse-like texture or small moulds of poultry or fish purée whipped with cream and served hot or cold.

Mount (monter) To add butter to a sauce, waiting until each small piece is incorporated before adding the next, to thicken it and give it a velvety texture and a rich sheen.

Noisette Hazelnut. Used also to describe a quantity, eg a nut of butter, or a shape. A noisette of lamb is a neat round taken from the best end.

Panade A mixture thickened with flour and used as the base of a soufflé or cake.

Papilotte An oiled paper or foil case that envelops food while it is cooking and contains its aroma or flavour.

Parboil To boil briefly. *See* Blanch.

Poach To cook gently in barely trembling water.

Pound To reduce to a paste or a powder with a pestle and mortar.

Praline Almonds and sugar pounded together and cooked to a toffee. Used to coat cakes and puddings.

Prove To rise, of yeasted dough.

Purée To press through a fine meshed sieve or otherwise reduce food to a smooth, soft consistency.

Quark Very soft, almost liquid white cheese made from skimmed milk.

Quenelle Finely pounded food, most commonly fish, mixed with egg whites and cream to a very smooth paste over ice, formed into sausage shapes and poached in water or light stock.

Ragoût A stew made from even sized pieces of meat, fish or sometimes vegetables. They are usually sautéed first, then simmered gently in stock. Cuisine Vivante chefs have developed lighter types of ragoût that need less cooking.

Ramekin Small ovenproof dish used for cooking tiny individual portions.

Reduce To boil, uncovered, so that the liquid evaporates. It strengthens the flavour and improves the appearance of liquids to be used as sauces.

Refresh To stop vegetables continuing to cook and losing their colour by submerging them briefly in cold water after they have finished cooking.

Relax To put pastry in the fridge in between rollings. The gluten in the flour will have expanded during rolling and this allows it to contract so that there is less danger of shrinkage in the oven.

Render To reduce fat to a liquid by melting over a gentle heat.

Rest Batter is set aside to rest so that the starch can expand. This makes it lighter when cooked.

Ribbon trail When a mixture has been whisked, it leaves a ribbon trail in the bowl when the whisk is raised out of the mixture. The thickness of the ribbon trail and the time it takes to disappear are indications of the consistency of the mixture.

Roast To cook meat in the oven by the action of direct heat and its own vapour.

Rouille Emulsion of garlic and oil for flavouring Mediterranean soups.

Roux An amalgamation of butter and flour cooked over a gentle heat and used as the basis for many sauces. Flour-based sauces are not favoured by chefs of the Cuisine Vivante, as they are heavy and tend to mask the flavours of the other ingredients.

Salmis Jointed poultry or game, roasted in the oven until almost done, then cooked in a rich wine sauce.

Salpicon Finely diced meat, fish or vegetables, bound with a savoury sauce and used to make rissoles, croquettes or stuffings for meat, vegetables or pastry cases.

Sauter Literally 'jump'. To fry food lightly in butter or oil, shaking and tossing it frequently.

Scald Mainly used of milk. To heat until just below boiling point.

Seal, sear, seize To brown the surface of meat quickly over a high heat to prevent the juices escaping during cooking.

Simmer To cook in liquid that is not quite boiling, so that only the occasional bubble rises to the surface.

Skewer To hold in place with metal or wooden sticks, pointed at one or both ends. Prawns etc. can be threaded onto a skewer or brochette and grilled over charcoal.

Slake To mix flour to a paste with water.

Steam Light method of cooking food over boiling water much favoured by Cuisine Vivante.

Suprême Poultry breast.

Sweat To cook gently in a closed pan without browning, either in butter or in the food's own juices.

Terrine A loaf-tin shaped baking dish. Also the food cooked in it — pâté or other minced mixtures baked or steamed and usually eaten cold and sliced.

Timbale Food cooked or served in a castle shaped mound.

Tomalley The liver of a lobster. Especially prized by the chefs of the Cuisine Vivante.

Tournedos Thick beef steaks from the narrow end of the fillet.

Turn Technique of cutting around vegetables to make them of even size and attractive in appearance.

Zest Finely grated lemon or orange rind. The coloured part only is grated and used for flavourings.

INDEX

ACKNOWLEDGEMENTS

The publishers wish to thank the
following for the loan of china, glassware,
kitchen equipment and provisions:

The Reject China Shop, Beauchamp Place,
   London SW1
David Mellor (kitchen supplies), Covent
   Garden, London WC2
Moulinex Ltd.
Magimix Ltd.
Mr John Lawless, City Herbs, London
Mr Terry Connelly, Woodhouse Hume
   Ltd., London
L & E Fisheries Ltd., London
Donaldson's, London